ALBERT
Prince Consort

ALBERT
Prince Consort

Hector Bolitho

THE BOBBS-MERRILL COMPANY, INC.
A Subsidiary of Howard W. Sams & Co., Inc.
Publishers • INDIANAPOLIS • KANSAS CITY • NEW YORK

To Muriel and Sydney Box

Copyright © 1964 by Hector Bolitho
All rights reserved
Library of Congress Catalog card number: 64-66283
Printed in the United States of America

Contents

Foreword

Albert the Good, my biography of the Prince Consort, was published in 1932. It was my first, untutored attempt at research and this fact is painfully obvious to me now. But I enjoyed remarkable advantages in my task. I was living at the Deanery in Windsor Castle while I was writing the book. The Duke of Saxe-Coburg-Gotha had already allowed me to copy all the letters his grandfather, the Prince Consort, had written to his brother, Duke Ernest, during the twenty-two years of his married life in England. These documents were kept in the archives in the Veste Coburg and had not been seen by Theodore Martin when he wrote his official biography. They revealed the truth of the Prince's heart and mind more than any other letters written during his life.

I also enjoyed the help of three surviving children of Queen Victoria – the Duke of Connaught, Princess Louise and Princess Beatrice. They often came to the Deanery and they trusted me with stories about their father. There were other elderly people living in the Castle and in the Thames Valley who could remember the Prince Consort. One of them, General Sir George Higginson, who lived until he was a hundred years old, recalled stories of the royal family going back to King George iv and King William iv.

I was allowed to work sometimes in the library of the Castle, which the Prince Consort had rescued from its old disorder. But there were disadvantages in these privileges, for I was almost

too near the man I was writing about. I became more interested
in the Prince Consort as a human being than in his tasks in relation to political and international history. His personality grew
and deepened so that I began to believe almost that I had known
him.

This was a dangerous state of mind for pure scholarship,
which was then beyond my circumstances and my talent.

When it was decided to republish *Albert the Good*, I had not
read the book for many years and I did not realize that even its
title was 'dated'. When I did read it again, I realized that I
would have to face the task of rewriting it, adjusting decisions
and opinions to suit my own, older mind, and with the hope that
I might interest the younger generation in the story of a remarkable, essentially good, man.

Reading the early book and writing a new one from it has
been an absorbing task. I find that I admire the Prince Consort,
with my older and calmer judgment, even more than I did
when I wrote about him thirty-odd years ago. His few faults
were the natural fruit of his virtues. He was too pure in his intentions, and he was therefore easily denounced as dull. He set
an example that intimidated ordinary people, and he kept all
the Ten Commandments as the simple law of his life. The only
serious fault in his behaviour was in the treatment of his eldest
son, and this was based on a besetting fear. The Prince Consort, because of his aggressive virtue, was haunted by the examples of history; the gay immorality and irresponsibility of
the Hanoverians, and the untidy morals of his own father and
brother in Coburg. He was afraid that his eldest son would
ignore the example of his own parents and yield to the older
inheritance. This his son did, though the Prince Consort tried
in every way in his power to prevent it. It was a conflict between
his mind and his son's nature.

In his relationship with the Queen, herself a Hanoverian by
instinct, but ultimately quelled by her love for her husband into
comparative obedience, the Prince Consort was a patient, wise
saint. Love, in the terms that appealed to her, was alien to his

almost celibate nature. He was, in this relationship, as in all others, 'Albert the Good'.

Queen Victoria wrote to King Leopold of the Belgians, on 29 October, 1844, 'They say *no* Sovereign *was more* loved than I am,' and she explained this was because of their '*happy domestic home* – which gives such a good example.' Her husband was similarly pleased; he wrote in a letter to his old mentor, Baron Stockmar, 'Here, after four years, is the recognition of the position we took up from the first. You always said that if Monarchy was to rise in popularity, it could only be by the Sovereign leading an exemplary life, and keeping quite aloof from and above party.'

The Prince Consort was – strange among princes – both an intellectual and an artist. His mind governed almost every action of his life, from when, as a student in Bonn, he bought Dürer and Van Dyck drawings, to his seeking out musicians and painters almost immediately after his arrival in England; from his sober choice of young university friends who talked of philosophy and jurisprudence, also at Bonn, to his disregard of the English aristocracy and his relaxed delight in the company of scholars. It will be observed, all through his story, that he enjoyed the trust of the politicians so soon as they realized the honesty of his intentions, and that their often tortuous habits of thinking were simplified when they came to appreciate the clarity of his mind. Men as coldly cynical as Lord Palmerston acknowledged his talents in the end, and became fond of him. All that was second-rate wilted in his presence.

*

Perhaps the time may come when thoughtful men will appreciate more fully the Prince Consort's place in the long spaces of history. He was born into the age when monarchs still thought they possessed the 'divine right' to do as they pleased; when princes schemed for power and made wars to increase their territory and grandeur. He was not such a prince. He sincerely tried to create a bridge between the mystery of royal omnipotence and the people. That bridge was his own conception of duty, and it is largely because of him that there is still a bond between the Sovereign and her 'subjects'. No thinking man can deny that this exists, especially with some of the Commonwealth countries otherwise separated and independent of Britain. The bond depends upon an exchange of accepted customs, quiet reason and manners, which help to save a State from falling into anarchy.

The Prince Consort's most enduring realistic achievement, beyond this nourishing gift to the tradition of the monarchy, was the Great Exhibition of 1851. It was a symbol of his belief that war and national rivalry might be lessened by peaceful industry and pursuit of the arts. The good results of the Exhibition are still enjoyed in our own time. We may criticize the actual design of the Victorian museums, institutes and colleges that survive in South Kensington and which were built out of the profits made from the Crystal Palace. But the collections in the museums, and the scholarships awarded each year by the Commissioners, are a constant memorial to the Prince's beliefs and plans.

*

There was no considerable example in Britain's history for Prince Albert to follow when he agreed to marry Queen Victoria, except Queen Anne's stupid husband who had been made a peer and who was never an influence for good in either the Court or the country. Prince Albert had to accept his responsibilities without any official position to compensate him for his sacrifices. He complained, in the first year of his marriage, to his friend Prince Löwenstein, 'In my whole life I am very happy and contented; but the difficulty of filling my place with proper dignity is that I am only the husband and not the master in the house.' He was to become the master, but through conflicts that ultimately hastened his death. His story is certainly that of the triumph of character and virtue over every possible barrier. His victories were gained because the Queen was so deeply in love with him that she slowly submitted to his quiet will. She was heir, not only to the faults of the Georges, but also to their mental instability. When the Prince Consort died, and for some years later, she was afraid that she would go mad. She tapped her forehead and said, 'My reason! my reason!' She admitted her fear. This the Prince was able to watch and subdue during his life, and his long patience with his wife had a saintly touch.

It is interesting to observe that throughout the Prince Consort's years in England nobody who came to know him failed to admire him. Lady Augusta Bruce wrote of him, when the Duchess of Kent died, 'I never saw such tenderness – such gentleness, such tact as His – oh! He is one in millions – well might She love Him as She did. I was so struck with his appreciation of Her. It was so true, and for One who is supposed to place intellect and reasoning powers above all, so remarkable.' This was the opinion of princes, statesmen, and servants. Even the Emperor Napoleon iii, after walking with the Prince in the gardens at Osborne, wrote, 'One goes away from him . . . more disposed to do good.'

This is a theme that may be unattractive in the 1960's, but it is important in the broader spaces of human history, and it continues as an influence, and will be respected and acknowledged in time.

*

It is surprising, as one reads the Prince Consort's letters and speeches, to trace what might be called a 'left-wing' tendency in his thinking. He wrote of, and argued for, 'that class of our community which has most of the toil and least of the enjoyments of this world.' On 18 May, 1848, when he was chairman at the meeting of the Society for Improving the Condition of the Working Classes, he reprimanded the capitalists; he warned them to be careful 'to avoid any dictatorial interference with labour and employment'. He told them that it was only ignorance that prevented the two classes from having confidence in each other, and that 'any real improvement must be the result of the exertion of the working people themselves'.

As late as November 1857, Lord Carlingford wrote in his diary, 'Prince Albert thinks poorly of the English aristocracy as ignorant & bigoted; knows they don't like him; he likes the professional classes.' The Prince went beyond this and sought every opportunity to help the workers and the poor. He wrote of Negro emancipation and of regulating factory labour; he corrected the essays written by the young farm workers on the estate at Windsor. He was more like a squire than a prince in the relationship with his servants. One of the most sincere and confident friends among them was Cart, the valet he had brought from Coburg. When Cart died, the Prince Consort was in tears.

Baron Stockmar, who served princes most of his life, once said to Lord Granville, 'My dear Lord, have you yet to learn that in the case of Royalties, so soon as one is neither useful nor amusing, one's only course is to disappear?'

This was not true of Prince Albert's relationship with Stockmar, who had guided him from boyhood. He was always kind to his old mentor, for he denied the tradition that royalty can never afford the emotion of gratitude. The Prince wrote constantly to Stockmar to the end of his life, and he enjoyed the rare privilege of being a quiet hero to all who served him.

It is to be remembered that the name 'Albert the Good' was given to the Prince by the ballast heavers whom he helped when he was appointed Master of Trinity House. When he died, they wrote to the Queen, 'Before he came to our rescue we could only get work through a body of riverside publicans and middlemen, who made us drink before they would give us a job. . . The consequence was that we were in a pitiable state. . . We got no help until we sent our appeal to your late Royal Consort. . . He at once listened to us. . . At once our wrongs were redressed and the system that had ruined us swept away.'

We take such gestures for granted in the mid-twentieth century. The human quality that inspired the Prince must be compared, not with what has happened since, but with what went before. One hundred years ago, his action was rare and remarkable.

*

The time will come when historians will compare Prince Philip, Duke of Edinburgh, with the Prince Consort – his great-great-grandfather – for their tasks have much in common, and they are rare and similar figures in English history. The contrast in their circumstances is a key to the immense changes that have come to the functions of monarchy during a century. The Prince Consort was a melancholy introvert and a dilligent intellectual, but Prince Philip would not lay claim to any of these disadvantages or virtues. He is a cheerful extrovert and a conformist in all questions of learning and taste. But he shares with his ancestor a lively interest in science and its application to the life of the country, and in his care for the young and under-privileged.

On 9 September, 1859, the Prince Consort wrote to his brother, from Balmoral, '. . . I am going to Aberdeen, to preside at the meeting of the British Association for the Advancement of Science, where I am to give the opening speech. For weeks I have been trying to arrange something popular about science, which is not to be tedious. . .'

Prince Philip might have written the same letter when he was to give the presidential address to the same Association in 1951. He makes many statements that seem to echo the Prince Consort's thinking, such as, 'The only thing you can learn from another country is their techniques. You can't learn an attitude of mind from another country. After all, the difference between an Englishman and a Frenchman; the difference between a Frenchman and a German, is a difference of attitude of mind.'

Prince Albert was never rewarded with the honours and position accorded to Prince Philip. Although a Regency Bill was passed in his favour before Queen Victoria's first child was born, he had no recognized place in the Constitution. He was subjected to waves of suspicion, even of panic, and he had to wait seventeen years for the title of Prince Consort. Even then it was no more than a consolation prize, without real meaning. In contrast, Prince Philip is a Peer of Parliament; he is eligible to be a Councillor of State, and he has precedence over all the Queen's subjects, including the heir to the throne.

The Prince Consort never enjoyed such advantages, yet he served Britain and his Queen with wise patience, to the limit of his talents and his strength. But, as he confessed, he did 'not cling to life'; and the story of his willingness to die is the tragic end to a career of almost absolute unselfishness.

HECTOR BOLITHO

REFERENCES
I have tried wherever possible to weave sources and dates into the narrative, to avoid the endless footnotes that spoil the pleasure of the average reader who does not wish to dart back and forth from asterisks in the text to references at the foot of a page, or at the end of the book. The small number of notes I have made throughout the text refer to those sources that are new or unusual. The list of the principal books which I used during my research is given in the Bibliography on pages 237–239.

ACKNOWLEDGMENT
I wish to thank Professor Asa Briggs for reading the manuscript of this book and for his many wise suggestions which will, I hope, make it more acceptable to the younger generation.

H.B.

CHAPTER ONE

1817-1819

At the beginning of the nineteenth century, the plan to draw the small principalities of Germany into the Prussian net was a remote dream. Prince Bismarck, who was to realize this dream, was not yet born. The little states still kept their separate identities and were independent of the ambitious power in the north. Two of them were the neighbouring duchies of Coburg and Gotha. Their rulers were neither royal nor grand, and they lived mostly in quiet castles built on high hills.

Duke Francis of Saxe-Coburg, who died in 1806, was an amiable old libertine with seven children, the eldest of whom, Ernest, succeeded to the dukedom at the age of twenty-two. His neighbour, the Duke of Saxe-Gotha, was a kind but foolish man, with an only daughter, Louise.[1] It was natural, in the close pattern of their lives, that the two families should unite in marriage; and early in 1817 Princess Louise was betrothed to Duke Ernest of Saxe-Coburg. He was then thirty-three years old : she was only sixteen, and described as 'radiating gracefulness . . . bewitching her surroundings'.

On the day of Princess Louise's betrothal, her father gave a thousand loaves of bread to the poor and there was a great feast for the 'good-mannered of all ranks'. And on 31 July, when she was married to Duke Ernest, thirty-six cannon shots announced the glorious event to the town and countryside.

The bride and bridegroom drove from Gotha to Coburg, along a road that was decorated all the way. When they arrived in Coburg there was a concert at which the people sang, 'Hail Duke! Hail Duchess! Soon you will rock Princes in your lap.' This amused the sixteen year old bride: she wrote to Augusta von Studnitz, her dearest friend back in Gotha, 'Is that not funny? I had to think quickly of the Holy Trinity.'[2]

The most interesting member of the Coburg family who welcomed Louise was her mother-in-law, the Dowager Duchess. Many years later, Queen Victoria wrote of her as a 'remarkable woman, with a most powerful, energetic, almost masculine mind, accompanied with great tenderness of heart and extreme love for nature'.

This 'tenderness of heart' guided the Dowager Duchess in her judgment of the young bride: she wrote of Louise in her diary, 'She is a charming, tiny being, not beautiful, but very pretty, through grace and vivacity. Every feature of her face has expression; her big blue eyes often look sad from under her black lashes, and then again, she is a happy, wild child... I hope she will still grow, as she is very short... I had half the town to tea because everybody wished to congratulate me.'

Among the Coburg princesses who received the young Duchess were her husband's widowed sister, Princess Victoria of Leiningen, and her daughter Feodora, then ten years old. Louise thought the mother 'very beautiful . . . most charming and natural'. And the child was her 'whole joy'.

Almost ten months later, the widowed Princess was married again, in Coburg, to the Duke of Kent. And almost twenty-two years afterwards their daughter, Queen Victoria, married Prince Albert, the Duchess Louise's second son.

•

There were no more than sixty thousand people in the little duchy of Coburg. On the crest of the mountain that overlooked the town was the old castle with its lofty turrets and battlements, and within, the room in which Luther had translated the Psalms. The family no longer lived there: they divided their year between Schloss Ehrenburg in the town, and Rosenau, a pretty house four miles away in the country.

After the first celebrations of the wedding, Duchess Louise wrote to her friend in Gotha, 'Oh! it is too beautiful. It is like being in Paradise, and it is also not wanting in an Angel.' She mixed seriousness with girlish pleasure: on the fourth day, after she had been with her husband to the ducal chapel, she wrote, 'We had a bad sermon, which contained nothing but praises for my Prince, with no religious thought . . . such a thing is not suitable in church. Then there was a big dinner at which I appeared in a pink and silver-embroidered dress, with a train.'

In the evening they drove out to Rosenau, which was to be the setting for the few happy years of their story. On this first visit, Duchess Louise was entertained by dancers in Chinese costumes and nymphs who came out of grottoes, with poetic addresses to present to her. Later, when she walked down the stairs to the ballroom, there were beautiful children standing on pedestals, dressed as Gods of Love, scattering flowers as she passed.

Duchess Louise shared all her pleasures with Augusta von Studnitz, her friend in Gotha. She wrote, 'You will get a fright, precious Augusta, when you receive this letter. . . You will count the pages and cry out again, "The Gossip! Will she never hold her tongue?" I risk all this, and the thought gives me pleasure, to talk and joke with you, to tell you how happy and contented and joyous I am . . . if one loves an Angel, one's master and husband, one is much softer and more tender, more susceptible and warmer also for friendship.'

Even when she sat in the garden with her husband in the evening, holding his hand, the Duchess still yearned for her young friend. She said to Ernest, 'If only Augusta could enjoy this quiet and beautiful evening with me. With you, and her, it would be too lovely!'

The Duke calmed her, and Louise wrote later, 'He thinks you will surely come to me. Can I hope?'

She described Rosenau: the window panes all of coloured glass, decorated with coats of arms; her own sitting-room, with its beautiful bronze furniture; her bedroom, with mock poles and trellis-work on the walls, and convolvulus vines and flowers painted on them. Her boudoir was sky-blue, with silver stars. It was in this room – she confessed to Augusta – that she 'liked being and thinking of you'.

She wrote also, 'I always accompany my husband to the chase, which amuses me very much. Every afternoon I go with him to the forest, to hear the tender calling of the stags. They roar and bellow until their wives arrive; then they go away proudly. If another stag comes, they fight with each other until one dies or succumbs. The wife follows the conqueror, voluntarily. A very bad trait in our sex!'

•

There was one prince of the Coburg family, Leopold, who had not been contented with the small prizes offered him within the duchy. He was encouraged by the wise advice of Dr Christian Frederick Stockmar, son of a lawyer in Coburg, and together they satisfied their different ambitions. Prince Leopold wished to be a king and Stockmar enjoyed the quiet, watching part of being a king-maker.

Prince Leopold was almost twenty-seven years old when his brother, Duke Ernest, married Princess Louise. He was already the most famous member of his family: he had been an officer in the Russian army when he was eighteen; as a cavalry general he had distinguished himself in the battles of Lützen, Bautzen and Leipzig, and he had entered Paris with the Allied sovereigns. Then Prince Leopold came to London and met Princess Charlotte, only child of the Prince Regent and heiress to the throne. They were married in May 1816. On 6 November, 1817, the Princess died in childbirth, and when the news reached Coburg, the Dowager Duchess wrote in her diary, 'Charlotte is dead! Good God! I cannot realize the gigantic tragedy. I cannot bear it. Poor, poor Leopold! She is dead, the beautiful, charming good woman; the hope of the large population over which she would have ruled. Her death ruins the whole life happiness of Leopold.'

It might have seemed that the house of Coburg had lost all hope of success in England. But another royal marriage corrected this – the marriage of the Duke of Kent to the widowed Princess Victoria, sister-in-law of the Duchess Louise.

The Duke of Kent was the fourth son of King George III. He had served with the Royal Fusiliers in Gibraltar, where he fell in love with the wife of Baron de Fortisson; and when the Duke went with his regiment to Quebec, in 1791, he took the Baroness with him. Their relationship was so tolerated that, on 2 July, 1792, the Bishop did not object when they were chosen as godparents for the christening of the baby son of one of His Majesty's Justices of the Peace. (This is recorded on the certificate of baptism in the registers at Beauport, Canada.)

After Baron de Fortisson was killed while fighting at Fort Royal, in 1794, his widow and the Duke of Kent were secretly married; and they lived in harmony together, with their children, for almost twenty-four years, the Baroness using her maiden name of Madame de St Laurent.

The long story of their happiness ended in the expediency and ambition from which princes seldom escape. When Princess Charlotte died, in November 1817, the Duke of Kent decided to marry a suitable consort, as he now stood nearer to the throne. A month later, the Duke met Thomas Creevey in Brussels and laid down the terms upon which he would be willing to abandon his morganatic wife and marry in the hope of presenting an heir to the English crown.[3]

The story moves back to Coburg. In January 1818, the Dowager Duchess of Saxe-Coburg wrote, 'In a few moons perhaps, Victoria becomes the wife of a man she hardly knows. . . The English Minister, Mr Taylor . . . brings the glad news that the Regent and the Queen of England, as well as the people, desire the marriage of the Duke.' On 26 May she wrote, 'We had hardly sat down at table when his equerry arrived with the news that the Duke would follow in a few hours. . . We waited with strained curiosity, and poor Victoria with beating heart; she had only seen him once. The first moment, Kent was a little shy, however much he is a man of the world, to drop like a bomb into such a large family.' The Dowager Duchess thought his tall figure had 'something noble about it': the 'simple, blunt manner of the soldier combined with the delicate good-breeding' made his conversation 'very agreeable'.

Stockmar was more critical and less gracious. He thought the Duke's face 'betrayed calculation', but he yielded to the charm of the bride. He wrote of Princess Victoria as 'naturally truthful, affectionate and friendly, unselfish, full of sympathy and generous'.

On 29 May, 1818, they were married according to the Lutheran rites in the Giants Hall in Schloss Ehrenburg. The bride wore a fair dress, trimmed with white roses and orange blossom, and the bridegroom looked well in the uniform of an English Field-Marshal, with an 'incredible cocked hat'. They came to England for a second, Anglican ceremony, on 11 July, in the drawing-room of the palace at Kew. Then they returned to Europe; but in the following spring, when their baby was to be born, they hurried back to England – the Duke himself on the box of the carriage – so that the event – the realistic purpose of his marriage – might be realized in his native land.

The child, Princess Victoria, was born in Kensington Palace on 24 May, 1819, 'as plump as a partridge', with, as witnesses, the Archbishop of Canterbury, the Duke of Wellington, and Mr Canning.

*

During this changing pattern in the life of the royal family in England, there had also been changes in the lesser pattern in Coburg. On 21 December, 1817, the Duchess Louise had celebrated her seventeenth birthday. Her mother-in-law wrote, 'God grant that she may celebrate her eighteenth being just as happy and jolly. Her extreme youth and delicate body make me very afraid for her condition in the hour of becoming a mother. Oh, Charlotte's death makes me so despondent. I don't trust fortune, and the poor little thing seems to be only a lovely vision. So often the happy child, free from care, suddenly becomes so pensive and gloomy . . . there is such a thoughtful and sad look in her big eyes, as of an alarming threat.'

The 'thoughtful and sad look' was not imagined. Louise pleaded with Augusta von Studnitz, 'My longing for you is really great . . . come and stay with me for a few months . . . fly into the arms of your ever-loving and hopeful friend. . .' But Augusta did not come and Louise began to complain because Duke Ernest spent so many hours shooting woodcock, while she was left alone. There was a relief from her sadness on 21 June, 1818, when the Dowager Duchess wrote, 'God be praised and thanked. Louise has been successfully delivered of a healthy boy.' They named him Ernest, after his father.

The summer of 1818 passed happily, but there were signs that Duke Ernest was often weary of his wife's girlish enthusiasms, from which he escaped into his own selfish pleasures. His mother wrote, early in 1819, 'I only see Ernest in the evening at parties, and Louise is too young to be a companion to me. I often think of the dear past with painful sadness. . .'

The sad theme was interrupted again in August 1819, when the Duchess Louise drove out to Rosenau, where her second baby was to be born. On the 27th, her mother-in-law wrote to the Duchess of Kent, then living happily with her husband and daughter in London, 'I am sitting by my Louisechen's bed. She was yesterday morning safely and quickly delivered of a little boy. . . The quiet of this house, only interrupted by the murmuring of the water, is so agreeable.'[4]

As soon as she was well enough, the young Duchess wrote to Augusta von Studnitz, 'My affectionate thanks for your dear letter. . . You should see him: he is pretty as an angel; he has big blue eyes, a beautiful nose, quite a small mouth, and dimples in his cheeks. He is friendly and he smiles the whole time. . . Ernest wishes to give him the old Saxon name of Albert.'

CHAPTER TWO

1819-1831

For some months, the two families, in Coburg and in Kensington Palace, wrote only of their growing children and seldom of the possible perils and duties of the future. Prince Albert's grandmother described him as being 'quick as a weasel', with 'large blue eyes and limpid cheeks . . . very handsome, but too slight for a boy; lively, very funny, all good nature and full of mischief.' There was no hint, yet, of the solemnity of mind and habits that were to be the essence of his character; nor of his destiny, which the old Dowager Duchess prophesied innocently when she wrote 'The little fellow is the pendant to the pretty cousin.'

The 'pretty cousin' was taken by her parents to a damp, lonely house in Sidmouth, to escape what the Duke of Kent described as 'the months of the year that are so odious in London'. Their companions were John Conroy, one of the Duke's oldest friends, and Baroness Lehzen, who had been brought from Amorbach to superintend the education of Princess Feodora – the child of the Duchess's first marriage – and then of Princess Victoria. The Duke liked to walk along the promenade beside his daughter in her perambulator, and he would stop strangers and ask them to look at her asleep. He wrote, 'My little girl thrives under the influence of the Devonshire climate.'

The Duke was less fortunate in the bracing air of Sidmouth. One day, in January 1820, he returned from a walk with his boots soaking wet. He would not change them : he preferred, he said, to sit beside Princess Victoria and watch her smile. That night he complained of a chill, but he would not take the potion of calomel or the James's powder that were offered him. In the morning his chill was worse; and during the next four days the Duchess stayed beside his bed, wearing the same dress, placing leeches on his brow, and watching him anxiously. He died on 23 January, in a state of forgiveness and virtue. Of the Prince Regent, who had behaved abominably to him, he said, 'If I could now shake hands with him I should die in peace.' He turned to his wife, in the last moment, and said, 'Do not, do not forget me.'

If the Duchess of Kent had taken Princess Victoria back to Coburg, she might have lived in modest security; but she stayed in England, in circumstances of loneliness and penny-pinching that were a shame to both the royal family and the government. She had to depend on money allowed her by Prince Leopold,[1] and she inherited her husband's debts, which were not paid until seventeen years later, when her daughter came to the throne.

Six days after the Duke of Kent died at Sidmouth, King George III died at Windsor, and the Duchess and her daughter were left to the cold mercy of George IV. His wish, as Leopold reminded Queen Victoria twenty years later, was 'to get you and your Mama out of the country; and I must say, without my assistance, you could not have remained.'

The Duchess of Kent stayed in her rooms in Kensington Palace, with good intentions that were often misdirected because of her lack of authentic advisers and her persistent need of money. She relied on Prince Leopold's purse to bring up Princess Victoria, and she estranged herself from the royal family and almost everyone else who had the power and means to help her. She lived through bitter years, with her daughter sleeping in the little white bed next to her own, depending on the self-interested advice of John Conroy, who was too small in mental and ethical stature to be a good influence in training the heiress to the throne.

*

In Coburg, there were threats of a different kind of unhappiness. In July 1820, one of the ladies-in-waiting was guilty of what Duchess Louise described as a 'stupidity beyond all bounds'. She wrote to Augusta von Studnitz, 'You will laugh when you hear it, but it has made me cry. She accused me of loving Count Solms [the Court Chamberlain] and scolded him because he was in love with me. It made him die of laughter.'

The Duke was told and Louise wrote, 'If he had been sensible, he would have laughed also, but he took it seriously and was angry with me. We talked about it and it all ended in tears. . . Now he watches me, which he has never done before . . . and he misconstrues everything. . . How is it possible, dear Augusta, that people can thus have such fancies and make such thrusts?'

A court of princes and their entourage can often be a hive of selfish intrigue, jealousy and gossip that is beyond the comprehension of good and ordinary people living in a house. While the Duke, a middle-aged profligate, was hunting in the hills about Coburg and philandering in the town, young Louise, in spite of the innocent attractions of her two baby sons, let her heart wander. She had been married only five years when she was entranced by a good-looking, seventeen year old boy, Baron Stillfried, who lay at her feet, and climbed an apple tree to look in at her window. She confessed to Augusta, in a letter, 'He . . . did a thousand pretty, amorous things, that amused me very much.' There was also an Austrian cavalry officer who 'sighed and languished like a turtle dove'.

In March 1824, when Prince Albert was four and a half years old, Louise wrote to Augusta of another 'good-looking' young man, with 'black curly hair . . . shining bright eyes and a resolute manner'. He was Lieutenant Alexander von Haustein of the Coburg Battalion, whom she afterwards married.

*

Many biographers, during the past century, have claimed that Prince Albert was illegitimate because of the infidelity of his mother. In 1921, Herr Max W. L. Voss, author of *England als Erzieher*, wrote, 'Prince Albert of Coburg, the Prince Consort, is to be described without contradiction as a half Jew, so that, since his time, Jewish blood has been circulating in the veins of the English Royal Family. . .' Lytton Strachey, in his *Queen Victoria*, refers thus to the divorce of the Duchess Louise: 'There were scandals: one of the Court Chamberlain's, a charming and cultivated man, of Jewish extraction, was talked of.'

Even if Count Solms or Alexander von Haustein had been of Jewish extraction, the letters of Louise, the diaries of her mother-in-law and the divorce papers all prove that there was no hint of infidelity before Prince Albert was born.[2] He was already a growing boy when the short, unhappy marriage ended; when Lieutenant von Haustein's 'resolute manner' conquered Louise. She wrote to Augusta von Studnitz, 'Don't damn me completely, but go on loving me. I have sacrificed everything, but don't also let me lose your friendly heart.'

The Duke and Duchess parted: he went to his summer castle at Ketschendorf, and Louise to Rosenau, and the arrangements for the divorce[3] were left to Colonel Szymborski, an adjutant to the Duke, who 'had a thorough knowledge of the intrigues in the court'. He made the cold, formal arrangements, and Louise wrote, 'The Duke was friendly towards me; we came to an understanding and parted, in tears, for life.'

The citizens of Coburg then intervened with a strange demonstration. The Duchess wrote to Augusta, 'The people love me to a degree of worship. . . They . . . went in thousands to Rosenau. Everything there was peaceful and still. As I stepped into my carriage they burst through the hedges and railings, cut the ropes, harnessed themselves to the carriage, and pulled me from Rosenau, with unceasing shouts and hurrahs, through the town and stopped before the castle. . . The love was most touching, and they were all armed. When I arrived at the castle I went on the balcony and thanked them all for their love. After shouts and hurrahs, they solemnly sang "Now thank we all our God". It was touching to hear these thousands of voices. . .'

Many years later, a witness recalled the episodes in this public attempt at reconciliation.[4] He wrote, 'I was caught up with the procession . . . pushed through the crowds and grabbed at a rope. . . At last we reached the castle. The Duchess alighted, and soon after appeared on the balcony . . . she waved her white scarf. Her face was bathed in tears.'

Cries were heard 'all over the palace' – 'We wish to see them both together! Let us also fetch the Duke! They must be reconciled! We wish to have unity and peace again in the dynasty!'

The Duke was still in the country at Ketschendorf, with his mother and Princes Ernest and Albert. The 'deputation' from the townspeople went to him and at last he 'gave way'. 'He would not agree to have his carriage pulled, but drove himself, with the princes, back to the castle.'

Later in the evening, 'the wish of the populace was granted at last,' and the Duke and Duchess appeared together on the balcony. 'The hurrahs were repeated and, with growing confidence that everything was now going to be smoothed out and come right, the people dispersed and nothing else disturbed the quiet of the courtyard or the town.'

But the peace was brief, and the reconciliation failed. Days of tumult followed, during which the crowd tried to destroy Szymborski, crying 'Knock him down dead, this grinder of peasants.' He escaped, but his arrangements for the divorce succeeded. A few days later, Duchess Louise wrote to Augusta von Studnitz, 'I signed the deeds of separation. . . I often went for drives, being greeted with shouts and hurrahs. . . On 4 September, at the stroke of midnight, I left Coburg . . . and took the road for Brückenau. . . Leaving my children was the most painful moment of all. They have whooping-cough, and they said, "Mama cries because she has got to go, when we are so ill!" The poor little lambs, God bless them!'

Louise had to wait almost two years for her divorce. On 31 March, 1826, she married Alexander von Haustein and their attempt at happiness began. But she was haunted by all that she had rejected. She wrote to Stockmar, 'Speak sometimes with Prince Leopold about me. I would not like him to forget me completely.' And her stepmother wrote of her to Duke Ernest, 'The thought that the children have quite forgotten her, worries her deeply. She wishes to know if they talk about her. I told her that it was impossible for them to forget their mother, but that they were not told how much she suffered, as that would make them suffer too.'

In March 1831, five years after their marriage, Louise and Alexander von Haustein were in Paris. One evening they went to see Taglioni dancing at the Opera House and during the performance Louise was carried from the theatre, suffering from a haemorrhage. She died of uterine cancer, on 30 August – four months before her thirty-first birthday – so suddenly that she could not even say good-bye to her husband, who was in the next room.

CHAPTER THREE

1826-1836

In 1826, the character of the 'bright little girl of seven' in Kensington Palace was already clear. She recollected when she was older, 'I was naturally very passionate, but always most contrite afterwards.' Her sympathies and her will were as definite and strong as when she was an old, obdurate monarch, at the end of the century.

Princess Victoria treated servants and poor people with uncritical generosity; but she could be ruthless with anyone in authority who tried to thwart her. When she saw a tramp sheltering from the rain, outside the Palace, she said to the footman, 'Run to that poor man with an umbrella; he is very old and will catch cold.' But when her music master used the word 'must', she closed the lid of the piano, assured him there was no such word, and walked away.

The first episode led to her unreasonable indulgence with servants in her Court. They could do no wrong. Late in her reign, when the man who tended the lamps at Windsor was so drunk one evening that he fell, dropped a lighted lamp, and thus endangered the Castle, the Master of the Household sent the Queen a written report of the accident. She merely wrote 'Poor man' in the margin.[1] She recalled, in 1872, 'I was taught from the first to beg my maid's pardon for any naughtiness or rudeness towards her; a feeling that I have ever retained. . .'

The second incident, with the music teacher, revealed the stubborn self-will with which, in her seventy-first year, she accepted Gladstone's resignation, 'with a coldness that disturbed him', and then chose Lord Rosebery as Prime Minister, without consulting anyone. From her schoolroom to her death, her decisions, though sometimes unwise, were seldom hesitant or confused.

Although Queen Victoria recalled her childhood as having been 'melancholy', it did not appear so to strangers passing by. Charles Knight, in his *Passages of a Working Life*, wrote of a day in 1827 'when the sun was scarcely high enough to have dried up the dews of Kensington's green alleys'. He saw 'a group on the lawn before the Palace . . . a vision of exquisite loveliness. . . The Duchess of Kent and her daughter, whose years then numbered eight, are breakfasting in the open air, a single page attending them at a respectful distance. The màtron is looking on with eyes of love, while the fair, soft English face is bright with smiles. The world of fashion is not yet astir. . .'

This was an outsider's sentimental glance at a mother and child whose relationship was not all sunshine – indeed, seldom so. The Duchess still kept the Princess in seclusion, especially from the royal family. She still 'considered that the surroundings of a Court, and especially *such* a Court' as that of King George IV, 'were not the best possible atmosphere in which to bring up a child'.

Sometimes, the 'corpulent Adonis' tried to be an amiable uncle to his niece. There had been the day in 1823: Princess Victoria was only four years old when her mother took her to see him at Windsor – three years after his accession. The Princess had not liked kissing his painted cheek, but when he said, 'Give me your little paw,' she did so. He presented her with a miniature of himself, set in diamonds, and next day, when he met the Princess and her mother again, he stopped the carriage and said, 'Pop her in.' They drove to Virginia Water and fished from a barge, followed by a second barge carrying a band that trailed merry tunes over the lake, as they made their way through the extravagant setting of trees and temples and sham stone ruins. They had tea, with peaches, and still more entertainment when they returned to Royal Lodge. The day ended in an innocent victory for Princess Victoria. When her uncle asked what she would like the band to play, she said, 'God Save the King.'

There was no hint in these two scenes, before the Palace in Kensington, and at Windsor, of the 'melancholy' childhood which the Queen recalled and resented when she was older. The most dramatic reason for the way the Duchess kept her daughter always at her side was suggested many years later. It seems incredible to mid-twentieth century thinking that the mother had all her daughter's food tasted before it was served, because she was afraid of poison. She believed that the Duke of Cumberland had planned the death of Princes Charlotte, as she was the barrier to his succession to the throne.[2] The Duchess of Kent feared that the 'wicked uncle' would repeat his sin; that he was capable of any crime that would give him the crown.

Princess Victoria was, of course, unaware of these suspected perils; nor could she comprehend the unhappy pattern of intrigue in her mother's household. She had enjoyed the companionship of her half-sister; but Princess Feodora was twelve years older, and she soon escaped from her mother's ruthless supervision, to Germany, where she was married in 1828. There was also John Conroy's daughter, but over the friendship with her hovered the ogre of John Conroy himself. In his position as Comptroller to the Duchess, he began infections of discontent whenever he meddled in her affairs. Prince Albert wrote, many years later, 'Mama here would never have fallen into the hands of Conroy if Uncle Leopold had taken the trouble to guide her.' But Prince Leopold was still preoccupied with his own ambitions, and, for a few years, with his mistress, the actress Caroline Bauer, whom he had brought from her theatre in Potsdam to the genteel pattern of a house in Regent's Park. He had time only to call now and then at Kensington Palace, and the Duchess was too confused to heed his advice. Princess Victoria thought that she loved him : he was the remote substitute for a father, and she wrote, 'To hear dear Uncle Leopold speak on any subject is like reading a highly instructive book.' But Uncle Leopold was seldom near, and the Duchess of Kent was left to the devices of Conroy, while Princess Victoria trusted Baroness Lehzen more than her mother.

They were four strangely different characters, at conflict, in Kensington Palace: the Duchess, who annoyed her daughter by making her pin a sprig of holly to the neck of her dress, to force her to sit up straight at table; Conroy, who was always ambitious; and Baroness Lehzen, who was dedicated to her difficult task. The bewildered Princess recalled that she 'adored' the Baroness, but that she was 'greatly in awe of her also'.

Princess Victoria began to notice that when she was out walking, gentlemen raised their hats to her, and she asked why. Baroness Lehzen broke the secret and told her of her place in the succession.[3] The legend is that Princess Victoria answered, 'I will be good'; and more than half a century later she passed this version of the incident in the manuscript of Theodore Martin's biography of the Prince Consort. But many years afterwards, when one of her ladies asked if it was true, Queen Victoria answered, 'Of course not! How could I say such a thing!'[4]

*

On 26 June, 1830, when King George IV clasped his doctor's hand and said, 'My boy, this is death,' Princess Victoria was eleven years old and one step nearer to the throne.

There was no such ominous shadow over the schoolroom in the little court in Coburg. In 1823, when Prince Ernest was five years old and Prince Albert four, they had been taken from the nursery and given to the charge of Christoph Florschütz, a gifted, sensitive scholar who became Prince Albert's friend for life.[5] Florschütz afterwards recalled that although the princes went hand in hand in all things, there was a difference in their dispositions. Ernest was physically active and less imaginative than his younger brother, to whom he was obedient. The tutor wrote of Albert, 'Every grace had been showered by nature on this charming boy.' He was more fanciful than Ernest, sympathetic, unselfish, and inclined to sadness and self-analysis. Although he was 'rather delicate than robust', he was 'remarkable for his powers of perseverance and endurance. . . To do *something* was with him a necessity.'

In games with his brother, Albert's was the directing mind. Yet the diary which he began to keep when he was five-and-a-half years old reveals that he was nervous and prone to tears. On 23 January, 1825, he had written, 'When I woke this morning I was ill. My cough was worse. I was so frightened that I cried.' Three days later he cried again because he could not remember his lesson. One evening he wrote, 'After dinner we went with dear Papa to Ketschendorf. There I drank beer and had bread and butter and cheese' But most of the entries reveal his shyness, from which he never really escaped.

The neighbouring Duchy of Gotha was added to the estates and titles of the house of Saxe-Coburg in 1826; and in November, Duke Ernest rode into the town with his two sons. After this they went to Gotha for part of every year, to the castle where the unhappy Louise had spent her childhood. Their step-grand-mother still lived there, and she was a wise influence in the story of the young Princes. After they had been to stay with her one summer, she wrote to their father, 'I have gratified their ardent wish to have another goat, which has been sent today. I entreat that they may be allowed to keep them, all three. . . Albert wishes to drive the little goat. Happy children! How much are they to be envied for the power of being pleased with so little. . . Do not let them take much medicine nor hear much about their health; it only makes them nervous.'

When Prince Albert was older he rode his English pony into the Thuringian forest, among the larch and pine trees. He enjoyed the still, gold light, but it was as a dreamer and a student that he made these journeys. He said later, 'I don't understand people making a business of shooting, and going out for the whole day.' He preferred to make lists of his geological specimens, to dust them, and to reproach himself whenever he was idle.

Thirty-two years later Prince Albert's uncle, Count Mensdorff, recalled these years of the boy's life. He wrote, 'It was
only what he thought unjust or dishonest that could make him
angry. One day he was playing at the Rosenau with boys of his
own age. Some of them were to storm the old ruined tower on
the side of the castle, which the others were to defend. One of
the boys suggested that there was a place at the back by which
they could get in without being seen. . . But Albert declared that
this would be most unbecoming in a Saxon knight. . . So they
fought for the tower, honestly and vigorously. . .'

Count Mensdorff wrote also, 'Albert was never noisy or
wild. . . He had a natural talent for imitation and a great sense
of the ridiculous . . . but he was never silly or ill-natured. . .
From his earliest infancy he was distinguished for perfect moral
purity in word and in deed.'

Prince Albert's virtues were flowering too solemnly and too
soon. He was a stranger, within a family where his father was
repulsively dissolute, his mother sadly unfaithful and banished,
and his brother destined to be heir to all their follies.

*

Towards the end of 1831 the Dowager Duchess died, and her
lively, intelligent help was withdrawn from Albert's life. His
father's influence also weakened. In 1832 he married his second
wife, Princess Marie of Württemberg, but the union soon broke
under the shadows of spite and infidelity. Nor did the step-mother
bring any strength or happiness to the two young Princes. She
upbraided Prince Albert for his neglect: she wrote,[6] 'You think
of me no more; you do not love me properly; and you do not
consider my advice as being well-intentioned.' He pleaded, 'This
doubt of our enormous love for you, and our gratitude, down-
right affection and care, cannot do otherwise than disturb us. . .
I do not know how we can possibly have earned this.' Yet she
did not attend the Confirmation of the Princes, in 1835, with

the excuse that the season was 'inclement' for her to make the journey.

Prince Albert had to depend for real affection and guidance on his three foster parents – his tutor Florschütz, who loved and admired the boy; his uncle Leopold, who in June 1831 had become King of the Belgians; and the ever-wise Stockmar, now raised to the rank of Baron, who continued to encourage the greatness of others. Many of his contemporaries wrote of him as the 'dear Baron' – though Gladstone later described him as 'a mischievous old prig'. He wrote of himself, 'I seem to be here to care more for others than for myself, and am well content with this destiny.' An old friend completed the comments on Stockmar's character when he said, 'It is good that you are so often ill, or there would be no bearing your exuberant spirits.'

King Leopold, handsome, self-assured and talented, was closely and faithfully bound to Stockmar. Their friendship had been sealed in a promise made when Princess Charlotte died. Stockmar recalled Leopold 'kneeling by her bed': he 'kissed her cold hands, and then raising himself up, he pressed me to him and said, "I am now quite desolate. Promise me always to stay with me." '

These were the two men, with no doubt or jealousy in their relationship, who were designing Prince Albert's future. They were ambitious for him, but they were ambitious also for the power of the Coburgs – as they watched the declining influence of the Hanoverian kings, one following the other, on the English throne. To King Leopold and Stockmar, the reign of the aging King William IV was a golden opportunity for preparation, and they saw the way for Princess Victoria and Prince Albert as absolutely clear.

About this time, King Leopold wrote, 'Albert is a fine young fellow, well grown for his age, with agreeable and valuable qualities; and who, if things go well, may, in a few years, turn out a strong, handsome man, of a kindly, simple, yet dignified demeanour. Externally, therefore, he possesses all that pleases the sex, and at all times and in all countries must please. It may prove, too, a lucky circumstance, that even now he has something of an English look.'

King Leopold's next concern was Prince Albert's mind. He wrote, 'On this point, too, one hears much to his credit. . . He is said to be circumspect, discreet, and even now cautious. But all this is not enough. He ought to have not merely great ability, but a right ambition, and great force of will as well.' The King wrote also of the plan to marry Princess Victoria : 'If he does not, from the very outset, accept it as a vocation of grave responsibility, on the efficient fulfilment of which his honour and happiness depend, there is small likelihood of his succeeding.'

*

King Leopold was equally free with his advice to Princess Victoria. He thought many Englishmen were 'humbugs and deceivers', and he warned her against hypocrisy, 'a besetting sin at all times.' He urged her to 'self-examination . . . every evening to recapitulate the events of the day and the motives which made one act oneself, as well as to try to guess what might have been the motives of others.' And he warned her against selfishness and vanity : 'Nothing is so great and clear a proof of unfitness for great and noble occasions than a mind which is seriously occupied with trifles.'

This advice must have been merely confusing to Princess Victoria. In July 1833, Princess Lieven wrote to Lord Grey, 'The squabbles that have been going on in Kensington Palace do not surprise me. The cause is that German *morgue* and little-mindedness which is rampant in that quarter; those people are wrong-headed to the utmost degree, all of which, however, is a great pity, for, after all, the future of England is placed in their hands.'

In pursuing that future, the unfortunate Duchess of Kent made many mistakes, and she even planned – with Conroy's encouragement – that if King William died soon enough, she should be appointed Regent until Princess Victoria came of age. Greville wrote in his diary of the Duchess choosing to 'set herself in opposition to the King', and said that he 'would like to have to deal with her impertinence for a little while'.

The King dealt with the 'impertinence' himself – in August 1836, when his seventy-first birthday was celebrated with a dinner in Windsor Castle. The Duchess of Kent was sitting next to him when he made his speech, in which he said, 'I trust in God that my life may be spared for nine months longer, after which period, in the event of my death, no Regency would take place.' Then, pointing to Princess Victoria, he said, 'I should then have the satisfaction of leaving the royal authority to the personal exercise of that young Lady, the Heiress presumptive of the Crown, and not in the hands of a person now near me, who is surrounded by evil advisers and who is herself incompetent to act with propriety in the station in which she would be placed.' He added that he would insist on Princess Victoria being more at Court in future.

The Princess burst into tears and her mother 'sate in silence'. When the dinner was over the Duchess ordered her carriage and 'was with difficulty prevailed upon to remain at Windsor for the night'. The Duke of Wellington's comment on the episode was brief and perfect: he said, 'Very awkward, by God!'

It was in this world of untidy manners and animosity that Princess Victoria had to form her own ideas and judgments; and to realize that she would need a refreshed and modified conception of royal behaviour to meet the tasks ahead of her. For both Prince Albert and herself, in their separate worlds, it must have already been obvious that their own principles and laws of conduct would not come through inheritance or family example, but from within themselves. There were signs that these principles were already being nourished. Florschütz recalled that Prince Albert had 'a real and living faith, giving colour to his whole life', and that religion was 'engraved in his very nature'. The Princess he was to marry was similarly righteous in all her intentions. She had revealed this after she was confirmed, when she wrote in her journal, 'I felt deeply repentant for all that I had done which was wrong and trusted in God Almighty to strengthen my heart and mind; and to forsake all that is bad and follow all that is virtuous and right.'

CHAPTER FOUR

1836-1837

Early in 1836, when Prince Albert was sixteen-and-a-half years old, he went to stay with King Leopold in Brussels. His horizon was spreading beyond the dark forests of Thuringia, with the example at hand of what his uncle had achieved; of what the Belgians were beginning to enjoy under his liberal rule. The next step was to send Prince Albert to England, so that he might meet the Princess he was to marry.

King William IV had other plans and he had already brought foreign princes to England, to meet his niece. When he learned that Prince Albert, his father, and his brother Ernest, were all coming to England to meet Princess Victoria, he was angry. He said that the Saxe-Coburgs should not be permitted to set foot in the country, and as a gesture of defiance he invited the Prince of Orange and his two sons and Duke William of Brunswick to be his guests at the same time, so that the Princess might have the opportunity of meeting all the young men together. But King William was only impetuous and his designs for his niece were frustrated by her Uncle Leopold, who held the advantage in that he had planned everything during years of watching. He wrote to Princess Victoria on 13 May, reminding her that slavery had been abolished in the British colonies, so why, therefore, should the King keep her, 'a white little slavey, for the pleasures of the Court', when he had never 'spent a sixpence' on bringing her up?

The Princes arrived, in spite of the King's ill-temper, in June

1836. Princess Victoria thought her cousins were the 'most delightful young people'. She wrote that they were 'very amiable, very kind and good, and extremely merry, just as young people should be'. But she added that they were also 'extremely sensible and very fond of occupation'.

Princess Victoria and Prince Albert sat on a sofa in Kensington Palace and turned over the pages of a book of drawings; they danced and walked together, and they played the piano. The Princess made the important decision that Albert was 'extremely handsome', and added that Ernest was 'certainly not'. She sent King Leopold a letter that must have satisfied his patient ambition. She wrote, 'Allow me then, my dearest Uncle, to tell you how delighted I am with him and how much I like him in every way. He possesses every quality that could be desired to make me perfectly happy.'

Prince Albert was less spontaneous. He yawned when he had to stay up until two o'clock in the morning, listening to a concert. He wrote to his step-mother, 'You can well imagine that I had many hard battles to fight against sleepiness during these late entertainments.' On the last morning, when the Princes departed, Princess Victoria 'cried bitterly, very bitterly'; and she wrote to King Leopold, 'I have now only to beg you, my dearest Uncle, to take care of the health of one now so dear to me and to take him under your special protection. I hope and trust that all will go on prosperously and well on this subject now of so much importance to me.'

Prince Albert returned to his studies. He wrote that the Channel crossing had given him 'a disgust of the sea', and that he had found Princess Victoria 'very amiable'.

*

For ten months after their visit to England, Prince Albert and his brother lived with their uncle in Brussels, and devoted most of their time to learning. Prince Albert wrote to his step-mother, 'The masters selected for us are said to be excellent, so that everything is favourable to our studies, and I trust there will be no lack of application on our part. . . After all our fatigues and amusements we are now settled in our new home. . .' Sometimes he left his books to shoot sea-gulls or to watch field days with King Leopold's army. But he seemed to resent all diversions: when his father summoned him to Coburg for Christmas, he answered, 'I am afraid we must deny ourselves that pleasure. Such an expedition would require five or six weeks and our course of study would be quite disturbed by such an interruption.'

While the Princes were at their desks, King Leopold crossed to England to instruct his niece. It was certain that King William IV would not live very long; every idea that Princess Victoria absorbed was therefore doubly important. She wrote in her journal that her uncle Leopold was 'so good, so dear, so distinguished', and she listened to his theories on the art of government, his laws for the behaviour of a good wife and mother, and his ideas on science and art. Then her uncle went back to Brussels, to watch over his nephews and to wait for King William's death and his niece's accession.

There was one terrible disruption before the King died. The Lord Chamberlain arrived at Kensington Palace with a letter; the Duchess of Kent held out her hand to take it, but the Lord Chamberlain had been ordered to give it only to the Princess. It was King William's final gesture: he offered his niece £10,000 a year, to be spent as she chose. He died before the gift could be made, but he had estranged mother and daughter more than ever. The Princess was further strengthened in her independence by a letter from her uncle in Brussels, who told her to be 'courageous and firm', and by the presence of Stockmar. 'You now have the Baron at your elbow,' wrote King Leopold; '*Speak sometimes with him* . . . my object is that you should be no one's tool. Keep your mind *cool* and *easy*; be not alarmed at the prospect of becoming, perhaps sooner than you expected, Queen.'

In a letter written on 17 June, 1837, King Leopold advised the

Princess 'on the subject' of what was to be done 'when the King ceases to live'. He wrote, 'The moment you get the official communication of it, you will entrust Lord Melbourne with the office of returning the present Administration as your Ministers. You will do this in that honest and kind way which is quite your own, and say some kind things on the subject.' He added that as her immediate successor was the Duke of Cumberland, this would frighten the Ministers 'into the most violent attachment' to her. Three days later, on 20 June, King William IV died, mumbling, 'The Church, the Church.' Victoria was Queen.

*

Prince Albert was at Bonn University when news came of the death of King William IV. He wrote to his cousin, 'Now you are Queen of the mightiest land of Europe. In your hands lies the happiness of millions. . . I hope that your reign may be long, happy and glorious. . . May I pray to you to think likewise sometimes of your cousins in Bonn and to continue to them that kindness you favoured them with till now. Be assured that our minds are always with you. I will not be indiscreet and abuse your time. Believe me always, Your Majesty's most obedient and faithful servant, Albert.'

From this restrained comment on an event that was to influence all the rest of his life, Prince Albert turned to his studies, and simple pleasures, in the beautiful little university town on the Rhine. The choice of Bonn was interesting. After the Congress of Vienna, King Leopold had written of the Prussians as 'that godless crew'. The prejudice was remembered in choosing a university for the Princes: Stockmar had dismissed the suggestion of sending them to Berlin because its influence would be 'formal and priggish'. Prince Albert might already have seemed to be 'formal and priggish', and when he walked with his friend Prince William of Löwenstein, 'juridical principles or philosophical doctrines were thoroughly discussed'. But after the lectures he mimicked the professors, for the delight of the other students. Also, his interest in art began. He had already collected some early German wood carvings, in Coburg. From Bonn, he drove to Cologne and bought a Dürer drawing, and one of a negro's head by Van Dyck. He sketched pleasant landscapes, played the organ and composed careful music. He fenced and practised the use of the broadsword, and he went for long walks, followed by his two fine greyhounds. One of them, Eos, he cared for so much that he afterwards brought her to England.

Florschütz was still with the two Princes, guiding them into seriousness that was natural to Albert, but tiresome to Ernest, who was pleased to escape on a walking tour with his brother in the autumn of 1837. They went to Switzerland and Northern Italy, and enjoyed the last holiday they were were to share. Prince Ernest was to drill himself, as best he could, to become Duke of Saxe-Coburg-Gotha. Prince Albert was soon to emerge into a bigger and more dangerous world. He paused one day and sent Queen Victoria a scrap of Voltaire's writing and an alpine rose.

Prince Albert loved his brother, beyond all moral criticism and in spite of the differences in their character, which were to increase as they became older.[1] Next year, when they were to travel apart, for the first time, Prince Albert wrote to Prince William of Löwenstein, 'Ernest is now going to Dresden in order to . . . throw himself entirely into a military existence. . . The separation will be frightfully painful to us. Up to this moment we have never, so long as we can recollect, been a single day away from each other! I cannot bear to think of that moment!'

CHAPTER FIVE

1837-1839

Queen Victoria's behaviour on the day of her accession was almost ruthless. At last she was free of her mother's rule and she used the word 'alone' in her journal as if it were a declaration of independence. She had been called at six o'clock in the morning to receive the Archbishop of Canterbury and Lord Conyngham, after their hurried drive from the death chamber at Windsor. The young Queen wrote afterwards, 'I got out of bed and went into my sitting-room (only in my dressing-gown) and *alone*, and saw them.'

The Queen ate her breakfast with Baron Stockmar, alone. (She had already written to her uncle Leopold that the Baron possessed her '*most entire* confidence'.) Later in the morning she received Lord Melbourne, her Prime Minister, as she wrote, 'Of course *quite alone*.' The emphatic underlining and double underlining, that was to add force to her letters, for more than sixty years, had begun.

When the Queen held her first Council, she faced her Ministers *alone*. She then received four Ministers of State, each *alone*. In the evening she dined *alone*, although her mother was still in Kensington Palace; and that night, for the first time in her life, she slept in her own bedroom.

There was personal humbleness mixed in with this proud, royal certainty. The Queen wrote in her journal, 'I shall do my utmost to fulfil my duty towards my country. I am very young and perhaps in many though not in all things, inexperienced,

but I am sure that very few have more real good will and more
real desire to do what is fit and right than I have.'

Her courage was surprising: she kept her 'dearly beloved,
angelic Lehzen' near, but she soon banished John Conroy, with
a baronetcy and a pension as consolation prizes. The Queen said
to Lord Melbourne, 'How is it possible that I can have any confidence in my mother when I know that whatever I say to her is
repeated immediately to that man?'

A month after her accession, the Queen moved to Buckingham Palace, where she gave her mother a suite of rooms – far
away from her own. It was Baroness Lehzen who was nearest;
and Stockmar, accepted by Lord Melbourne as 'one of the
cleverest fellows' he had ever seen; a 'most discreet man, the
most well-judging, and most cool man'.

The gap between the Queen and her mother widened, and for
some years the Duchess had to ask for an audience with her
daughter when she wished to see her, as formally as any minister. The exiled widow, who had fought for her rights with such
misdirected will, became silent and sad. She fell asleep over her
playing cards in the evening, and had to refresh her memory
with smelling salts when she played duets with her lady-in-
waiting.[1]

Queen Victoria knew immediately whom to love and trust
among the strangers coming into her life, and the first of these
was Lord Melbourne. Fate made its first, wise gesture to the inexperienced monarch in bringing him, then a man of fifty-eight
and at the height of his intellectual powers, to advise and encourage her. He was brilliant, and all that he did was laced with
integrity. After his first audience, on the morning of her accession, the Queen wrote, 'I like him very much, and feel confidence in him. He is very straightforward, honest, clever, and a
good man.' She wrote later, 'There are not many like him in this
world of deceit... He is my friend and I know it.'

The wise Duke of Wellington was also 'very dear and nice'
to the young Queen. When Lord Melbourne asked if there was
anyone she 'preferred to be associated with in the care of the

sovereignty', she answered, 'There is one individual for whom I entertain a decided preference, and that individual is the Duke of Wellington.'

*

Queen Victoria came to the throne against a background of political anxieties she could not yet comprehend. The country was disturbed, and journalists wrote of the 'appalling state of commercial distress'. One figure from the statistics of the year reveals the frame of mind in which England was governed and led at the beginning of the reign. In the entire country, only twenty thousand pounds of public money was spent on education. There had been a promising light in 1832, when the first Reform Bill was passed, but its benefits were to come very slowly; and trade and industry, already the roots of England's being, were still barely represented in Parliament.

The Second British Empire, which was to be the foundation of Queen Victoria's fame and popularity at the end of the century, was remote from her mind and unimportant to the mass of her people. Those who thought at all remembered what happened to the American colonies, and they did not wish to repeat such an experiment. The first of the many campaigns during her reign, which were to force the immense pattern of her empire into being, was fought and won in the year of her accession – when the French settlers revolted in Lower Canada. Australia was still, in most English minds, 'a criminal colony'; and the Union Jack had not yet been hoisted in New Zealand. Cape Colony was little more than a trophy won from the Dutch; and India was still governed by the East India Company. Some of the countries that were to form Queen Victoria's empire had not even been discovered in 1837. The only valuable island fortress in her realm, when she was crowned, was Gibraltar, where her father had been governor, thirty-five years before.

Many of the lands to be conquered in the nineteenth century – and, mostly, to be abandoned in the twentieth century – were mere names on the map to the Queen. She had been taught to consider Britain as an island drawn inevitably into the pattern of wars and politics in Europe; and she was quite unaware, when she went to stay in Windsor Castle in the summer of 1837, that she would reign over her country during the greatest age of its growth and power.

*

Queen Victoria soon learned that freedom also brought independence. While she was at Windsor, enjoying 'the pleasantest summer' she had 'ever passed' in her life, King Leopold came to stay. Lord Melbourne was also there, and the Queen wrote, 'The sound observations they make and the impartial advice they give me would make a most interesting book.' When her uncle returned to Brussels she wrote, 'How I shall miss your conversation!' But a second thought began to form: there was a point where advice became interference, so she wrote to him, at the end of the year, 'You must not, dear Uncle, think that it is from want of interest that I, in general, abstain from touching upon these matters in my letter to you; but I am fearful, if I were to do so, to change our present delightful and familiar correspondence into a formal and stiff discussion upon political matters, which would not be agreeable to either of us and which I should deeply regret.'

On 28 June, 1838, Queen Victoria was crowned. She had been worried lest the people in the streets might be 'crushed or squeezed' as her coach drove to and from Westminster Abbey; but the day passed without mishap and her 'subjects', released from the unpredictable behaviour of the Hanoverian kings, cheered her as a symbol of escape, youth and refreshment. Within the Abbey, she glanced at Baroness Lehzen, not her mother, for a smile of encouragement; and she was pleased afterwards to remember the 'fatherly' look from Lord Melbourne as the crown was placed on her young head. When they met again in Buckingham Palace after the long day of ceremony, there were tears in Lord Melbourne's eyes as he said, 'And you did it beautifully – every part of it, with so much taste, it's a thing you can't give a person advice upon; it must be left to a person.'

Prince Albert was still at Bonn University at the time of Queen Victoria's coronation, and he described his thoughts in a letter to Florschütz. He wrote, 'From all one hears . . . it must have been a sight never seen before. She was the only person not in the least tired by the ceremony.' Then, on the prospect of his marriage, 'Papa had a little conversation himself with Victoria in which she told him, with some slight embarrassment, "*Mes sentiments sont toujours les mêmes; mais çela ne se pourra que dans deux ou trois ans.*" This last sentence was, I think, quite superfluous. There is great danger in the long delay, but the Baroness relieved Papa's anxiety by saying that she thought V. regarded herself as fully pledged.'

Prince Albert confessed his depression over his future: he wrote, 'I am to go into society, learn the ways of the world and vitiate my culture with fashionable accomplishments, the last of which would appear to be an extraordinary good testimonial in V's eyes. And I will do it. . . I shall suffer sometimes when I look at myself in private; but I hope it will be only a veneer which will not corrode the kernel.'

At the end of this letter to Florschütz, the Prince wrote, 'V. is said to be incredibly stubborn, and her extreme obstinacy to be constantly at war with her good-nature; she delights in Court ceremonies, etiquette and trivial formalities. These are gloomy prospects, but they would not be so bad if there were not such a long interval for them to harden, so that it will become impossible to modify them. She is said not to take the slightest pleasure in nature and to enjoy sitting up at night and sleeping late into the day. Now Uncle Leopold is going to England. I hope much from his presence. Although he is said to be no longer in high favour, his mere appearance will restore him to it.'

Prince Albert's possible task of having to adapt his serious habits to Queen Victoria's love of pleasure would not be easy. She was enjoying her freedom with the delight of a debutante.

On her nineteenth birthday she had danced until four o'clock in the morning; and she wrote, 'How different to last year! Everybody was so kind and so friendly to me.' She revelled in the 'vortex of society', which Prince Albert shunned.

Queen Victoria had become afraid that her independence would be lost in marriage: the sentimental scenes with Prince Albert two years before, and her tears when he left Kensington Palace, were forgotten. Before her accession they had exchanged many affectionate letters, but her doubts since her coronation were so disturbing that she had not written to him again. She explained this in a letter to King Leopold, on 15 July, 1839, 'Though all the reports of Albert are most favourable and though I have little doubt I shall like him, still one can never answer beforehand for *feelings*, and I may not have the *feeling* for him which is requisite to ensure happiness. I *may* like him as a friend, and as a *cousin*, and as a *brother*, but not *more*; and should this be the case (which is unlikely) I am *very* anxious that it should be understood that I am *not* guilty of any breach of promise, for I never gave any.'

*

While the Queen was clinging to her freedom, perhaps through fear as much as pleasure, Prince Albert was travelling in Italy again; this time with the ubiquitous Baron Stockmar and an English officer, Sir Francis Seymour, a subaltern in the 19th Regiment with whom he was immediately friendly. There was one foolish episode, in Rome, described by the Prince in a letter to Florschütz that proves he was not without a sense of humour, as is so often supposed. He wrote, after their visit to Pope Gregory XVI, in March 1839, 'He received me very kindly and I kissed his hand. I was bidden to sit down by him and we conversed for more than half an hour on Etruscan art. . . Herr Plattner flung himself on his knees to kiss the Pope's foot. He had already brought his lips within reach of the shoe when the Pope took a step backwards and turned round to pull the bell for the door to be opened for us. Thereupon P. lost his balance and fell on his face. Nevertheless he crawled after His Holiness on his stomach and grasped his raised foot. The Pope, a very stout, heavy man whom one foot only could not support, began to stagger and made violent efforts to free himself, which made him kick Plattner's mouth, outstretched to kiss, ten times at least. Seymour was on the point of bursting out laughing at this extremely comic scene when Herr von Stockmar pushed him out through the door. Herr P. was much moved by the Pope's graciousness!'

It seemed that the Prince was trying to change his habits to suit his future. From Florence, he had written to Prince William of Löwenstein, '. . . I am often quite intoxicated with delight when I come out of one of the galleries.' Then, of the very different picture of the 'whirl of society', he wrote, 'I have danced, dined, supped, paid compliments, have been introduced to people, and had people introduced to me. . . You know my *passion* for such things, and must therefore admire my strength of character, that I have never excused myself – never returned home till five in the morning – that I have emptied the carnival cup to the dregs.'

The Prince wrote also of the more serious prospect of marriage; that he was willing to submit to 'delay', but that 'if after waiting, perhaps for three years . . . the Queen no longer desired the marriage', it would place him 'in a ridiculous position' and would, to a certain extent, 'ruin' all his 'prospects for the future'.

Baron Stockmar watched Prince Albert, day by day, during these months of pleasure and conflict. The Prince wrote that the 'society of a man so highly distinguished . . . was most precious and valuable'. Stockmar wrote of his pupil, recalling first the Duchess Louise, who had died eight years before. He thought Prince Albert bore 'a striking resemblance' to his mother : the likeness, in Stockmar's opinion, was 'both physical and mental'. In the Prince he saw 'the same nobility and readiness of mind, the same intelligence, the same over-ruling desire and talent for appearing kind and amiable to others.' But he also thought Prince Albert had become lazy, and he regretted his recent tendency to spare himself. He complained because his pupil showed not the slightest interest in politics or women; and he wrote, 'On the whole, he will always have more success with men than with women, in whose society he shows too little *empressement*, and is too indifferent and retiring.'

The Baron would also never comprehend the strange love that Prince Albert kept for his brother, and the reassurance he enjoyed from their letters. When Prince Albert returned to Coburg, he walked along the road between Rosenau castle and the town; he climbed the lonely hills, and watched the changing colours in the fields. He wrote to his brother in Dresden, 'You cannot imagine how empty it seems to me since you left.' Then, 'This is the first separation; it will not be the last. But I console myself with the old saying, "There must be a valley between two hills." ' Then the practical advice, 'Do take care of your health'; and then the sentimental suggestion that they should bind their letters into books, at the end of each year.[2]

CHAPTER SIX

1839-1840

When Queen Victoria corrected and added to the manuscript of Theodore Martin's biography of the Prince Consort, published in the late 1870's, she passed the reference to the 'dazzling and continuous excitement' of her early years, admitting that they were 'detrimental to all natural feelings and affections'; and that 'those who had her welfare most at heart were anxious to secure for her, without longer delay, a husband's guidance and support'.

There had developed in the young Queen 'a great repugnance to change', but the need for guidance and support became obvious early in 1839, when the Lady Flora Hastings scandal antagonized the aristocracy and diminished the cheers of the people.

Lady Flora, a sister of the Tory Marquess of Hastings, and a lady of the bedchamber to the Duchess of Kent, returned from a holiday and complained of feeling ill. She went to the Court physician, Sir James Clark, who suspected from her 'appearance' that she might be pregnant. She became the subject of such unhappy rumours in the Court that Lord Melbourne induced the Queen to approve of a further medical examination. Lady Flora's innocence was proved, but the flame of gossip spread so far that her family demanded reparation. The Queen then made the first grave error of her reign: she apologized privately to Lady Flora, but she refused to censure Sir James Clark and allowed him to continue in office. Greville wrote, on 2 March, 'It is inconceivable how Melbourne can have permitted this disgraceful and mischievous scandal, which cannot fail to lower the character of the Court in the eyes of the world.' The attitude of the Tory aristocracy was expressed by the Duchess of Montrose, who hissed the Queen in the enclosure at Ascot races. The attitude of the London crowd was expressed when Lady Flora Hastings died, less than five months after the second examination – of a malignant tumour which Sir James Clark had failed to diagnose. Stones were thrown at the royal carriage that was sent to accompany the funeral procession on its way from Buckingham Palace.

The scandal was proof enough – though not to the Queen herself – that she needed the affection and advice of someone nearer than Lord Melbourne and Baron Stockmar. The need was emphasized in May 1839, when the Whig government gained such a small majority on the Jamaica Constitution Bill that they were obliged to resign. Queen Victoria was miserable at the prospect of accepting that 'cold, odd man', Sir Robert Peel, and his Tory colleagues, in place of the daughter and father relationship she had enjoyed with Lord Melbourne. Her reaction was entirely selfish : she was not yet twenty-one years old, and her kingdom and the world beyond were still a remote myth to her; she could think only of her own comfort at Windsor and within Buckingham Palace.

For her the issue was simple : she liked the Whigs, led by Lord Melbourne, because she knew them; and she disliked the Tories because they were strangers to her. (She was a girl of only sixteen during Sir Robert Peel's first ministry, from November 1834 to April 1835; and she had been brought up to mistrust all that his party stood for.) Lord Melbourne was kind, but also clever with his advice; he suggested that the Queen might be allowed to keep the ladies-in-waiting appointed during his ministry. When the Queen demanded this concession from Sir Robert Peel, he protested. Her letter to Lord Melbourne describing the scene was unconstitutional, and it revealed the dangers of her will. She wrote on 9 May that Sir Robert had 'behaved very ill'. He had 'insisted on my giving up my Ladies, to which I replied that I never would consent, and I never saw a man so frightened'. Then, 'I was calm but very decided, and I think you would have been pleased to see my composure and great firmness; the Queen of England will not submit to such trickery.' She added, 'Keep yourself in readiness, for you may soon be wanted.'

Her stubbornness led to a dangerous victory: when Sir Robert Peel came to see her again, he said he regretted that unless she accepted his choice of at least some of her ladies, he could not form a government. So Lord Melbourne remained in power, and, with the illusion that she could impose her will on all circumstances, the Queen enjoyed her selfish achievement.

*

The prospect of matrimony became strangely frightening to Queen Victoria. She told Lord Melbourne that she 'had no great wish to see Albert', as the whole subject of marriage was 'odious'. Prince Albert had become equally cold upon the matter; but he set out for England once more, with his brother, on the mission that King Leopold had forced upon him. He wrote later, on 6 December, to his friend Prince Löwenstein, that he had gone to Windsor 'with the quiet but firm resolution to declare, on my part, that I also, tired of the delay, withdrew entirely from the affair.'

King Leopold took the precaution of arming Prince Albert with a letter for the Queen, in which he described her cousins as 'good and honest creatures', deserving of her 'kindness'. He wrote, 'I recommend them to your *bienveillance*.'

On 10 October, 1839, the Princes drove into the upper quadrangle of Windsor Castle; and when Prince Albert looked up, he saw Queen Victoria waiting for them at the top of the stairs. They were unable to dine with her that evening as their correct clothes had gone astray during the journey, so they ate in another room and went into the drawing-room after dinner. The first self-conscious moments passed with the help of Lord Mel-

bourne, who gallantly leaned forward and told the Queen that
he was struck with the likeness between herself and the Prince.
When she retired she wrote in her journal, 'It was with some
emotion that I beheld Albert, who is beautiful.'

During the days that followed, they rode together through
the glades of Windsor Forest. On 11 October, the Queen wrote,
'Albert is, in fact, so fascinating and looks so handsome; he has
such beautiful blue eyes. . . His figure is fine, broad at the
shoulders and slender at the waist.' Then, 'I have to keep a tight
hold on my heart.' On the 12th she wrote to King Leopold,
'Albert's *beauty* is *most striking*, and he is so amiable and un-
affected – in short, very *fascinating*; he is excessively admired
here.' Next day she described him in her journal as 'dearest
Albert'; and on the 15th, she sent for him. At half-past twelve
o'clock he went to her room and they were alone. Prince Albert
described the scene in a letter to Florschütz: 'I was summoned
to a private audience at which, in the kindest and most gracious
manner, she confessed her love and her resolve to share her life
with me. . . The only people who know at present are Lord
Melbourne and Mme Lehzen. My Aunt as yet knows nothing
and is not to be told until a few days before we leave.'

King Leopold was also told: the Queen wrote to him on 29
October, 'Oh! dear Uncle, I *do* feel so happy! I do so adore
Albert! He is quite an angel, and so very, very kind to me, and
seems so fond of me, which touches me very much. . . I cannot
bear to part from him, for we spend such happy, delightful
hours together.'

Prince Albert wrote to Florschütz more quietly, 'Victoria is
so good and kind to me that I am often at a loss to believe that
such affection should be shown to me. . . I have attained the
height of my desire. . . Alas, my days in my beloved home are
numbered.' His letter to his step-grandmother in Gotha was
more revealing: he wrote, 'My future position will have its
dark sides and the sky will not always be blue and unclouded.
Oh, the future! Does it not bring with it the moment when I
shall have to take leave of my dear, dear home, and of you?' In

a later letter to Prince Löwenstein he confessed, 'My future lot is high and brilliant, but also plentifully strewn with thorns.'

For King Leopold and Stockmar, almost twenty years of ambitious planning were bringing their good reward. The Baron sent Prince Albert one more realistic letter of advice, to which he replied, writing of 'nobility', 'resolution' and 'courage', and admitting, 'In regulating my actions, good advice is the one thing needful; and that you can give me better than anyone, if you will only make up your mind to sacrifice your time to me, at least for the first year of my being here.'

In the letter to Prince Löwenstein, which was written after he left Windsor, the Prince added, 'While I shall be untiring in my efforts and labours for the country to which I shall in future belong . . . I shall never cease to be a true German; a true Coburg and Gotha man.'

*

On 23 November, 1839, with a miniature of Prince Albert set in a bracelet upon her arm, the Queen faced eighty-three members of the Privy Council at Buckingham Palace and told them of her betrothal. She wrote that she felt her 'hands shake', but she 'did not make one mistake'. When she left Buckingham Palace to return to Windsor Castle, there was the kind of celebration which is the habit of the twentieth century, but which was a surprise on the winter day in 1839 – a London crowd outside the Palace, cheering the monarch as she drove through the gates. Queen Victoria was described as 'radiant and bowing'. It might have seemed that her future was to be safe and beautiful, but there were still many doubts and political menaces to delay her happiness.

Prince Albert's position was unique, with no precedent to help in deciding the rank he should enjoy. There was only the example of Queen Anne's husband, whom Queen Victoria described as 'very stupid and insignificant'. He had been made a peer. But Prince Albert would not accept such a humble prize, especially because he would then have to give up his privileges in Coburg, where, if his brother died without legitimate children, the ducal rights would come to him.

The next doubt came after the Queen had announced her betrothal at the opening of Parliament, on 16 January, 1840. The Tories, who were soon to come into power, pointed out that the word 'Protestant' had not been used in describing Prince Albert. Was he a Catholic? His uncle Leopold, while still accepting his allowance from the English government, had become one as the first King of the Belgians. The Queen wrote to the Prince, 'A few stupid people here try to say you are a Catholic; but nobody will believe it.' She asked him for a short history of the Coburgs, which he sent, proving that there had not been 'a single Catholic Princess' married into the family 'since the appearance of Luther'. The Queen was able to assure the anxious that the Prince was 'particularly Protestant' in his beliefs and opinions.

There was also the humiliation Prince Albert had to endure over his yearly allowance, which, under pressure from the Tories, was finally reduced from the proposed fifty to thirty thousand pounds. Greville wrote of 'the mortification of the Prince', and that there was 'something mean and sordid in squabbling for all they could get'.

To the Queen, the Whigs could do no evil while her 'kind Lord Melbourne' was at the head of them; and the Tories could do no good. She wrote, with simple but dangerous prejudice, 'Do what one will, nothing will please these Tories.' Like her forbears, and unlike the monarchs who were to follow her, political bias was part of her inheritance. She had no example of neutrality between the crown and politicians, such as is expected from royalty in the mid-twentieth century.

The strong political prejudice of the time was to influence also the choice of Prince Albert's secretary – George Anson, a devoted Whig, who was already Lord Melbourne's secretary. The Prince complained in a letter to the Queen, 'Think of my position, dear Victoria, I am leaving my home with all its old associations, all my bosom friends, and going to a country in which everything is new and strange to me. . . And it is not even to be conceded to me that the two or three friends, who are to have the charge of my private affairs, shall be persons who already command my confidence?'

His protest was ignored. George Anson was appointed to the important and personal office, with only the one concession that he would not continue to work for Lord Melbourne.

Her youth is the only excuse for the Queen's show of ruthless independence. Because the once-loved Duke of Wellington had opposed the amount first suggested for the Prince's allowance, she had to be 'induced to invite him to her wedding'. The Queen was reported to have said, 'I won't have that old rebel!'

Nor was King Leopold spared. When he sent the Queen some advice that she thought ungracious, she wrote to Prince Albert, 'Dear Uncle is given to believe that he must rule the roost everywhere.' Reports of such conflicts must have made Prince Albert realize that his path was already 'plentifully strewn with thorns'; but he wrote to the Queen, 'All I have to say is that while I possess your love, they cannot make me unhappy.'

The Duchess of Kent was almost forgotten during these storms – except by Prince Albert. He had always been fond of his 'Dear Aunt Kent', in spite of her liking for gossip. He wrote to her of his 'dread of being unequal' to the future tasks, and of the 'multitude of emotions' that beset him. He sent her a ring she had given him long ago. 'It has your name upon it,' he wrote; 'but that name is Victoria's too.' She replied with a pathetic letter, trying to draw herself back into the picture with her description of the Queen, sitting in her room, 'silent and sad', thinking of the Prince.

The words 'silent and sad' were not true. Queen Victoria continued her war against all interference and advice. She even answered Lord Melbourne, when he suggested that it would be improper for her to invite Prince Albert to stay with her before the wedding, that he was talking 'foolish nonsense'. She wrote in her journal that she had said to him, 'laughing', that she would show how she 'could sometimes' have her own way, though she was 'so seldom allowed to have it'. Lord Melbourne laughed also. Greville wrote, on 27 November, 'If she has already shaken off her dependence on Melbourne, and begins to fly with her own wings, what will she not do when she is older, and has to deal with Ministers whom she does not care for, or whom she dislikes?'

Prince Albert again became the victim of her will, after he had written suggesting that, when they were married, they might enjoy a quiet honeymoon at Windsor. The Queen answered, on 31 January, 1840, 'I am the Sovereign,' and she reminded him that she was 'never easy a moment' if she was not 'on the spot'. Everybody, including her aunts, who were 'very knowing in all these things', agreed that she should 'come out after the second day'. Then the intimidating sentence, 'This is also my wish in every way.'

The struggle, between her love of independence and her love of the Prince, was to continue into their marriage for some time, before the Queen recognized and accepted the guidance of his superior mind.

Prince Albert turned to Coburg and his own people for solace. They celebrated his betrothal with balls, trumpets and wine. During one banquet, the Duke rose and cried, 'God Save the Queen,' and the Coburg Artillery fired a salute outside. The Prince looked up and saw the muslin curtains billowing into the room. One of them was caught on a bracket of candles and it burst into flames. The fire rose to the ceiling and the festivities had to be abandoned until the blaze was subdued.

After such public occasions, the Prince returned to read the depressing letters from the Queen. She wrote that her 'good old' Prime Minister would dine with them three or four times a week; almost always on Sundays. She reminded him that the Court was still in mourning for King William iv, and that it would not be 'reckoned right' for her to give 'dinners on Sunday', so they would eat with Lord Melbourne alone.

The Prince once allowed ten days to pass without writing to the Queen, and she confessed to King Leopold that she was 'quite miserable'. When he did write, he told her, 'How often my thoughts are with you. . . I cannot even yet clearly picture to myself that I am to be indeed so happy as to be always near you; always your protector.'

King Leopold was still alarmed when the Princes paused to stay with him in Brussels, on their way to England for the wedding. He sent a letter to the Queen, ahead of them, to warn her that Prince Albert was 'much irritated' by what had happened about his annuity. The King wrote, on 4 February, 'He does not care about the money, but he is much shocked and exasperated by the disrespect of the thing.' He warned her that the Prince was 'pretty full of grievances', and he explained, 'Albert is quick, not obstinate in conversation, and open to conviction if good arguments are brought forward. When he thinks himself right he only wishes to have it *proved* that he *misunderstands* the case, to give it up without ill-humour. He is not inclined to be sulky, but I think that he may be rendered a little melancholy if he thinks himself unfairly or unjustly treated.'

The young Queen received a last letter of advice from her uncle: he recalled Princess Charlotte and the rule of his brief married life with her – 'never to permit *one single day* to pass over *ein Miszverständnis*, however trifling it might be.' He advised his niece to do the same, and added, 'Albert is gentle and open to reason.'

*

Queen Victoria and Prince Albert were married on the morning of 10 February, 1840. She wrote him a note, which she folded in *billet* form, that ended, 'Send one word when you, my most dear beloved bridegroom, will be ready.' She signed it, 'Thy ever-faithful Victoria R.'

On this morning of his marriage, Prince Albert wrote to his step-grandmother in Gotha, 'In less than three hours I shall be standing in front of the altar with my dear bride. In that solemn moment I must once again ask your blessing, which I am well assured I shall receive, and which shall be my protection and my joy. . .' With a touch of anxiety, he added, 'May God help me !'

The day was grey with rain, but the people surged outside Buckingham Palace, climbed the trees and covered the fences, to see the processions. First came Prince Albert, dressed as a British Field-Marshal, with his father and his brother. They were heralded with trumpets as they drove to St James's Palace. The Queen followed, wearing a vast white dress, with a train that was carried by twelve ladies as she stepped from her carriage and entered the chapel. *The Times* reporter wrote, 'Ladies more beautiful never graced palace, ball or country green.' At the close of the service Queen Victoria stepped away from Prince Albert, to kiss the Queen Dowager; then they drove back to Buckingham Palace. There was one cheer on the way louder than for them, and this was for the Duke of Wellington.

Later in the afternoon the bride and bridegroom drove to Windsor Castle. Greville described this beginning of their brief honeymoon sadly. He wrote that they travelled 'in a very poor and shabby style': instead of 'the new chariot in which most married people are accustomed to dash along', they were 'in one of the old travelling coaches, the postillions in undress liveries...'

The Times reporter was waiting near the Castle to describe the scene. The rain had fallen in torrents early in the day, and the ancient walls and the town looked dull and miserable; but later in the afternoon 'the sun shot forth its beams, and the bells, as if awakened from slumber, burst out in joyous chimes.' It was already dark when the old travelling coach arrived in the town, and by then the walls of the houses 'glowed with crowns, stars, and all the brilliant devices which gas and oil could supply.'

At eight o'clock Queen Victoria and her husband drove into the upper quadrangle of the Castle; into the shelter of almost eight centuries of English history, to which, in time, they were to make their own, separate and new contribution. Within the Castle and the quiet of her room, the Queen wrote in her journal, 'I and Albert, alone.'

CHAPTER SEVEN

1840

Queen Victoria and Prince Albert were up and walking about early in the morning after their wedding. The Queen wrote to King Leopold that she was 'the happiest, happiest being that ever existed'. Of her husband she wrote, 'He is an angel, and his kindness and affection for me is really touching. To look in those dear eyes, and that dear sunny face, is enough to make me adore him.' Then, 'I was a good deal tired last night, but am quite well again to-day, and happy.'

There is no record of Prince Albert's emotions during the first day of the honeymoon. He was able to walk through the rooms of the Castle, with their untidy, precious trophies of many centuries. In the library were folios of hundreds of Leonardo da Vinci and Holbein drawings; in the cupboards were thousands of documents, uncatalogued and unidentified. Here was an opportunity for his scholarship and his tidy mind that was to occupy him in the years that followed. He walked in the park and gardens, which were shabby from neglect. Here also was opportunity. But, while he observed this first pattern of tasks awaiting him, the politicians in Westminster were still arguing over his precedence and his right to become a Privy Councillor. Among those who watched him at Windsor was the Duchess of Bedford. She thought that he was 'not being happy', and later told Greville that the Queen was 'excessively in love' with the Prince, 'but he not a bit with her'.

The Prince denied this in his first letter to Florschütz, a week after the wedding. He wrote, 'I could wish for no happier family life than has been granted me. The unpleasant incidents in Parliament before our arrival, of which you will have read, will have made you very angry on my account. But the people themselves are doing everything to show their sympathy in the Queen's domestic happiness and their approval of her choice . . . the change in my life is very great, but I am beginning to adapt myself to it.'

The Queen was not shy about her first pleasures in marriage. On the third night of her honeymoon she collected a party in the Castle, some from London, for dancing. Greville wrote of this as 'more strange than delicate'. Her 'best friends' thought that she should continue 'for a short space in that retirement, which modesty and native delicacy generally prescribe.'

Queen Victoria was Hanoverian enough not to be prudish, in the English sense of the word. Being happily married, she wished everyone to know it. The entries in her journal, describing her delight in her first marital relationship, were so frank that after she died, more than sixty years later, her youngest daughter, Princess Beatrice, destroyed the honest pages.[1] But there was one later, revealing passage that described the independence of her mind, in spite of the obedience of her heart. She wrote, 'I thought it was ten to one that I should agree with nobody.' She admitted that before her marriage she had enjoyed her 'own way'; and she had confessed her fear of Prince Albert, ' . . . suppose he should endeavour to thwart me, and oppose me in what I like, what a dreadful thing it would be.'

From such independence the Queen turned quickly to sentiment. When Prince Ernest was to return to Coburg, she found Prince Albert 'pale as a sheet', and she wrote, 'Oh, how did I feel for my dearest, precious husband, at this moment. . . All has he left, all, all for me. . . What is in my power to make him happy, I will do.'

But these were spontaneous words for an occasion, and she soon forgot them as she returned to her tasks as monarch. At first Prince Albert was never in the room when she met her

Ministers, and all that he did at her desk was to hold the blotting-paper. Stockmar had returned to Germany, and the Prince was alone with strangers. He told Lord Melbourne that the Queen would not let him see any official documents, or discuss affairs of state with him. When Lord Melbourne talked of this to the Queen, she explained that the neglect was only because of her 'indolence'. But she did nothing to correct it. George Anson, the Prince's secretary and already his trusted friend, wrote a memorandum on 25 May in which he recorded that Lord Melbourne had urged the Queen to take the Prince into her confidence; but that the Prime Minister's 'private opinion was that the Queen feared that her domestic harmony might be disturbed if Albert differed from her opinion on public matters'. About the same time, the Prince wrote to his friend Löwenstein, 'In my whole life I am very happy and contented; but the difficulty of filling my place with proper dignity is that I am only the husband and not the master in the house.' Many weeks and many conflicts were to pass before Prince Albert wrote to his brother, on 22 August, that King Leopold agreed everything in the Court was 'going on so much better' since the marriage, and that 'Victoria' had 'changed much to her advantage'.

*

The domestic strains and trivial political squabbles continued, though neither the Queen's journal nor Prince Albert's letters suggest that they yet comprehended the wider problems of Britain and the world. There were arguments when the Queen wished the Prince's name to be introduced into the Liturgy, and complaints from the Duke of Sussex because the banners of the Knights of the Garter in St George's Chapel had been moved, to make room for Prince Albert's. There was no hint yet of the sense of public responsibility that was to become the enduring inspiration of the reign.

One glances aside from the small jealousies, at the state of the country. Harvests had been bad since 1836 and trade was in the

doldrums. There was talk of revolution in many parts of Britain.
The Duke of Wellington said that even in war he had never seen
a town subjected to such violence as Birmingham, in 1839. In
Ireland, crime was raging : in 1838 there had been two hundred
and seventy-seven committals for murder in eleven Irish coun-
ties, but only three convictions. There was still revolt from the
French colonists in Canada, and possible threat of war with the
United States of America. In the East, British ships were being
held up by the Chinese, who went on with piracy and destruc-
tion of cargoes so ruthlessly that the government was forced to
retaliate with a series of actions that were to lead to the treaty
of Nanking, in 1842.

Such tragedies and alarms were still remote from the Queen
and the Prince. In the early summer they toured England. They
went to Epsom on Derby Day, and, for the first time, the sovereign mingled with the crowds between the races. They visited
the English aristocracy in their country mansions, and were
received graciously, but coldly. Prince Albert was thought to be
too German and too punctilious in his manner. This view of
him never wholly changed among the secure, deep-rooted English upper class. Some years later the Queen and the Prince
stayed with Lord Leigh. His daughter, afterwards Lady Jersey,
recalled, 'The Queen was more than gracious and at once won
the hearts of the children, but we did not equally appreciate the
Prince. . . Assuredly he was excellent, but he was very stiff and
reserved.'²

The Queen and the Prince were to become popular, slowly,
but with the mass of people rather than with the aristocracy. The
popularity began with the first of many attempts at assassination.
On 12 June, 1840, Prince Albert wrote to his brother,

> You will not yet know that you very nearly lost your brother
> and sister. I will hurry to tell you what happened.
>   The day before yesterday, Wednesday, we drove as usual at 6
> o'clock in our small carriage, with four horses and two postillions.
> I sat to the right, Victoria to the left. We had hardly gone one
> hundred and fifty paces from Buckingham Palace . . . when I saw

a small, disagreeable looking man, leaning against the railing of Green Park, only six paces from us, holding something towards us. Before I could see what it was, a shot cracked and it was so dreadfully loud that we were both quite stunned. Victoria, who had been looking to the left, towards a rider, did not know the cause of the noise. My first thought was that, in her present state, the fright might harm her. I put both arms around her and asked her how she felt, but she only laughed. Then I turned around to look at the man (the horses were frightened and the carriage stopped). The man stood there, in a theatrical position, a pistol in each hand. It seemed ridiculous. Suddenly he stooped, put a pistol on his arm, aimed at us and fired; the bullet must have gone over our heads, judging by the hole made where it hit the garden wall. Now the many onlookers came forward. They had been almost petrified before, and cried, 'Kill him, kill him.' I called out to the postillion to drive on.

We went to see our Aunt [the Duchess of Kent] and then we drove through the parks, where we were most enthusiastically greeted by the people. All the rest you will find in the newspapers. . .

During the days that followed, the Queen and the Prince were applauded whenever they drove from the Palace; and when they went to the opera, 'the whole house rose and cheered, waved hats and handkerchiefs'. The Queen recorded this in her journal, and added, '. . . Albert was called for separately and much cheered.'

*

In July 1840 there was another sign that the prejudice against Prince Albert might fade. On the 17th he wrote to his brother, 'Yesterday a Bill of especial importance for me was brought into the House and accepted without any debate after many intrigues had been tried against it. This is the Regency Bill. In case of Victoria's death and her successor being under eighteen years of age, I am to be Regent – *alone* – Regent, without a Council. You will understand the importance of this matter and that it gives my position here in the country a fresh significance.' He added, 'Victoria is most satisfied with this arrangement.' Lord Melbourne was also delighted, and he told the Queen that the Bill was passed entirely because of the Prince's character. 'Three months ago,' he said, 'they would not have done it for him.'

As the pattern of his responsibilities increased, Prince Albert slowly learned how to influence the Queen's mind and to lessen her political prejudices. He had revealed his own mind as early as 15 April, 1840, when he wrote in a memorandum, 'I do not think it is necessary to belong to any party. Composed as party is here of two extremes, both must be wrong. The exercise of an unbiased judgement may form a better and wiser creed by extracting the good from each. . . My endeavour will be to form my opinions quite apart from politics and party, and I believe such an attempt may succeed.' Thus, two months after his marriage, at the age of only twenty, he defined the duty of the monarchy and the changing significance of the crown.

*

The Prince was already blessed with patience, and he was free of rancour. When the Duke of Wellington came to dine, there was no recollection of his part in cutting down the amount of the annuity. Prince Albert treated the great man with such warmth that the Duke told Greville afterwards he 'never saw better manners, or anybody more generally attentive'. Greville added in his diary, 'There is something like sunshine in the Palace now.'

The only important enemy of this sunshine was Baroness Lehzen, the companion, but also the power, in Queen Victoria's childhood, and now a dangerous rival for Prince Albert's confidence. When Theodore Martin wrote his biography of the Prince, Queen Victoria allowed him to say that Baroness Lehzen was 'very probably blinded . . . to the obvious truths, that her former influence must, in the natural course of things, give way before that of a husband, especially of a husband so able and so deeply loved. . .' Prince Albert was obliged, through necessity, to encourage her eclipse.

The first important victory over Baroness Lehzen came in August 1840. Prince Albert wrote to his brother, 'On the 12th Parliament will be closed. In spite of Lehzen and the Master of the Horse, I shall drive *with* Victoria in a carriage to the House, and sit beside her, on a throne especially built for me.'

This was not his only achievement in clearing the Court of selfish influences. The Prince was able to 'boast' that he had 'driven' the Lord Chamberlain and other officials out of their rooms and back into St James's Palace, where they could not interfere so much with the Queen's personal affairs.

One more barrier, most important of all, was broken down six months after the marriage. The Queen yielded at last to the advice of King Leopold and Lord Melbourne: she allowed the Prince to read the Foreign Office dispatches and to be present when she received her Ministers.

Later in the year Prince Albert wrote an undated letter to his brother, describing the bonds of matrimony. 'The heavier and tighter they are, the better for you. A married couple must be chained to one another, be inseparable, and they must live only for one another. I wish you could be here and see in us a couple united in love and unanimity. Now Victoria is also ready to give up something for my sake; I everything for her sake. Become as happy as we are; more I cannot wish for you.'

This comment on marriage was Prince Albert's attempt to guide his brother in his own search for a wife. He added, 'For me, here, it will not be favourable if you marry a Catholic. But I shall not make my happiness a consideration, when your happiness is concerned.'

*

Queen Victoria, in the first year of her reign, had celebrated her freedom by enjoying London – Buckingham Palace, and all the pleasures it brought her. One of Prince Albert's next victories was to teach her to enjoy escape into the history and quiet of Windsor Castle. The archives fascinated him and, with the help of librarians and a bookbinder, he began to tidy the tremendous store of papers. He ordered the planting of trees, he became interested in the farms, and he supervised the stables. He wrote to his brother, 'I feel as if in Paradise in this fine fresh air.' At his heels walked Eos, the greyhound he had brought from his student days in Bonn. He complained, 'The late hours are what I find most difficult to bear'; but, slowly, he taught the Queen to share his own pattern of pleasure. The long nights of dancing until dawn came to Buckingham Palace, were forgotten: within a year the Queen wrote in her journal, 'Since the blessed hour of my marriage, and still more since the summer, I dislike and am unhappy to leave the country.' She confessed that the 'thick, heavy atmosphere' of London now depressed her.

After his day of tasks was over, Prince Albert often played the organ. One evening, some time later, Lady Lyttelton listened to 'dear Prince Albert playing . . . and with such master skill.' Later, at dinner, she spoke to him of her pleasure, and he said, 'Oh, my organ, a new possession of mine. I am so fond of the organ! It is the first of instruments; the only instrument for expressing one's feelings.'

'How strange he is!' Lady Lyttelton wrote. 'He must have been playing just while the Queen was finishing her toilette, and then he went to cut jokes, and eat dinner, and nobody but the organ knows what is in him, except indeed, by the look of his eyes sometimes.'

The Prince's inward resources were revealed more deeply at Easter, when he took the Sacrament at Windsor, with the Queen beside him, for the first time. He asked that they should dine alone the night before, and that they should observe all the discipline associated with the religious act.

The strength of his Christian feelings was revealed again later in the year, when a member of the Court proposed to the Prince that a sentence should be added to the Liturgy: a prayer for the Queen's first baby, soon to be born. Prince Albert answered, 'No, no; you already have one in the Litany – "All women that be with child". You pray already five times for the Queen.' The courtier asked, 'Can we pray, sir, too much for Her Majesty?' and the Prince answered, 'Not too heartily, but too often.'

In November 1840 the Queen and the Prince were back in Buckingham Palace. On the 21st, the Duchess of Kent wrote to her nephew, Prince Ernest, 'Our good angel Albert remains at the side of his beloved.' Later the same afternoon, she continued, 'A daughter was born at two o'clock. Mother and child are as well as they can be, God be praised!'

Prince Albert wrote a postscript, telling his brother that Queen Victoria was 'well and happy'. He added, 'Albert, father of a daughter! You will laugh at me!'

CHAPTER EIGHT

1840-1843

In his preface to *The Coburgs*, Edmund B. d'Auvergne wrote that they had 'made monarchy respectable'; that before their time 'the King's trade seemed fit only for gilded libertines and gloomy tyrants'. He claims, 'Leopold of Belgium and Albert of England changed all that. They introduced middle-class standards into the Palace. They were excellent husbands and fathers, and showed the bourgeois that a king could be a respectable married man as well as he.'

The Duke of Wellington told Greville, in September 1841, that it was the 'Prince who insisted on spotless character (the Queen not caring a straw about it)', and that he was 'extremely straight-laced and a great stickler for morality, whereas she was rather the other way'. This was true at the beginning; but after the troubles of the first two years of the Queen's marriage were solved, she learned, slowly, to make concessions to her husband's principles. Their domestic example suited the changing pattern of English life – the rise of the middle classes, who approved when they learned that Prince Albert had given up playing chess on Sundays, because it offended the Sabbatarians.

Such genteel behaviour pleased the mass of people, but it offended many of the aristocracy. They missed the gaming tables and the surfeit of wine when they were invited to the Palace; and they were annoyed by the Queen's insistence that the gentlemen should join the ladies at the end of dinner, after only five minutes over their port and their stories.

The rooms in the Pavilion at Brighton,[1] where King George
IV had caroused with his mistresses, were deserted and left to
the dust sheets. When the Queen and Prince Albert agreed to go
there for the first time, with their daughter, the Regency ghosts
must have been alarmed. In the music room, where 'Prinny'
had sung *Glorious Apollo*, fired with his air-gun and stumbled
against a table when he was tipsy, Queen Victoria sang an air
from an opera by Costa. She sat to Sir David Wilkie for her
portrait, and to Pistrucci for her head to be sculpted for the new
coinage. But she disliked Brighton, because there was no
privacy; because, as she wrote, 'the people are very indiscreet
and troublesome'. Like the Prince she preferred the glades and
seclusion of Windsor.

In his study in the Castle, overlooking Spenser's 'Sweet
Thames' flowing softly in the valley below, Prince Albert wrote
to his brother, who was soon to be married. His letters were
heavy with advice and with descriptions of his own ideas and
tasks. After his first daughter was born, he wrote, 'You can
imagine that I have my hands very full, as I also look after V's
political affairs. I should have preferred a boy, yet as it is, I thank
Heaven.'

Soon after his marriage, Prince Albert had taken a course in
the Laws and Constitution of England, from a scholar who
arrived at Windsor Castle each day, like a tutor. When the
Prince had mastered the subject he induced the Queen to read
Hallam's *Constitutional History of England* with him, in the
evenings.

Thus the Queen and the Prince prepared their minds for the
turn in politics that came in May 1841, when Lord Melbourne's
government was defeated on the Budget. The elections that followed gave the Tories a majority of ninety-one; and in September Sir Robert Peel became Prime Minister, with Lord Aberdeen
as Foreign Secretary and the Duke of Wellington as leader in
the House of Lords.

At first the Queen forgot the lessons she had learned from
Hallam during the quiet evenings at Windsor, and she resented

the idea of receiving that 'bad man' who had made her so un-happy in May 1839. Lord Melbourne's conduct was beautifully above party politics, and he sent Peel advice as to how he could break down the Queen's stubbornness. She was 'not conceited', he told his successor. 'She is aware there are many things she cannot understand and she likes to have them explained to her elementally, not at length or in detail, but shortly and clearly.' Lord Melbourne then assured the Queen that he had the 'highest opinion' of Prince Albert's 'judgement, temper and discretion', and that, in retiring, he found 'a great consolation and security in the reflection' that he left her with the 'inestimable advantage of such advice and assistance' as her husband was able to give her. During his last audience as Prime Minister, he reminded her, 'You said when you were going to be married that he was perfection, which I thought a little exaggerated then, but really I think now that it is in some degree realized.'

*

In this first political crisis since her marriage, the Queen ad-mitted and finally appreciated her husband's guidance. She wrote to King Leopold, 'Albert is indeed a great comfort to me. He takes the greatest possible interest in what goes on, feeling with me and for me, and yet abstaining as he ought from bias-sing me either way . . . his judgement is, as you say, good and calm.' This judgment, and Lord Melbourne's advice, helped Queen Victoria to meet Sir Robert Peel without apparent ran-cour, and she admitted that the first audience had 'gone off well'. Manners and reason governed all concerned in the com-plicated changes of government. Peel had told Anson that he would make any personal sacrifice 'except that of his honour', and that he would 'waive every pretension to office' rather than bring any 'personal humiliation to the Queen'. Stockmar said that Peel had shown a 'fairness and delicacy, an uprightness, conscientiousness and circumspection, such as are not likely to be met with again in similar circumstances.'

Under the rules of political change, the pattern of the Court also changed. Lord Melbourne no longer came to dinner three nights a week, and, slowly, the Queen's young resentment of anything to do with the Tories began to disappear. The most interesting relationship was between her husband and the new Prime Minister. Peel, who had been among those who fought against the Prince's annuity, was 'not a little touched', now that he was in office, to find that no 'shade of personal soreness could be traced' in the Prince's attitude towards him. Prince Albert soon came to appreciate the 'stately and upright commoner', who was the chief sponsor of great changes in English government; and in return, Peel appreciated the Prince's character, so that they soon reached a state of mutual frankness and trust. The Prime Minister described the Prince to Lord Kingsdown as one 'of the most extraordinary young men' he had ever met.

*

During this second year of his marriage, Prince Albert had two burdens that were personal, and separate from his success. The first was the conduct of his brother, which he would never improve; and the second was the chicanery of Baroness Lehzen, whose removal had now become necessary for the peace of the Court.

Prince Ernest had inherited all his father's vices, and he was being punished, physically, for his philandering. On 18 April, 1841, Prince Albert wrote, '. . . for a man of honour there is only the bird's-eye view, standing firmly above the low actions of the world. . . It is right that you drink Marienbad water, but keep quiet while doing so. That is the evil of your sufferings. They seem to be totally cured; you feel quite well, and suddenly they appear again. Should it happen after your marriage, I should consider it the total ruin of your health, honour, moral and home happiness. Therefore, for God's sake, do not play with your health.'

The Prince added that he still kept all his brother's letters and 'put them in a book, with a lock'; but the boyhood sharing of summer days at Rosenau was becoming a sad memory. When he wrote to his brother again, on 29 July, he recalled a scene during Prince Ernest's previous visit to England, when Queen Victoria had been 'frightened' by his behaviour. As she was soon to give birth to her second child, Prince Albert did not wish his brother to come again. He wrote, 'Your presence would not be desired.' He repeated this in his next letter, on 1 August, following the elections and the prospect of Melbourne's fall from power. 'I must say,' he wrote, 'that nothing would be more disagreeable at present than your visit, or *any visit* . . . at *present* we do not wish you to visit us.'

From this unhappy cleavage with his brother, Prince Albert turned to deal, slowly, with the problem of Baroness Lehzen. Twenty years later, when the Duchess of Kent died and Queen Victoria was reading her mother's diaries, she wrote, 'OH! I am so wretched to think how, *for a time, two people most wickedly estranged us.*' The two people were Conroy, whom she had dismissed when she became Queen, and Baroness Lehzen, to whom she clung. She still clung to her during the first three years of her marriage, and she allowed her to enjoy the last spell of her tyranny even over Prince Albert, who described her to Stockmar as 'the House Dragon, spitting fire'. Not only the Prince, but everyone near the Queen, realized that the influence should end, and that the time had come for Baroness Lehzen to retire. In 1842, she left England for ever, and went to live in Hanover, with her store of royal souvenirs. Sixteen years later, when the Queen and Prince Albert were in Germany, they saw the exile waving to them with her handkerchief, from a little railway station outside the city. They waved back, but they did not pause to meet her.

Without the Baroness, always meddling dangerously in memory of her early position of power, Prince Albert's life in England became more his own. When he wished to escape into the past he could talk to Cart, his Swiss servant, who had at times carried him up the stairs in Coburg when he was a boy, and to whom he was devoted.

*

In less than two years, Prince Albert had broken down much of the prejudice against him. The only one who seemed displeased was Baron Stockmar, who sent him one of his moralizing letters on 17 May, 1841. He wrote, 'Let us cleave devoutly but unceasingly to high thoughts and noble purposes.' Prince Albert was required 'not to spare' his own flesh, but to 'cut into' his 'own faults as well as other men's.' He was urged to 'moral excellence' and told that, through a touch of weakness or vanity, he was inclined to 'rest satisfied with mere *talk*, where *action* is alone appropriate, and can alone be of value.'

The criticism was unjust, and Prince Albert was able to turn to George Anson for encouragement. In January, four months before Stockmar's reproving letter arrived, Lord Melbourne had said to Anson, 'The Prince is bored with the sameness of his chess every evening. He would like to bring literary and scientific people about the Court, vary the society, and infuse a more useful tendency into it.' He added that, unfortunately, the Queen had 'no fancy to encourage such people'. More than this, she was anxious lest Prince Albert should have any interests beyond her comprehension. In the same memorandum in which he recorded Melbourne's conversation Anson had written of a talk between himself and the Queen, who said one evening that she was pleased by 'the Prince's utter indifference to the attractions of all ladies.' When Anson bravely answered that 'these were early days to boast', the Queen was 'rather indignant'. Anson added in his memorandum, 'I think she is a little jealous of his talking much even to men.'

Anson wrote again of the Prince, in July 1841 – ten weeks after Stockmar's dour letter – of the Cabinet Ministers treating him 'with deference and respect'. He added, 'Art and science look up to him as their especial patron . . . the good and wise look up to him with pride and gratitude.'

This was a thoughtful compliment from the Whig secretary whose very appointment Prince Albert had resented, before he was married. The Prince now had his own advisers, who enjoyed his mind and his integrity. Sir Robert Peel drew him into a deeper knowledge of politics, for which Stockmar had once complained that he showed 'not the slightest interest' when he was young. George Anson encouraged also the humanist in him; the qualities of sympathy that helped to create a bridge between the monarchy and the workers that had never existed before. In June of the following year the Prince wrote to Lord Ashley, who was trying to improve labour conditions in the coal mines, that he was 'horror stricken' by what he had heard. He was always to be haunted by this concern for the poor. In November 1843, when he and the Queen were staying with Sir Robert Peel near Birmingham – a storm centre of radical politics – Prince Albert said that he wished to visit the city and to see some of the workers. The Prime Minister and the Home Secretary objected at first, because they feared violence; but the Prince was allowed to go, and to visit some of the factories. Anson wrote that 'nothing could exceed the good humour and good feeling' of the thousands of people in the streets; and the mayor even said that he would 'vouch for the *devoted loyalty* of the whole Chartist Body', and that the Queen 'had not more loyal subjects in her dominions'.[2]

Prince Albert was quietly estranging the monarchy from the aloof aristocracy, and creating an image of the Queen more real to the middle and lower classes than to the proud, ancient families to whom England had belonged; to whom the rise of the masses, and the rule of a 'respectable' monarchy, were slightly repulsive.

CHAPTER NINE

1841-1843

Soon after her first child was born, Queen Victoria had written to King Leopold of the 'great inconvenience' of a big family, 'particularly for the country'. She added, 'Men never think, at least seldom think, what a hard task it is for us women to go through this very often.'

The Queen was similarly depressed when she realized that she was to bear her second child. Prince Albert wrote that she was 'not very happy' about it. But when the baby was born, in Buckingham Palace on 9 November, 1841, the Queen seemed to lose her depression over the 'inconvenience'. She wrote to King Leopold, on 29 November, 'Our little boy is a wonderful large and strong child, with very large dark-blue eyes, a finely formed but somewhat large nose, and a pretty little mouth.' Later, she wrote, 'You will understand how fervent are my prayers, and I am sure everybody's must be, to see him resemble his father in *every every* respect, both in body and mind.' Her wish was not realized: it was soon apparent that the boy was to grow up in her lively image, rather than that of his grave, correct father.

The Court was at Windsor when Christmas came with its celebrations. In the churches, bishops called down blessings on 'the young Sovereign and her cradled babe'. The Queen and Prince Albert gave every poor adult in Windsor town '4 lbs. of beef, 2 lbs. of bread, 1 lb. of plum pudding, a peck of potatoes and 2 pints of ale'. Children were given half this quantity, and there was a sack of coals for each family. The Windsor newspaper described a ball in the town hall, where there was 'a profusion of everything that could be desired'; and there were parties, 'tastefully decorated and illuminated with appropriate transparencies'.

Queen Victoria wrote that during the day-time she was 'a good deal occupied' with her first child, the Princess Royal, who was beginning to 'assume companionable qualities'. Prince Albert went for a run with his beagles, rode to Ascot to meet the royal staghounds, and 'enjoyed the sport of shooting'. On Christmas Eve he wrote to his father, 'Today I have two children of my own to give presents to.' He added that they were 'full of happy wonder at the German Christmas tree and its radiant candles'.

*

There were two menaces to the peace of Christmas and the promise of the new year. One was the momentary jealousy among the kings and princes in Europe, as to which of them should be godfathers to the baby Prince. King Leopold of the Belgians could not be invited because he was a Catholic. For reasons of policy, the King of Prussia was chosen, much to the annoyance of Prince Albert's father, who wished to have the King of Saxony instead. But he also was a Catholic and had to be rejected. There was an exchange of angry letters that had no effect on Queen Victoria's will: the child had already been created Prince of Wales, on 4 December, 1841; and on 25 January, 1842, with the King of Prussia present, he was baptized in St George's Chapel and given the names his parents had chosen – Albert, after his father, and Edward, after the Queen's father, the Duke of Kent. Very soon, he was called 'Bertie' by his family, and he kept this name for his intimates all his life.

The second menace was the continued correspondence between the Queen and Lord Melbourne. This was less easy to resolve. In December 1841, Stockmar was visiting a house in London when a stranger said to him, 'So I find the Queen is in

daily correspondence with Lord Melbourne... Don't you believe
that Lord Melbourne has lost his influence over the Queen's
mind!' Stockmar answered, 'I don't believe a word of it.' But
there was further proof of this unconstitutional leaning on the
old Prime Minister's opinions; this sharing of a confidence in
which even Prince Albert had no part. Sir Robert Peel became
aware of it and he told Stockmar that if he ever learned of the
Queen taking Melbourne's advice, he would not remain in office
another hour, whatever the consequences of his resignation
might be. Stockmar was so alarmed that he wrote to Lord Melbourne, on 23 November, 1841, 'Would you have it said that Sir
Robert Peel failed in his trial, merely because the Queen alone
was not fair to him, and that principally you had aided her in
the game of dishonesty?'

Prince Albert was patient over this disloyal but affectionate
bond between the Queen and 'dear Lord Melbourne'. He continued his virtuous way, with quiet insistence; and Queen Victoria continued her correspondence with Lord Melbourne until
he died, in November 1848, soon after he had received her last
letter, which, he wrote, had been 'a great comfort and relief' to
him in his loneliness.

•

While Queen Victoria risked Sir Robert Peel's anger with her
letters to Lord Melbourne, Prince Albert strengthened his
friendship with the Tory leader, who became a companion for
his mind. They exchanged books, and they corresponded on the
Nibelungenlied. In October 1841, after Peel had announced the
choice of the Prince as President of the Fine Arts Commission,
he wrote that there was 'cordial satisfaction' in every quarter of
the House. The Prince was now 'more intimately acquainted
with some of the most distinguished men of the day'. He was
stepping into a field where the Queen was not yet eager to
accompany him; a field in which the serious dreams of his student days in Bonn could flourish. When Charles Eastlake, the

artist and later President of the Royal Academy, went to see him at Buckingham Palace to discuss the work of the Fine Arts Commission, he noticed none of the stiffness of which the aristocracy had complained. The Prince 'stood, kneeling with one knee on a chair', and Eastlake recalled, 'We were at close quarters and in a strong light, which showed his beautiful face to great advantage... There was nothing in his exterior so striking as his face... He soon put me at ease by his pleasing manner... Two or three times I quite forgot who he was, he talked so naturally and argued so fairly...'

*

There was still no evidence that the Queen and the Prince were seriously concerned with alarms beyond England's shores. They did not seem to realize that the rebellions in Ireland, at the Cape and in the West Indies were warning of greater disasters to come. Nor did their letters show understanding over the threat of war across the Atlantic. After sixty years of independence, the Americans were still disputing the boundary between Maine and Lower Canada; and at one time it seemed that British troops would be needed to keep the peace. Relations with the United States were further strained by Britain's war against slave traders. The government claimed the right to search and identify vessels, and to hunt out British slave traders sailing under foreign flags. This the Americans refused, until Lord Ashburton visited the United States in 1842 and settled both these problems with the Webster-Ashburton Treaty, signed at Washington on 9 August, which fixed the frontiers of Maine, and recorded the agreement of both nations to maintain patroling squadrons off the African coast.

These were questions for diplomats to solve, and they were remote from the daily life of ordinary British people. But, in January 1842, there came a more personal disaster. Almost 4,500 men of an Anglo-Indian army, together with thousands of camp followers, including English women and children, had died or been butchered by Afghan tribesmen as they were making their way back to India from Kabul, under the sly promise of safe conduct. There had been peace in most of India since 1826, but there was always the fear that Russia might push her armies across Afghanistan and threaten – perhaps destroy – the power of the British in the sub-continent. That danger seemed near after the massacre of January 1842, and a war of revenge was considered to be inevitable. The punitive advance through the Khyber Pass began on 5 April, and ended, after more than five months of terrible killing and privation, on 16 September, when the British flag was raised in the great fort within Kabul and the bands played 'God Save the Queen'.

Queen Victoria's soldiers returned to India with their empty victory. The glory of knowing that the National Anthem had been sung in Kabul had to be paid for – in the grief of bereaved families; in the feelings of men like Greville that the 'massacres and havoc' perpetrated by the expeditionary force were 're-garded with universal contempt and abhorrence'; and in the realistic fact that the campaign had swelled the deficit in Britain's revenue to five million pounds.

The Queen gave a lead in response to the fiscal measures in-troduced by Sir Robert Peel's government. When Peel an-nounced a tax of sevenpence in the pound on all incomes above one hundred and fifty pounds a year, the Queen declared that she wished also to pay the tax, and her example helped to silence the grumblers. It was a surprise in the history of the relationship between the monarchy and the people; a hint that, in the future, monarchs might share the life of their subjects instead of merely exploiting them; that they might rule less through power and more through example.

It is fair to believe that the Queen's action was influenced by Prince Albert's vision and diligence. He was by nature senti-mental, but also practical, and his realism found its opportunity in the way that he dealt with the management of the royal houses. In both Buckingham Palace and Windsor Castle there were curious inefficiencies and extravagances. The Lord Chamberlain's department cleaned the inside of all the windows, and the Woods and Forests department cleaned the outside. Queen Victoria had never enjoyed the simple pleasure of looking at her gardens through clear glass, because the two departments never did their work at the same time. Also, one department laid the fires in the Palace rooms, and another department lighted them. Prince Albert ended such ridiculous habits. As was the custom in most great houses, candles in the Palace were never lighted a second time. Hundreds of them, with the tips slightly burned, were filched by the servants each morning. The Prince changed all this, and at the same time introduced economies in the kitchens and the cellars. He wrote to Stockmar, on 27 December, 1842, 'It always seems to me as if an infinitude of small trivialities hang about me like an ever present weight; I mean by these the domestic and Court arrangements, and to these I have chiefly applied myself, feeling that we never shall be in a position to occupy ourselves with higher and graver things, so long as we have to deal with these trifles. . .'

After two years the Prince was rewarded for his care and parsimony: he had saved enough money from the Queen's income to pay about two hundred thousand pounds for Osborne House, the 'marine villa' to which they were to escape for rest, in the Isle of Wight.

The Queen watched Prince Albert treading his cautious way and she constantly thanked God for the blessing of her marriage. She wrote in her journal, 'I *know what* REAL *happiness* is.' Only italics and capitals could celebrate her gratitude. Soon after the Prince of Wales was born, Lady Lyttelton was brought into the Court to take care of him, and she remained until he was seven years old. She wrote of the 'vein of iron' running through the Queen's 'extraordinary character'. But this hardness lessened, as her fears lessened; as she allowed her affection to govern her actions, and as she learned to accept the fact that Prince Albert's intellect was greater than her own. Even Stockmar came to acknowledge the achievements of his pupil. During his visit to England, early in 1842, Lord Aberdeen told him how gratified ministers were 'to perceive that the Queen leant upon the Prince's judgment, and showed an obvious desire that he should share her duties'. At last he enjoyed some of 'the moral status and influence to which he was entitled'.

There had been one more, private encouragement, in February 1842. Prince Ernest had announced his betrothal to Princess Alexandrine of Baden, and Prince Albert wrote his brother more affectionate and improving letters. 'Do not leave your wife alone at home, while you go out after your own pleasures. Married, and with your own wife, there is more chance of success for you here. . . I meant to give you a centrepiece as a wedding present, but as you wish to have a travelling carriage, I shall have it made at once and see that it is made very well. Victoria and I intend giving Alexandrine some fine jewels.'

It seemed that the marriage might save Prince Ernest from his sins. When he brought his bride to England, in July, Queen Victoria wrote to Lord Melbourne that she was 'a most amiable, sensible and gentle creature, and without being really handsome, very pretty and pleasing.'

Between the marriage of his brother in Coburg, and the visit with his bride, there had been another attempt to shoot the Queen, by a 'thorough scamp' named John Francis. On 29 May, she was driving with the Prince from the Chapel Royal, between lines of spectators, when the man stepped out and aimed his pistol. Prince Albert described the 'dreadful occurrence' in a letter to his father: he wrote, on 1 June, 'He was some two paces from us. I heard the trigger snap, but it must have missed fire. I turned to Victoria, who was seated on my right, and asked her, "Did you hear that?" She had been bowing to the people on the right, and had observed nothing.'

They returned to the Palace, but, while the man was at large, he was still a danger, so they drove out again next day, hoping that he would repeat his folly and betray himself to the police. Prince Albert continued in his letter, 'You may imagine that our minds were not very easy. We looked behind every tree, and I cast my eyes around in search of the rascal's face. . . On our

way home, as we were approaching the Palace . . . a shot was
fired at us about five paces off. It was the same fellow with the
pistol – a little swarthy, ill-looking rascal. The shot must have
passed under the carriage, for he lowered his hand. . . The cul-
prit was instantly taken off to the police station. The populace
are in a state of extreme indignation. He is not out of his mind
but a thorough scamp. . . I hope his trial will be conducted with
the greatest strictness. . .'

Again, on 3 July, a 'hunch-backed wretch' tried to shoot the
Queen while she was driving with Prince Albert and King
Leopold. The pistol missed fire and a boy of sixteen tore the
weapon out of the man's hand. After scuffles and attempts at
escape, he was arrested and later tried and imprisoned.

Sir Robert Peel was in Cambridge when he received news of
this second shooting. He hurried to Buckingham Palace, and
when the Queen walked into the room, he bowed to her and
wept.

Assassination was a risk shared by both the monarch and her
ministers. On the afternoon of 20 January, 1843, Daniel
M'Naghten, a crazy, twenty-seven year old Irish Protestant, fired
a shot at Edward Drummond, one of Peel's secretaries, mistak-
ing him for the Prime Minister. Drummond died, and
M'Naghten became famous as the reason for the judicial
opinion on which rests the law 'as to the criminal responsibility
of the insane' – the 'M'Naghten Rules', which have endured as
part of English legal practice.

The bond of similar danger drew Sir Robert Peel closer than
ever to the Queen. All her old resentment faded, and in February 1843 she wrote of him to King Leopold as 'a great statesman, a man who thinks but little of party, and never of
himself.'

*

In June 1842, the Queen had shared a happy occasion with
Prince Albert, which fulfilled his wish to bring more musicians

and artists into the Court. One afternoon Mendelssohn came to play and sing with them, at Buckingham Palace. Mendelssohn wrote afterwards to his father of the Queen coming into the room where he was already standing with the Prince, near the organ. 'She said she was obliged to leave for Claremont[1] in an hour, and then suddenly interrupting herself, exclaimed, "But Goodness, what a confusion!" for the wind had littered the whole room . . . with sheets of music. As she spoke she knelt down and began picking up the music. Prince Albert helped, and I too was not idle. . . I begged that the Prince would first play me something so that, as I said, "I might boast about it in Germany"; and he played a Chorale, by heart, with the pedals, so charmingly, and clearly, and correctly that it would have done credit to any professional. . . Then it was my turn and I began my chorus from *St Paul* – *How lovely are the Messengers.* Before I got to the end of the first verse they both joined in the chorus. . .

'The Queen asked if I had written any new songs, and said she was very fond of singing my published ones. "You should sing one to him," said Prince Albert, and, after a little begging, she said she would try. . .'

They went to the Queen's sitting-room, where there was a piano, and where they were joined by the Duchess of Kent. Queen Victoria sang 'quite charmingly, in strict time and tune, and with very good execution'. Mendelssohn wrote, 'I thought to myself; one must not pay too many compliments on such an occasion, so that I merely thanked her a great many times, upon which she said, "Oh! if I only had not been so frightened. Generally I have such long breath!" Then I praised her heartily and with the best conscience in the world.'

Prince Albert also sang, and then they asked Mendelssohn to improvise. He was in 'the best mood for it', and wrote, 'They followed me with such intelligence and attention that I felt more at ease than I ever did when improvising to an audience.'

This visit was typical of many occasions that were to follow. Prince Albert became Mendelssohn's friend and the sponsor of composers as surprising, at the time, as Wagner. It was through the Prince's incentive and enthusiasm that *Lohengrin* was first performed in England – at Windsor Castle.

The afternoon with Mendelssohn, in 1842, was a sign that the Queen might also wish for the company of artists and thinkers. As President of the Fine Arts Commission, Prince Albert had asked the painters who were adding frescoes to the House of Commons to introduce a moral into their pictures. Then he encouraged them by designing a pavilion in the garden of Buckingham Palace, in which Landseer and his contemporaries were to paint the panels, with subjects that were also to be 'both moral and beautiful'.

The pavilion was built, and the artists came to add the frescoes. Among them was Thomas Uwins, who was painting the lady in *Comus*. He observed the Queen and the Prince, and commended them because they breakfasted early, heard morning prayers, and were out in the gardens 'before half-past nine o'clock – sometimes earlier'. He saw them also in the evenings, while he was still painting his panel, enjoying 'each other's society in the solitude of the garden'.

Uwins talked alone with Prince Albert sometimes, and he wrote of him, 'He is really an accomplished man, and withal, possesses so much good sense and consideration that, taken apart from his playfulness and good humour, he might pass for an aged and experienced person, instead of a youth of two or three and twenty.'

*

During her reign, Queen Victoria spent less than five weeks in Ireland and almost seven years in Scotland. She gave her heart to the Highlanders and withheld it from the Irish, for the simple reason that she comprehended and enjoyed the one and was unable to appreciate the unpredictable nature of the other. Her choice, made in all innocence at the time, seriously affected the future. If she had chosen Ireland for her castle of escape, some of the political tides of the next half century might have changed their way.

The Queen and the Prince, with their two children, went to Scotland for the first time in the summer of 1842. They sailed from Woolwich on 29 August and landed at Granton pier, Edinburgh, on 1 September. Sir Robert Peel was with them, and he afterwards described the tour to Greville as 'very nervous, inasmuch as they went through all the disturbed districts'; but that 'loyalty and interest in seeing the Queen triumphed over every other feeling and consideration', and that 'all went off as well as possible'.

The conquest was mutual. During the fourteen days of the visit, the Scots liked the sight of their sovereign, and the Queen began her love for them that was to become almost an obsession for the rest of her life. For Prince Albert, the landscape reminded him of his native Thuringia, and he wrote to his step-grandmother on 18 September, that he thought the Scottish people 'more natural, and marked by that honesty and sympathy which always distinguish the inhabitants of mountainous countries, who live far away from towns'. The Queen thought the Highlanders to be 'such a chivalrous, fine, active people'. When they went to the Palace of Scone, Prince Albert was given a pair of curling stones with which he played on the polished floor of the drawing-room. When they sailed on a lake, the boatmen sang them Gaelic songs. While the Prince made one or two expeditions alone, the Queen painted in water colours – the little huts, 'so low, so full of peat smoke', and the old women washing potatoes in the river, 'with their dresses tucked up almost to their knees'.

From such simple pleasures the Queen and the Prince returned to England and the confusion of tasks. There was the burden of Peel's income tax to pay for the futile expedition to Afghanistan, but also the solace of a good harvest in Britain for the first time in five years. And there was good news from the Far East where, after two years of conflict with the Chinese, Britain made a peaceful and profitable agreement that gave her access to five ports. The prize that was to endure was the cession of Hong Kong, confirmed in the Treaty of Nanking, on 29 August, 1842. So the island became an outpost of Queen Victoria's growing empire, with the promise that her name would be given to the capital, and to the highest peak. She ordered the striking of medals with her head on them – the first of the thirty that were to be won by her soldiers and sailors during her reign.

CHAPTER TEN

1843-1846

When Baron Stockmar came to England early in April 1843, he thought that Prince Albert seemed 'well and happy', though he frequently looked 'pale and worried'. Then came one of his solemn comments; that his pupil was 'full of the practical talent' which enabled him 'to see the essential points of a question'.

This 'practical talent' did not help Prince Albert when the Queen's third child was to be born and he had to take her place at the spring levées. Many of the English aristocracy decided to stay away rather than kneel before him. When the Queen told Sir Robert Peel that she would not allow any of them to snub her husband, he assured her that only 'a person of deranged intellect' could have such a 'hostile feeling' towards Prince Albert; but he suggested a compromise – that the proud ladies might be excused from kneeling and kissing his hand.

On 25 April, 1843, the Prince wrote to his brother, 'At four o'clock this morning, Victoria was confined with a little daughter. . . I have endless letters to write, to all parts of the world; therefore I must say good-bye.'

Even the ceremony of christening the baby – Princess Alice – was threatened by jealous bickering, among the possible royal guests. Prince Albert wrote a strange letter to his brother, telling him that his 'not appearing would probably be chosen', in his interest, 'not in ours'; and then added that Prince Ernest's present for 'little Princess Alice' should be some 'article in silver, with a value of about £50.'

The real disturber was Ernest Augustus, Duke of Cumberland and King of Hanover, who had been the chief villain in the strange pattern of plot and jealousy during Queen Victoria's childhood. He never missed a chance of making some petty and vulgar gesture whenever he came to England. On 2 June he arrived in a hackney carriage, an hour after the banquet following the christening of Princess Alice was over. At first, he was in 'good humour', but this did not last: a few weeks later, on 28 June, when Princess Augusta of Cambridge was married to the Grand Duke of Mecklenburg-Strelitz, in Buckingham Palace, the King was tiresome. On 2 July, Prince Albert described the astonishing scene: he wrote to his brother, 'It almost came to a fight. . . He insisted on having the place at the Altar, where we stood. He wanted to drive me away and, against all custom, he wanted to accompany Victoria and lead her. I was to go behind him. I was forced to give him a strong push and drive him down a few steps, where the First Master of Ceremonies took him and led him out of the Chapel.

'We had a second scene, when he would not allow me to sign the register with Victoria. He laid his fist on the book. We manoeuvred round the table and Victoria had the book handed to her across the table. Now the table was between us and he could see what was being done. After a third attempt to force Victoria to do what he commanded, but in vain, he left the party in great wrath. Since then, we let him go, and happily, he fell over some stones in Kew and damaged some ribs!'

Such incidents are unimportant now, except that they reveal the nourishment the monarchy gained from the eclipse of the arrogant Hanoverians; the advantage of Prince Albert's example, and his influence over the Queen. On 23 November, 1843, he wrote to his brother, 'Victoria has greatly improved and has become very reasonable and good-natured.'

With peace and order in the Court, Prince Albert was able to turn from the 'small trivialities' of which he had complained, and concern himself with 'higher and graver things'. The first of these was his wish to forbid duelling between officers in the services. He wrote to the Duke of Wellington, condemning this 'unchristian and barbarian custom', but the old warrior was not enthusiastic; nor were the Lords of the Admiralty and the Master of Ordnance. Nevertheless, the Articles of War were amended so that it became 'suitable to the character of honourable men to apologize and offer redress for wrong or insult committed', and equally suitable 'for the party aggrieved to accept frankly and cordially explanation and apologies for same'.

Prince Albert had won his first victory in reform. He was identifying himself with new thinking, rather than clinging to the past. In October 1843, he went to Cambridge to receive the honorary degree of Doctor of Laws. The undergraduates welcomed him with cheers, and Queen Victoria noted in her report of the day to King Leopold that they were all 'young people', who, in time, would 'have a certain part to play'. They were 'the rising generation'.

*

Early in September 1843, the Queen and Prince Albert extended their influence beyond the shores of England. They went to stay with King Louis Philippe in France, crossing the Channel in their new yacht, the *Victoria and Albert*. Their host met them at Le Tréport, in his barge. The Queen wrote, 'The good kind King was standing on the boat, and so impatient to get out that it was very difficult to prevent him. . . He got out and came up as quickly as possible, and embraced me warmly . . . the emotion which it caused I shall never forget.' During the visit, Louis Philippe 'repeated again and again his wish to become more and more closely allied with the English'.

There was plotting behind this amiable exchange, of which the Queen and Prince Albert seemed unaware, and which was to destroy the pleasant memories of the visit three years later. While the monarchs made their pledges of friendship, their ministers dealt with the harsh realities of their trade. One of the old causes of distrust between Britain and France was the future marriage of Queen Isabella of Spain. Concern with this question had begun in 1834, when she was a child of four, and it was still an alarm during the royal visit in 1843. The cynical grasping for power makes a long story : it is enough to recall that the British government encouraged the suit of Prince Albert's cousin, Leopold of Saxe-Coburg, a brother-in-law of Queen Marie of Portugal; while the French, resenting the prospect of increased influence for the Coburgs, sought an alliance between Queen Isabella – or her sister, the Infanta – and a son of Louis Philippe. It seemed that the vexing old question might be decided in France in 1843 between Queen Victoria and the King of the French, with Lord Aberdeen and Guizot as their advisers. They decided that if the British withdrew their support for the Coburg prince, Queen Isabella should be free to make her own choice, and that she should marry, and give birth to an heir to the Spanish throne, before Louis Philippe allowed one of his sons to marry the Infanta.

Queen Victoria and Prince Albert returned to England with what seemed like a quiet victory. Even Baron Stockmar was pleased : he wrote to Prince Albert, 'You have availed yourself, with tact and success, of the first opportunity that has come your way. The results are before us. Take then, in good part, my hearty congratulations upon them.'

They had to wait until August 1846 before they were disillusioned; before they realized that Louis Philippe and Guizot had tricked them.

*

Prince Albert returned to the pattern of life he enjoyed most. At Windsor, he had managed the home farm so well that it was making a profit. His children were happy, with Princess Victoria 'running and jumping in the flower garden', and the Prince of Wales growing up, according to the Queen, to be 'like his father'. In November 1843, when Prince Albert hunted with the Belvoir, he rode so boldly that the English aristocracy were momentarily pleased with him. The Queen wrote to King Leopold that her husband's performance 'had made such a sensation' that it had been 'written all over the country'. 'They' had made 'much more of it than if he had done some great act'. George Anson, also a fox-hunting man, wrote, 'The Prince rode admirably.'

The image was spoiled by an episode that Prince Albert described in his Christmas letter to his brother. He wrote of the trees ordered for the children, and then, 'It seems to me as if it was not long ago that we were enchanted at the sight of our trees, and especially you, enjoying the beloved quince-bread. Yesterday I had my first fall, while hunting, and I fell into a ditch near the railway station at Slough.'

*

Prince Albert's father died on 29 January, 1844, and his brother Ernest became Duke of Saxe-Coburg-Gotha. The Prince wrote to him, on 3 February, 'How I should like to be with you and weep with you and see the beloved face once more, though it is cold. We no longer have any home. . . This is a break that you cannot feel in the same way. . . Poor subjects; be a father to them. . . Victoria weeps with me; for me and for all of you.'

The old Duke's sins were forgotten for a moment under the extravagant signs of grief. Duke Ernest sent Prince Albert some relics of their father that gave him great pleasure; among them a fruit knife. 'How often,' he recalled, he had seen it 'in his hand'.

The Queen shared her husband's sorrow. Four days after he heard of his father's death, Prince Albert wrote to Stockmar, 'The relation in which we stand to one another leaves nothing to desire. It is a union of heart and soul and is therefore noble.' On 9 February, he wrote to Stockmar again, 'A new epoch has commenced in my life; not indeed in action and in aim, but in my inmost life. My youth, with all the recollections linked with it, has been buried...'

It was soon obvious that Duke Ernest II had neither the mind nor the character to rule the duchy wisely, so in March 1844 Prince Albert went to Coburg, alone, to give his brother advice. This was the first time he had been away from the Queen during the four years of their marriage, and his letters to her proved what he had already told Stockmar, of his happiness. While the ship was still in Dover Harbour he wrote, 'My own darling, I have been here about an hour, and regret the lost time which I might have spent with you... Poor child! You will, while I write, be getting ready for luncheon, and you will find a place vacant where I sat yesterday. In your heart, however, I hope my place will not be vacant... You are even now half a day nearer to seeing me again; by the time you get this letter, you will be a whole one – thirteen more and I am again within your arms...' Then he endured the sea journey that he always disliked: he wrote again from Ostend, on 28 March, 'I kept my seat on one spot all the way with my eyes shut, but I was far from easy in my mind, and I arrived at half-past eight stiff and cold.'

He wrote again from Cologne, where he had been so often in his 'student days', and told the Queen that her 'picture' was hung 'everywhere' in the Imperial Hotel, 'prettily wreathed with laurel.' From Gotha he sent her 'an auricula and a pansy' he had gathered at Reinhardtsbrunn; and then he went on to Coburg, from which he sent her 'a few sugar Easter eggs'. He wrote nothing of his brother's task, or of the real purpose of his journey: all was nostalgia, especially when he went to Rosenau, where he had been born and where he picked more flowers, from the garden of his childhood. Five days later he was back in England, and he wrote in his diary, '*Great joy.*'

He thought of his deep roots in Coburg again, on 6 August, 1844, when the Queen gave birth to her second son, Prince Alfred. It was then certain that Ernest would never be father of a legitimate heir, and that the next Duke of Saxe-Coburg-

Gotha would be one of Prince Albert's sons. When the baby was two weeks old, the Prince wrote to his brother, 'The little one shall, from his youth, be taught to love the dear small country to which he belongs, in every respect, as does his Papa.'

*

Prince Albert's letters during his early years in England had been mostly personal; the letters of a virtuous man bent on doing what was right. He did not seem yet to envisage the great spaces of the world or to enjoy power in the way that princes usually do. The year 1844 must have increased his vision and experience, for, with the Queen, he welcomed kings and princes from Russia, Saxony, France and Prussia, all of whom came to do homage to Victoria, but also to pluck at political advantage and to learn what lessons England could teach them.

In June, the King of Saxony came; a quiet, friendly monarch, whose chief pleasure was wandering through the old streets of London. About the same time, the Emperor Nicholas of Russia came; a more complicated and less predictable figure, who said to Stockmar, 'I know that I am taken for an actor, but indeed I am not.' His behaviour denied this: he upset the polite routine of Windsor Castle by avoiding the bed provided for him and sleeping on a mattress of straw, brought by his valet from the royal stables.

The Emperor was forty-eight years old, 'thoroughly straight-forward' according to his own boast. He said that he esteemed England 'highly', and assured Sir Robert Peel that he did not 'covet one inch of Turkish soil', but that he would not 'allow anybody else to have one'. This last declaration was aimed at France: he said, 'As to what the French say of me, I care not. I spit upon it.' When Sir Robert Peel and Lord Aberdeen refused to commit themselves on Near East policy, he resigned himself to the parades and ceremonies planned for his entertainment. There was a grand review of troops in Windsor Park, after which the Emperor, stirred by the bold programme, told Prince

Albert that he hoped some day they would meet on the battle-field. He added amiably that they must be 'on the same side'.

Prince Albert's answer is not recorded. His thoughts and feel-ings remained his own. It was noted at the review that when he rode past at the head of his regiment, he lowered his sword in full military salute to the Queen. Lady Lyttelton was near enough to see that he did it 'with *such* a look and smile'. She had never seen 'so many pretty feelings expressed in a minute'.

Queen Victoria's judgment of the Emperor showed that she was becoming less spontaneous, and wiser. She wrote to King Leopold of the 'great event' of the visit; then she described her guest. He was 'a *very* striking man; still very handsome; his profile . . . *beautiful*, and his manners *most* dignified and grace-ful. . .' She thought him 'extremely civil – quite alarmingly so', as he was 'so full of attentions and *politesses*'. The expression of his eyes was '*formidable* and unlike anything' she had seen be-fore. He seldom smiled, but when he did, 'the expression' was '*not* a happy one'. Later she wrote, 'Very clever I do not think him, and his mind is not a cultivated one. His education has been neglected.'

Louis Philippe came in October – the first time a king of France had landed in Britain since the Black Prince brought Jean II back as a captive, in 1356. Louis Philippe also disturbed Windsor Castle by his odd habits; eating only two meals a day, one of which had to include a bowl of chicken broth; and sleeping on a horsehair mattress and a plank of wood. He asked for no luxuries beyond a big table on which he could spread his papers. They were not likely to have included his plans for the 'Spanish marriages', which were to wreck all the good that might have come from the visit. He kept his dark scheme to himself and enjoyed instead the semblance of trust that had come with the solution of what was described as the 'Tahiti affair'.

Early in the year the British Consul in Tahiti had been seized by the French officials, and the outrage led to months of anxiety that continued until a few weeks before Louis Philippe arrived in England. The Queen had written to King Leopold, 'The good ending of our difficulties with France is an immense blessing.' There was no hint, while the King was at Windsor, that the 'blessing' was to be so brief. He delighted the Queen with his compliments to the Prince : she wrote to King Leopold, 'The King praised my dearest Albert most highly and fully appreciates his great qualities and talents – and what gratifies me *so much*, treats him completely as his equal, calling him *"Mon Frère"*, and saying to me that *my husband* was the same as me, which it is – and *"Le Prince Albert, c'est pour moi le Roi."* '

(In her wish that her husband should be treated on equal terms by the sovereigns of Europe, Queen Victoria overlooked the fact that the King of the French, as the heir to a revolution, also needed to be regarded as *'Mon Frère'* by the other rulers. The Emperor Nicholas of Russia never thought of Louis Philippe in this way.)

Prince Albert withheld his opinions until August 1846, when the engagements were announced, simultaneously, of Queen Isabella of Spain to the Bourbon prince, Don Francisco de Asis, and of her sister to Louis Philippe's son, the Duc de Montpensier. The plot behind this was cynical : the King of the French had proved that his desire for power in Spain was more important to him than the trust of England.

Don Francisco de Asis was an unfortunate young man who loved strutting before his looking glass and engaging in such feminine vanities that even his family called him 'Paquita' – the Spanish for 'Fanny'. Louis Philippe and Guizot had chosen Don Francisco for the Queen, knowing that her virtue would be unhappily safe and that he would never father an heir to the throne. (Prince Albert described him as 'impotent and half a fool'.) Thus, all power, and hopes for the Spanish succession, would belong to the Infanta and the Duc de Montpensier.

Louis Philippe's deceit hastened his own downfall : it subjected the Queen of Spain to a ridiculous marriage that lasted only seven months, and it killed his precarious friendship with Queen Victoria, and with Prince Albert, who wrote to his brother on 17 September, 'We have been shamefully betrayed and now the other party triumphs. A miserable triumph, to have betrayed a friend. . . The *bonne entente* has breathed her last.' On 2 April, 1847, when Queen Isabella and her timid husband had parted, Prince Albert wrote again, 'What will Louis Philippe have to answer for in Heaven!'

*

The first experiment of the Queen and the Prince in politics beyond the Kingdom was a failure; but the pattern of their life in England had already brought some prizes. The approval the Prince had enjoyed from the old ruling class by his riding with the Belvoir, was brief; his precise behaviour, his cold handshake and his caution, gave them no pleasure. Beyond Peel and Anson, he made few intimate friends. But the mass of people seemed to appreciate the example that he set. When he drove with the Queen along the crowded London streets to open the Royal Exchange, they were greeted with spontaneous cheers. The Queen wrote to King Leopold, on 29 October, 1844, 'They say *no* Sovereign *was more* loved than I am,' and she wisely explained the reason, that this was because of their '*happy domestic home* – which gives such a good example.' Prince Albert made a similar boast: he wrote in a letter to Baron Stockmar, 'Here, after four years, is the recognition of the position we took up from the first. You always said that if Monarchy was to rise in popularity, it could only be by the Sovereign leading an exemplary life, and keeping quite aloof from and above party.'

*

After Christmas at Windsor, in 1844, which Prince Albert described as 'German and *gemütlich*', the Court returned to London for the opening of Parliament. By this time the relationship with Sir Robert Peel had become warm and friendly: when his grandson was born, the Queen asked that she might be one of his godmothers. Prince Albert, with his love of learning, treated Peel as his tutor in politics, and on 4 February, 1845, he wrote of him to Stockmar as 'a sagacious, honourable Statesman'.

Peel's path in Westminster was not so easy as it was in the Palace, and he had been Prime Minister long enough to pass through the usual seasons politicians have to endure; from the enthusiasm of election, to the hazards of power. His party was big and restive, and contentious issues were likely to increase the strains within. Queen Victoria wrote, 'In these days, a minister *does* require some encouragement, for the abuse and difficulties he has to contend with are dreadful.' She asked him to accept the Order of the Garter, but he thought it wise to refuse.

The Queen's early, nervous haughtiness of manner was fading: her faith in Peel was related to the private security that she now enjoyed with her husband. Her fear, before their marriage, that Prince Albert might endeavour to 'oppose' her, had changed into a fear that he might not be exalted enough. In February 1845 she wished him to be created 'King Consort', and she wrote in her journal, 'He ought to be, and is above me in everything really, and therefore I wish that he should be equal in rank to me.' Her wish became gossip in Fleet Street, and the *Morning Chronicle* suggested that the conferring of such a title would be 'preliminary to a demand for an increased grant'.

No more was done: Prince Albert continued in his quiet way, drafting the Queen's letters to her ministers and being satisfied, as he wrote, that Sir Robert Peel regarded his 'present position as extremely good'.

CHAPTER ELEVEN

1845-1847

The Queen and Prince Albert are often blamed, personally, for the deluge of lace curtains, *jardinières*, lambrequins and *objets d'art* that are now dismissed as 'Victorian art'. Where learning and a sense of history were concerned, the Prince was sensitive and wise: he protested against covering and mutilating the early frescoes in Eton Chapel; he brought Italian primitive paintings from Coburg to England, and he purchased more of them, in London, at a time when they were out of fashion. But his knowledge of art remained distinct from the modes in decoration that he encouraged – later, at Balmoral, with its flood of tartan over the French gilt furniture; and in 1844 and 1845 at Osborne, where he could escape with the Queen from what he described in a letter to his brother as 'inquisitive and often impudent people' – like those who had spoiled their holidays in the Pavilion at Brighton.

Osborne House with its gardens, in the Isle of Wight, was a pleasant retreat, away from the Hanoverian ghosts that haunted Windsor and Buckingham Palace; away from the government departments that Queen Victoria described as 'the plague of one's life'. Prince Albert made terraces, summer houses and winding walks, overlooking the Solent. Wherever there was a view that pleased him, he placed a seat on which he could laze in the evening, with the Queen beside him; or sometimes they stood on the edge of the woods, where he whistled to the nightingales 'in their own, long peculiar note', and they 'invariably answered'.

When Lady Lyttelton was in waiting, she wrote 'It is pleasant to see how earnestly Prince Albert tries to do the best about this place, giving work to as many labourers as possible.' They were 'away from all the bitterness people create for themselves in London'.

Within the house were many surprises – the pseudo-marble pillars in the drawing-rooms; the tables crowded with hundreds of miniatures and objects, in wood, ivory or silver. In the passages were recesses, lined with Garter blue and crowned with gilded plaster shells, each framing a German avuncular bust. In the garden, Prince Albert ordered a Swiss chalet to be built, in which the children could play. There was also a model fortress where he taught them the more innocent secrets of war, as Uncle Leopold and Florschütz had taught him, twenty summers before.

A few miles from Osborne are the ruins of Carisbrooke, where crumbling ramparts and gaping arrow slits recall the time when King Charles I was a prisoner in the castle. Nearby is the grave of his daughter who had died there, 'consumed by a feverish distemper'. One of Queen Victoria's first gestures was to erect a memorial, as a sign of her own devotion to the Stuarts, and as 'a token of respect' for the Princess's virtues and of 'sympathy for her misfortunes'.

*

During the five years of their marriage, the Queen and Prince Albert had often talked of visiting Coburg together. Every birthday and Christmas, presents came to remind them of the little duchy and its tranquil landscape; drawings, boxes of German biscuits and even furniture made from the antlers of stags shot by Ernest in the forest. But the links were not all sentimental: on 10 May, 1845, Prince Albert wrote to his brother, 'The worm that is gnawing at your heart and which often robs you of all pleasure in life is *mistrust*. . . It presses itself between you and those who are dearest to you.' The time had come for

Prince Albert to take Queen Victoria to his birthplace – for his brother's sake as much as for hers. Soon after he wrote his frank letter to his brother, Sir Robert Peel assured the Queen and the Prince that the country was quiet; that even in Ireland the Catholics and the Protestants were enjoying a momentary truce; so they arranged to go to Coburg in August, by way of Brussels, Cologne and the Rhine.

Lord Aberdeen, Lord Liverpool, Lady Canning and Lady Gainsborough were to go with them, and Prince Albert warned his brother, in a letter written on 23 May, 'You need not fear that these people will make any pretensions. They have already travelled with us and last autumn they lived with us in a miserable, small house in Scotland. . . The principal thing will be to keep the whole English colony together. . . Do not separate us from them. . . We do not expect any festivities. We only wish to have an opportunity of seeing the neighbourhood and the family.'

On 13 June, Prince Albert wrote again, 'If *Strangers* wish to come, don't encourage them to remain. They would only wish to watch us. We are by no means expecting any grand festivals. What I think would give Victoria a great deal of pleasure would be to see the children's procession at the Gregorius Festival. . . Victoria likes to dance, especially at small *thé dansants*. You might arrange some. . . Regarding the English way of keeping Sunday and the scruples belonging to it, I must mention that on Sundays we would not go to a ball or to the theatre, but there is no reason why we should not be happily assembled.' A few days before they sailed, Prince Albert wrote again, 'You need not arrange a chase, as Victoria does not like such pleasures, and I prefer to stay with her. . .'

They arrived in Antwerp on 'a pouring wet evening', and Queen Victoria, who had never travelled so far before, wrote in her journal of all that she saw – the women in the streets, with 'their jugs of brass, going to market'; the streets of Cologne, which were sprinkled with *Eau-de-Cologne* to make her journey fragrant; and Bonn, where the stiff professors who had taught the Prince came now to congratulate him on his achievements. The Queen went with him to the house in which he had lived as a student; they stood together in the room where he had worked and dreamed. There was only one escape from nostalgia into humour: they attended the unveiling of a statue of Beethoven, and Queen Victoria had to note, 'Unfortunately, when the statue was uncovered, its back was towards us.'

They drove out to Brühl, where the King of Prussia was waiting for them in the splendid little palace – a miniature Versailles, with the finest rococo interior of all the Rhineland. At the banquet, the toast was 'Victoria', and when the King rang his glass against Prince Albert's, she wept a little; but she remembered to bend towards her host and kiss his cheek.

King Leopold came to see them on their way. Here, in the heart of Europe, he met again the niece and nephew whose destiny he had planned; the nephew of whom he had written, ten years before, 'If he does not, from the very outset, accept it as a vocation of grave responsibility, on the efficient fulfilment of which his honour and happiness depend, there is small likelihood of his succeeding.' There was no anxiety now; the harsh demand had been met and was being fulfilled.

Queen Victoria 'began to feel greatly moved – agitated indeed', as they came near the Coburg frontier. They drove into the town, where the streets were crowded with girls dressed in green and white. The sun shone and there were showers of blossoms. Among those who were waiting for them was the Duchess of Kent, who had come all the way from England to welcome them. She was nearer to her daughter now, through the healing influences of happiness and time.

The castle at Rosenau had been prepared for them and they drove there, past the harvesters in their blue blouses, the petunias hanging from the cottage windows and the chicory flowers in the dry grass. 'My Albert's birthplace; the place he most loves,' Queen Victoria wrote. He was 'so, so happy, to be there' with her. The menaces of responsibility did not intrude so far as this: it was 'like a beautiful dream'.

On the morning of Prince Albert's birthday, they went to the room where he was born twenty-six years before. He opened the window and they looked down on the fountain and the roses. In the afternoon they walked by the stream and came to a pool where Prince Albert made a drinking cup for the Queen with his hands, because she was thirsty. A peasant woman came along the path and said, '*Guten Abend.*' The Queen gave her some money and shook her hand. She wrote afterwards in her journal, 'I don't think she the least knew who I was.'

*

The year 1845 had begun well in Britain and trade had been nourished by the many new railways that opened up the country-side. This vigour and confidence were fading when the Queen and Prince Albert returned from their summer holiday, to endure an autumn of alarms and disasters. In New Zealand, where the Queen's flag had been hoisted in January 1840, there was savage fighting between the Maoris and the colonists. In India, after years of pretending to keep a treaty of friendship, the Sikhs invaded the territory of the East India Company, on 11 December; and thus began the first Sikh war, that lasted sixty-two days, during which they were defeated in four major battles. Nearer, and more alarming, was the threat of famine – in England, because of the poor harvest, and in Ireland, because of the potato blight that destroyed the crops overnight. On 11 November, Prince Albert wrote to his brother, 'The potato crops have turned out badly and will lead to the greatest political complication – it is impossible to argue with famished people.'

The blight had spread to Belgium, Holland, Sweden and Denmark, but their governments acted quickly : they opened their harbours and brought in cheap foreign corn. When Peel urged that Britain should copy the example of the European countries; when he said he was willing to introduce a measure 'involving the ultimate repeal of the corn laws' that shielded English farmers from foreign competition, his 'Protectionist' colleagues voted against him. On 5 December, he wrote to the Queen, assuring her that 'in the present state of affairs' he could render more service to her and the country 'in a private than in a public station'.

Sir Robert Peel went to Osborne, and the records of his meeting with the Queen and the Prince reveal their mutual sadness at the prospect of parting. Prince Albert wrote, '. . . he was visibly much moved and said to me that it was one of the most painful moments in his life, to separate himself from us.' The Prince, including Lord Aberdeen in his regret, added, 'On our side the loss of two so estimable men, who possess our whole and perfect confidence in public as well as in private affairs, and have always proved themselves true friends, leaves a *great gap*.' Peel's own feelings are revealed in his *Memoirs*: he wrote, 'I will not say more than that the generous support which I have uniformly received from Her Majesty and from the Prince, and all that passed on the occasion of the retirement, made an impression on my heart that can never be effaced.'

Prince Albert wrote of the realistic theme in their conversation: 'After we had examined what possibilities were open for the Crown, the conclusion was come to that Lord John [Russell] was the only man who could be charged with forming a Cabinet.' After the Queen had agreed, Sir Robert said that he would support Russell and use all his influence with the House of Lords to 'prevent their impeding his progress'.

The farewells were not yet necessary. On 20 December, Lord John Russell had to confess his failure to form a government, because of dissension between his colleagues; and so, as Benjamin Disraeli said, 'Lord John handed back with courtesy the poisoned chalice to Sir Robert.' Peel resumed office, and Prince Albert wrote to his stepmother, on Christmas Day, 'We are glad in soul . . . that we have survived the ministerial crisis and are now standing exactly where we stood before – upon our feet, whereas during the crisis, we were very nearly standing on our heads.' He wrote more seriously to Baron Stockmar, that the experience had been 'a source of real advantage to the Crown, by producing a widely spread feeling that amid all the general confusion and heat of the party, at least one person has remained calm and free from party spirit, this person being the Queen'.

During the crisis, Queen Victoria, with Prince Albert to guide her, had enjoyed her first victory over public opinion, as opposed to public emotion. The *Examiner*, one of the most Radical newspapers in Britain, forsook its grumbling policy to pay the Queen a compliment. The editor stated,

> In the pranks and bunglings of the last three weeks, there is one part which, according to all report, has been played most faultlessly – that of a Constitutional Sovereign. In the pages of history the directness, the sincerity, the scrupulous observance of constitutional rules, which have marked Her Majesty's conduct in circumstances the most trying, will have their place of honour. Unused as we are to deal in homage to royalty, we must add, that never, we believe, was the heart of a monarch so warmly devoted to the interests of a people, and with so enlightened a sense of their interests.

Sir Robert Peel wrote that he felt 'like a man restored to life'. When Parliament met in the new year, he made a succession of powerful speeches and, in spite of what Greville described as 'shouts of derision and gestures of contempt', he carried the Corn Importation Bill against the opposition of two-thirds of his own Tories, stirred by Disraeli, but with the support of Lord John Russell and the Whigs. The Bill passed the House of Lords on 25 June, 1846; but the same night, Peel was defeated in the Commons on the Irish Coercion Bill, by the combined opposition of the Whigs, 'Protectionists' and Radicals, who enjoyed the chance to oust him from power.

At two o'clock in the morning, Sir Robert wrote to the Queen, advising her 'to dissolve Parliament'. On 29 June, he went to Osborne to tender his resignation, 'much relieved', Prince Albert noted, 'in quitting a post the labours and anxieties of which' seemed 'almost too much for anybody to bear'.

●

After years of having felt 'so safe' with Sir Robert Peel and Lord Aberdeen, Queen Victoria was now obliged to accept a new political regime, with Lord John Russell as Prime Minister and Lord Palmerston as Foreign Secretary. She wrote to King Leopold, on 7 July, 1846, that the 'contrast' was 'very striking', and that there was 'much less respect and much less high and pure feeling'. She added that the new Government was *very* weak and extremely disunited'.

The Queen had to adapt herself to this political upheaval during the weeks following the birth of her third daughter, Princess Helena. The public troubles encouraged her into deeper appreciation of her private blessings, with five children and a perfect husband. She wrote to King Leopold, 'I pray God never to let me survive him.'

During the change of government, the Queen had written to her uncle, 'Albert's use to me, and I may say to the *Country*, by his firmness and sagacity, is beyond all belief in these moments of trial.' She wrote also, 'Everywhere my dearest Angel receives the respect and honours I receive.' But this was not true. He was still a minor German prince to the haughty English aristocracy, and when one of them – the Duke of Buckingham – deigned to carry the Prince's coffee to him 'after dinner on a waiter', the Queen was pleased, because it was known that the Duke was 'immensely proud'.

Many of the artistocracy clung to Lord Chesterfield's view that 'a man of fashion, who is seen piping or fiddling at a concert, degrades his own dignity', and they were chagrined because of Prince Albert's liking for scientists, artists and musicians. Queen Victoria had appealed to King Leopold for advice on this delicate problem, and he answered, 'To hope to *escape* censure and calumny is next to impossible. . . The dealings with artists, for instance, require great prudence; they are acquainted with all classes of society, and for that very reason dangerous.' But Prince Albert persisted in seeking the company of thoughtful and creative people. His sympathies went even beyond this, and he wrote of 'that class of our community which has most of the toil and least of the enjoyments of this world'.

The time had come for Stockmar to make another solemn report on the progress of his pupil. He thought that the Prince had made 'great strides'. He wrote, 'Place weighty reasons before him and at once he takes a rational and just view. . . He has also gained much in self-reliance. His natural vivacity leads him at times to jump too rapidly to a conclusion and on occasion he acts too hastily, but he has grown too clear-sighted to commit any great mistake. He will now and then run against a post and bruise his shins.' Stockmar added, sententiously, 'But a man cannot become an experienced soldier without having been in battle and getting a few blows.'

Stockmar wrote also of the Queen. 'She makes daily advances in discernment and experience; the candour, the love of truth, the fairness, the considerateness with which she judges men and things, are truly delightful, and the ingenuous self-knowledge with which she speaks about herself is simply charming.'

When Christmas came again, Prince Albert wrote to his brother, '. . . I am beginning to look at the accumulating years with mixed feelings. May the year 1847 bring us together again, so that we may enjoy a happy meeting. Our present consists of two pictures of us which are real pendants, not too large, painted by Winterhalter. So we hope you will like them.' He described the paintings: 'Victoria leads Bertie by the hand. I behave most decently, in black evening dress, and "elegantly wrapped in a cloak".'

*

Lord John Russell wrote of his family, which had helped to rule Britain since the age of the Tudors, that 'in all times of popular movement the Russells have been on the "forward" side'. He was fifty-three years old when he formed his first ministry, in 1846. Eight of his fifteen ministers were hereditary peers. Lord

Palmerston, also dedicated to politics, had been a minister when he was twenty-two: he was sixty-one when he became the Queen's Foreign Secretary. Palmerston was powerful and self-assured and his bold talents had won him the regard of the country. He enjoyed the dangers of his work almost as much as the prospect of solution. He was a brilliant cynic, with great experience of life, and he had neither the character nor the simplicity that would assure him the continued trust of the Queen and Prince Albert.

They began with a frank wish to conquer prejudice. On 9 August, 1846, Prince Albert begged Lord Palmerston never to hesitate in sending the Queen 'private communications', however unreserved they might be in their language. He said that it was 'their chief wish' that, by hearing all parties, they might 'arrive at a just, dispassionate and correct opinion upon the various political questions'. But it was not in the tradition of British party politics, nor in Palmerston's character, to be 'dispassionate'. In April 1847, the Queen reprimanded him for sending drafts to Lisbon without first submitting them to her. Lord John Russell also had to be scolded, for appointing a Physician in Ordinary without consulting his Sovereign.

This unhappy cleavage between the Queen and her ministers was to increase and add to the difficulties of the coming years, when Europe was to be devastated by revolution, and Ireland was to endure the darkest age of her history. The first warning of what was to happen in Europe had come in November 1846, when Cracow was seized by the Emperor of Austria and drawn into his empire, in defiance of the Treaty of Vienna. The Irish were still suffering the famine that brought them to the verge of civil war: within the next few years, the population of Ireland fell from eight to five millions; hundreds of thousands died of starvation, and thousands more escaped to America. In England, there was already such a shortage of wheat that it was selling at 102 shillings a quarter. The Queen wrote, 'The price of bread is of an unparalleled height, we have been obliged to reduce every one to a pound a day, and only secondary flour to be used in the Royal kitchen.'

*

Prince Albert continued his improving interests. In February 1847, he was elected Chancellor of Cambridge University, in preference to Lord Powis. Sixteen of the twenty-four professors voted for him, and nineteen of the thirty senior wranglers. Queen Victoria was delighted, but also angry with Lord Powis for daring to stand against her 'beloved Angel', and she never forgave him. Later, when they met, the Queen refused to speak to him.[1]

Queen Victoria went to Cambridge with Prince Albert for the proud occasion. The Prince advanced towards her, 'in his beautiful dress of black and gold', and read his speech. Baroness Bunsen described the 'admirable command of countenance of both', and noted that the Queen 'only smiled upon the Prince at the close, when all was over'.

Honour was not enough for Prince Albert. He was soon at his desk, examining the programme of studies at the University and deciding that classics and mathematics were pursued out of all proportion. He anticipated the mind of the twentieth century by urging that the study of political economy, psychology, geography, chemistry and astronomy should be increased. It was not easy for a foreign prince to dare to interfere with the aged University, especially as the Vice-Chancellor had already urged that a century should pass before new scientific discoveries were admitted into Cambridge. This 'dread of innovation' shocked Prince Albert, so, hoping to enforce his argument, he invited the Vice-Chancellor to stay at Windsor. He was reluctant: it was so hard, he said, to convince the heads of colleges that there was merit in change. But he returned to Cambridge, promising to act. A plan of reform was drawn up, allowing for extended fields of study and opportunities for more degrees. The scheme was described as 'broad enough to satisfy the demands of all moderate reformers', and it was adopted by a 'triumphant majority'.

The Vice-Chancellor admitted that the Prince's election had brought 'a new and glorious era' in academic history. *The Times*, which had always been cautious in praising the Prince, said that the nation owed him 'a debt of gratitude', as he had been the 'first to suggest, and the most determined to carry out' the changes. Even *Punch*, which liked making fun of him, allowed Leech to draw him 'taking the *Pons Asinorum*, after the manner of Napoleon taking the Bridge of Arcola'.

CHAPTER TWELVE

1847-1848

The Court went to Scotland in August 1847. When Prince Albert made a journey to the west coast, a reporter wrote that he 'looked pleased with everything and everybody, and with himself too'. The Prince quoted the sentence in a letter to the Duchess of Kent, and remarked, 'I must also confess that the reporter was right . . . is not that a happy state?' He added, 'Yesterday, my twenty-eighth birthday, we had a Highland gathering at which there were all sorts of ancient games of a warlike kind.'

This summer the Queen, Prince Albert and their five children stayed in a shooting-lodge at Ardverikie, where there were 'beautiful drawings' on the walls of stags by Landseer. The Prince tramped the moors for a day or two, but he was soon at his desk, writing of international politics. He made the surprising statement, out of keeping with his early teaching, that the 'political reformation of Germany' lay 'entirely in the hands of Prussia', and that Prussia had 'only to will, in order to accomplish these results'. He sent the King a letter, urging him to realize that the day was past when monarchs might make treaties without consulting the wishes of their people. He wrote also, 'The political horizon grows darker and darker. Italy, Greece, Spain and Portugal are in a state of ferment.'

Prince Albert still listened to his old master: late in September a letter arrived at Ardverikie in which Baron Stockmar wrote, 'Let your increasing study, your increasing occupation, be human nature in all its length and breadth, and consider politics only as a means of doing service, as far as in you lies, to the whole human race.'

Soon after the Prince received this advice, the Court returned to Windsor, where there was proof that the Prince's knowledge of 'human nature' had already yielded good. In the park, less than a mile from the Castle, was Frogmore, where the Duchess of Kent lived with her ladies. All rancour had gone from the once bitter relationship between mother and daughter: the Prince had brought them together in affectionate trust that endured to the end of the Duchess's life. Nine years later, Lady Augusta Bruce,[1] who was in almost constant attendance on the Duchess, wrote that the Queen's 'kindness', her 'anxiety' and 'tenderness' for her mother were 'too dear'. But it was Prince Albert who warmed the heart of this lesser court. He was shy, but they all admired his 'good sense and *feeling*'. Lady Augusta wrote, 'The *blessing* he is to the Queen and country . . . the good he does, his kindness, his well-conditioned mind and tastes, and his anxious desire to do what is right and encourage and develop in others all that is good. . .'

*

Early in the new year, 1848, Prince Albert had to look beyond his domestic peace and consider the tide of insurrection that was surging over Europe. The Austrian Chancellor, Prince Metternich, then seventy-four years old, wrote of the 'blood-stained tragedy', but he had known for decades that it would come. In March, he fled to exile in England, and in December his Emperor was to abdicate. Almost every country in Europe was torn by revolt; and in France, Louis Philippe and his Queen had already escaped from the Tuileries by a back door, to seek refuge, also in England. They landed at Newhaven on 3 March – pitiful victims, in part, of their own folly.

The spirit of revolution followed the exiles over the Channel: a few weeks later a crowd gathered in Trafalgar Square crying

'*Vive la République*'. They marched not to the Houses of Parliament, nor to No. 10 Downing Street, but to the grounds of Buckingham Palace, which they invaded far enough to wreck Prince Albert's skittle alley. They were led by a youth wearing epaulettes; when he was arrested, he cried.

Chartism flared again and there was a succession of disturbances, in the provinces and in London, as a protest against hunger and inequality. Prince Albert wrote to Baron Stockmar on 11 March, 'We had our revolution yesterday, and it went up in smoke. In London eight hundred special constables were on duty, but the troops were kept out of the way, to prevent any possibility of a collision. The law was victorious. I hope this will make a good impression on the Continent. In Ireland things look still more serious.'

During March, Queen Victoria was obliged to leave her desk and its tasks: on the 18th, her sixth child, Princess Louise, was born in Buckingham Palace. Prince Albert paused to report to the King of Prussia, that 'mother and child' were both 'quite well'; then he returned to his endless memoranda on the conflicts, at home and abroad. He wrote to Stockmar, 'My heart is heavy. I lose flesh and strength daily. European war is at our door... I have need of friends. Come, as you love me.'

On 10 April, Chartists from all over the country met on Kennington Common, with the plan to march on London. They were pacified by the special constables so successfully that when the crowd of 23,000 came to the Thames bridges, they agreed to send their 'petition' to Westminster in three hansom cabs. Three days later Greville wrote, hopefully, that the 'defensive demonstration' would 'produce a vast effect in all foreign countries, and show how solid is the foundation on which we are resting.' Elsewhere, in England and Scotland, there were more riots. On 6 May, Prince Albert wrote to Stockmar, that if the Chartists 'could, by means of their organization, throw themselves in a body upon any one point, they might be successful in a *coup-de-main*.' He added, however, that 'The loyalty of the country on the whole is, besides, very great; and, so far as the person of the Sovereign is concerned, can never have been greater.'

As early as February 1848 the fever of revolution had already reached Germany, and the Grand Duke of Baden had been forced to make his people liberal concessions, including trial by jury. Thus encouraged, the passion for emancipation spread, from Prussia in the north, to the quiet of Prince Albert's Thuringia. There were riots in both Gotha and Coburg. He had written to his brother on 14 March – four days before his 'little daughter' was born – 'The news that you sent me in your letter of the 8th, about conditions in Gotha, made me exceedingly sad... Such an outbreak of the people is always something *very dreadful*, and what will have to be done now, will probably have to be done hurriedly and therefore badly. The claims themselves do not seem to contain anything but what you have already proposed. The only difficult point is the question about the domains. Would it not be best to divide the domains? One part might be declared state property; the other, part of the family trust. Would not that solve the question best? ... I should also consider the hunting grounds as private property and declare myself ready to hold them.' He then described his plan for the new Constitution, and added, 'The laws for election should be liberal and extended.'

Prince Albert was adamant over the limitations of the rights of the army, a lesson he had learned in England. He wrote, in the same letter to his brother, 'In Germany and on the Continent the mistake is made as a rule, of looking upon the military as executors of the law, but the Army has, in reality, nothing to do with law, and it should be called in for help only when it is proved that law has been trespassed and that a state of anarchy has broken out. Only then is it the duty of the military power to step in and assist the lawful authority.' He added, 'Everything looks rather black in Germany just now, but I don't give up hope...'

Two months later, on 8 June, the Prince was still in despair over his brother's future, and he wrote, 'Should the Sovereignty fall from Coburg altogether (God grant it may not be the case), I don't see why my *eldest* son should not have the right of succession. . . I hear that Altenburg recommends that I and my children should be excluded from the succession in Coburg and Gotha. . . It will be worth while to keep your eyes on this question.'

When peace came, Duke Ernest lost only half his land; and his powers were reduced, but not wrecked, under the new spell that was being cast over Europe.

*

Some of Prince Albert's ideas were alarming to the old ruling class in Britain, but they pleased the mass of his listeners. On 18 May, 1848, when he took the chair at the meeting of the Society for Improving the Condition of the Working Classes, instead of damning the strikers, he reprimanded the capitalists. He warned them to be careful 'to avoid any dictatorial interference with labour and employment'. He told them that it was only ignorance that prevented the two classes from having confidence in each other, and that 'any real improvement must be the result of the exertion of the working people themselves'.

When the Prince went to see a new industrial machine, in York, he showed the experts where another wheel might be introduced, with advantage. One of them said afterwards, 'Not one man in ten thousand would have noticed the omission.' When he spoke to the Royal Horticultural Society, he delighted the Yorkshire farmers by saying, 'We agriculturalists of England.' The words were not empty, for the farms at Windsor showed an increasing profit under his direction. When he returned home from Yorkshire he shared his pleasure with Stockmar, to whom he wrote, on 18 July, 'I had to speak . . . and was immensely applauded for what I said. . . I only mention it because I believe it will give you pleasure, as you have often urged me to have more confidence in matters of this kind.'

A few weeks before, the Prince had written to his stepmother in Coburg, 'I never remember to have been kept in the stocks to the same extent as I am just now. The mere reading of English, French and German papers absorbs nearly all the spare hours of the day; and yet one can let nothing pass without losing the connection and coming in consequence to wrong conclusions.'

There was one bundle of newspapers that the Prince read with pleasure; they came from Brussels. King Leopold's years of planning, and the liberal views he had instilled into Prince Albert, were being tried and proved in Belgium. In the letter to his stepmother, the Prince wrote, 'Belgium and England stand up to the present time unshaken, and furnish useful standards of what constitutes real freedom.' On 9 July, he wrote again to Stockmar, 'Here everything goes on to a wish. The Government is weak, but it manages to get along, and the public is loyal and patriotic.'

On 9 August, Prince Albert wrote to his brother of the lull in Ireland's troubles: 'The leaders in the riots . . . have been caught, and the same people who applauded their addresses, will see them hanged with equal pleasure.' Fears that there would be a link-up between the Irish and the Chartists were dispelled in the meantime, but there were other menaces to spoil the peace of mind of both the Queen and the Prince. Rebellion continued in Europe, and in Whitehall there was the more personal cause for anxiety in the behaviour of Lord Palmerston. On 20 August, the Queen protested to him because a 'private letter', addressed to her, had been 'cut open at the Foreign Office'. She wrote, 'The Queen wishes Lord Palmerston to take care that this does not happen again.' More indignant letters followed: when Austria declined Lord Palmerston's offer to mediate in her quarrel with Sardinia – a 'step' to which the Queen had said she would not give her consent – he did not tell her; and on 4 September, she protested again, 'The Queen is surprised that Lord Palmerston should have left her uninformed of so important an event.'

The day following this protest, Queen Victoria prorogued Parliament. Her speech was reassuring: she reminded the

House, 'The strength of our institutions has been tried, and has not been found wanting. I have studied to preserve the people committed to my charge in the enjoyment of that temperate freedom which they so justly value. My people, on their side, feel too sensible of the advantages of order and security to allow the promoters of pillage and confusion any chance of success in their wicked designs.'

The Queen could not know that, within less than a century, most of the reforms the Chartists sought would become the policy and the law of Britain and that a large part of Ireland would become independent.

While the last scene of the parliamentary year ended, in Westminster, the royal yacht, *Victoria and Albert*, was already waiting at Woolwich. The same afternoon, the Queen and the Prince, with their six children, sailed down the Thames and then up the east coast to Aberdeen. Their goal was Balmoral, the small old castle they had rented and which they were to visit for the first time. But even on board the yacht, with the first illusions of escape, the Queen wrote a further protest to Lord John Russell, because Lord Palmerston was using the new *entente cordiale* with republican France 'for the purpose of wresting from Austria her Italian provinces by French arms'; and she commented on the very 'intemperate' tone of Palmerston's language. This was prophetic; the holiday was to be haunted by fear of what the unpredictable minister might do next.

*

On 11 September, Prince Albert wrote to his stepmother, 'We have withdrawn for a short time into a complete mountain solitude, where one rarely sees a human face; where the snow already covers the mountain tops, and the wild deer come creeping stealthily round the house. I, naughty man, have also been creeping stealthily after the harmless stags, and today I shot two red deer.'

The daily life at Balmoral was simple, compared with the huge patterns of Windsor and Buckingham Palace. The Highlanders on the estate – which was not yet their own – were so different from the English; so authentic and natural, and respecting the Queen's wish for quiet. The castle was small, with only two sitting-rooms, and there the Queen and the Prince lived with their children. Their eldest daughter, Princess Victoria, already revealing her father's virtues, was almost eight years old; and their eldest son, Albert Edward, Prince of Wales, who was to inherit some of the worldly faults of his Hanoverian forbears, was almost seven. There were already many letters regarding his future education, which was to help in estranging him from his parents; letters between them and Stockmar, all heavy with opinion. But in the meantime, he was as the Reverend E. W. Benson saw him, at the Braemar Highland Games – a 'fair little lad of rather a slender make, with an intelligent expression'.

The Queen and the Prince had a talent for separating their private, family pleasures from their royal duties. They spent part of the day on the moors or in the garden, but they always had to return to deal with the endless red boxes with their endless documents, that arrived each day from Whitehall. They brought reports of continued bloodshed and mistrust in Europe; of more violence in Ireland, and of the new aggression in India that led to the second war against the Sikhs, and to their defeat, at Gujrat, in the following spring.

These were alarms enough to make the Queen and the Prince realize that peace was a mere interlude in their lives. And there was the constant fear of the Foreign Secretary. On 19 September, the Queen had a conversation with Lord John Russell and she wrote afterwards, in a memorandum, that she 'felt really' that she 'could hardly go on' with Palmerston, and that she 'had no confidence in him'. She was 'seriously anxious and uneasy for the welfare of the country and for the peace of Europe' while he continued at the Foreign Office, and she 'felt uneasy from one day to another as to what might happen'.

From Balmoral the Court travelled to Osborne, and then to Windsor. Prince Albert seldom wrote, or spoke, of the history of his adopted country. Nor was he prone to listen to the ghost voices within the ancient castle, where King John had protested, 'By God's teeth I will not grant them liberties which will make me a slave,' and where King Richard 11 had declared, 'What we approve shall be granted, and what we think improper refused. For think not we are to be ruled by our people. That has never been.'

Such arrogance belonged to the dark spaces of history. Queen Victoria and Prince Albert were unconsciously creating a new form for the monarchy that would yield to the harsh realism of free, intelligent people. The Prince wrote more memoranda on more reforms at Cambridge University, and on the function of Bishops in the House of Lords. This latter document is a solemn proclamation of his mind at the age of twenty-nine; and it is astonishing for its ideas, in the light of what has happened in the century and more since he wrote to the Dean of Westminster:

A bishop ought to abstain completely from mixing himself up with politics of the day, and beyond giving a general support to the Queen's Government, and occasionally voting for it, should take no part in the discussion of State affairs. He should come forward whenever the interests of humanity are at stake, and give boldly and manfully his advice to the House and country (I mean questions like Negro emancipation, education of the people, improvement of the health of towns, measures for the recreation of the poor, against cruelty to animals, for regulating factory labour, etc. etc. etc.).

As to religious affairs, he cannot but take an active part in them, but let that always be the part of a *Christian*, not of a mere Churchman; let him never forget the insufficiency of human knowledge and wisdom, and the impossibility for any man or even Church, to say, 'I am right; I alone am right.' Let him therefore, be meek, and liberal, and tolerant to other confessions, but let him never forget that he is the representative of the Church of the Land, the maintenance of which is as important to the country as that of its constitution or its throne. Let him here always be conscious that the

Church has its duties to fulfil, that it does not exist for itself, but
for the people, for the country. . .

A Bishop ought to be uniformly a peace-maker, and, when he
can, it is his duty to lessen political or other animosities, and remind the Peers of their duties as Christians. . . He ought to be a
guardian of public morality, not, like the Press, by tediously interfering with every man's private affairs, speaking for applause, or
trampling on those that are fallen. . . He should likewise boldly
admonish the public even against its predominant feeling, if this be
contrary to the purest standard of morality (reproving, for instance,
the recklessness and wickedness of the proprietors of Railway
Shares, who, having no funds themselves, acquire riches at the
expense of others, their dupes).

Such high-minded memoranda continued to isolate Prince
Albert from the fashionable world, but he tried to please them
also with concerts and plays, in Buckingham Palace and at
Windsor. This Christmas, Mr and Mrs Kean brought their com-
pany to the Castle and staged *The Merchant of Venice* in the
Rubens room. They came for many years after, and thirteen
more Shakespeare plays and many less solemn pieces were pro-
duced, with the encouragement of both the Queen and Prince
Albert – in the Castle where Shakespeare had come to produce
The Merry Wives of Windsor for the first Queen Elizabeth.

In spite of the discords in the world beyond the Castle walls,
the Queen and the Prince created their own happiness. In
November 1848, when Lord Melbourne died, the Queen wrote
in her journal, 'Truly and sincerely I deplore the loss of one who
was a most kind and disinterested friend of mine, and most sincerely attached to me.' But even Lord Melbourne was the symbol
of years that she wished to forget. She wrote to King Leopold,
'God knows! I never wish that time back again.'

CHAPTER THIRTEEN

1848-1850

There were lessons in the history of Windsor that Queen Victoria and Prince Albert did not heed: none more melancholy than the theme of the relationship between the sovereigns and their heirs, who had lived in the Castle during almost eight hundred years. They might have paused by a wall on which, in the twelfth century, Henry 11 was said to have 'caused to be painted' an 'olde eagle with its body and eyes being scratched by four younger birds', in protest against his sons who, he said, 'cease not to pursue my death'. Or they might have recalled the bitterness with which King George 11 described his son as the 'greatest ass and the greatest liar and the greatest *canaille* and the greatest beast in the whole world.'

The Castle was heavy with warnings of the animosity that has almost always isolated royal parents from their eldest children. This old evil was to spoil Queen Victoria's relationship with her heir, especially after Prince Albert died. It began, innocently, when the time came to plan his education. He was slowly drawn into his own, separate world, from which he saw his mother and father as aloof and exalted persons; beyond the confidence of ordinary children who embrace their parents, in search of trust and affection.

In 1846 Prince Albert had written[1] to Florschütz, his old tutor in Coburg, 'We are all in excellent health, but the education of six such different children (for they are none of them the least like each other, in looks, mind or character) is a difficult

task. They are a great deal with their parents and are very fond
of them. I don't interfere in the details of their upbringing, but
only superintend the principles, which are difficult to uphold in
the face of so many women, and I give the final judgment. From
my verdict there is no appeal.'

The 'principles' that were to govern the training of the Prince
of Wales were inspired by a zealous prayer that he should grow
up in his father's image, and as unlike any of his Hanoverian
great-uncles as possible. Such 'principles' were absolutely alien
to the boy's nature.

Lady Lyttelton had taken care of all the children, when they
were very young. The eldest princess inherited her father's diligence and was quick to learn. The Prince of Wales was less so,
but he was the one who enjoyed Lady Lyttelton's heart. She
thought his 'childish dignity very pretty to witness', and she saw
'intelligence' in his 'large, clear blue eyes'. The differences between father and son were already obvious. When Prince Albert
was a child in Coburg he had cried with shyness at parties. The
Prince of Wales 'showed signs of social instinct' when he was
still a baby. The twentieth-century psychiatrist might analyse
all the different circumstances of father and son, and explain
why Prince Albert remained a German in mind and habits,
while his eldest son was to grow up disliking everything that
emanated from his father's country, and slowly giving his heart
to France.

On 11 July, 1848, when the fate of so many monarchs in
Europe encouraged Queen Victoria to think anxiously of her
own crown, she had written to King Leopold, '. . . I feel an uncertainty in everything existing. . . When one thinks of one's
children, their education, their future – and prays for them – I
always think and say to myself, "Let them grow up fit for *whatever station* they may be placed in, *high or low*." ' Lord Melbourne had once advised her, 'Be not over-solicitous about education. . . It may mould and direct character, but it rarely alters
it.' But Lord Melbourne was dead; and the Queen's mood of
'uncertainty', stirred by the fate of princes in Europe, soon

passed. Her son would become a king in time; and the counsel of Stockmar, and the model of her husband, were stronger than ordinary, human understanding.

In the spring of 1849, the Prince of Wales was taken from Lady Lyttelton's care and given his own tutor – Henry Birch, whom Prince Albert described as 'a young, good-looking, amiable man'. He thought that his son might become 'attached' to him, but soon decided that the degree of attachment was dangerous. The kind, sympathetic tutor became a symbol of romantic fondness that the boy did not seem to feel for his parents. The young Prince wrote affectionate letters to Birch, and, stealing into his bedroom, placed them on his pillow. Sometimes there was a present to prove his devotion.

After two years, Prince Albert decided that there were faults in Birch's religious teaching, and, with this excuse, the tutor was asked to resign and was given a living in Lancashire as consolation. Lady Canning watched the parting and wrote, 'It has been a trouble and sorrow to the Prince of Wales, who has done no end of touching things since he heard that he was to lose him. . . He is such an affectionate dear little fellow; his notes and presents which Mr Birch used to find on his pillow were really too moving.'

In Birch's place came Frederick Waymouth Gibbs, a precise intellectual of 'humble parentage' who was to stay with the Prince until he was seventeen years old. He was a disciplinarian, and he sought the confidence of the father rather than of the son. For this he was punished with the Prince's dislike and many scenes of his passionate temper. Gibbs's diary,[2] published a century later, reveals this unhappy conflict. On 26 January, 1851, the tutor wrote, '. . . he hangs his head, and looks at his feet, and invariably within a day or two has one of his fits of nervous, unmanageable temper.' Two days later, Gibbs wrote, 'On the terrace he quarrelled with, and struck P. Alfred, and I had to hasten home.' The drawing master was equally alarmed when the Prince of Wales pulled his brother's hair 'brandishing a paper-knife'.

Baron Stockmar confided in Gibbs that the Prince was 'an exaggerated Copy of his Mother'. There was little comfort in this for the tutor, who was struck by the Prince with 'a large stick' when he was 'in a passion'. The boy threw stones at Gibbs's face, 'made grimaces' and refused to learn. It is strange therefore that the tutor wrote, after two years, that 'if in the meantime it is possible to furnish him with that elementary knowledge, which is acquired only in childhood, his natural shrewdness and good sense will enable him to understand and efficiently discharge the duties he will be called upon to perform'.

While his elder sister enjoyed her learning, the Prince of Wales yearned for the company of the young, whom he never met. Someone must have mentioned this to his father, who tried to correct the dangerous loneliness by inviting boys from Eton to tea on Sundays. Prince Albert was curiously insensitive in the way he arranged these formidable afternoons in the Castle. The youngsters he brought from Eton were mostly sons of peers, chosen for their social perfection. And he was always present, to control them with his excellence. Sir Sidney Lee admits, in his biography of King Edward VII, that 'Prince Albert . . . inspired the boy visitors with a sense of dread'.

In time, the conquest came to the Prince of Wales. Some of these young Etonians, no doubt exchanging silent glances of fun and trust with him, of which Prince Albert was unaware, became his 'close friends for life'.

The differences between the father, whose plans were philosophical rather than human, and the son, for whom philosophy remained a mystery, were never to be bridged. About the time when Gibbs assumed the task of educating him, the Prince of Wales was taken to the Great Exhibition – the wonder his father was to create, in 1851. The boy was delighted by some waxwork models of the murderous Thugs of India. He wrote of them in his diary, which was always read by his father. Prince Albert reported the folly to Stockmar, who was shocked. He reminded the young Prince that he had been 'born in a Christian and an enlightened age in which such atrocious acts are not even dreamt of'. It is no wonder that Sir Sidney Lee wrote that 'King Edward looked back with pain on his educational ordeal'.

*

In December 1848 Queen Victoria had given her guarded approval when Louis Napoleon, who had emerged triumphant from the revolution, was elected President of France. She was more pleased early in 1849, when she learned that he was trying to bring stability to his country. She wrote to King Leopold, on 6 February, 'Everybody says Louis Napoleon has behaved extremely well in the last crisis – full of courage and energy, and they say that he is decidedly straightforward, which is not to be despised.'

Peace was slowly coming back to most of the countries of Europe, as each attempt to change the existing order was crushed by force; but the Pope, who had fled from Rome in November, was still a fugitive in Gaeta, and Prussia and Austria had not yet exhausted their anger. Compared with them, Britain was now a quiet and peaceful land. But there was another alarm from India, in the reports of reverses against the Sikhs in the Punjab. Hundreds of officers and men had been killed since the war began, in 1848, and there were many anxious families in Britain for whom the fate of the army in India was more important than the political struggles within Europe. The prizes of Imperial glory were costly for those who won them : in the battle of Chilianwala, in January 1849, the Anglo-Indian losses were so alarming that the results was interpreted by the British and Indian governments as a miserable defeat. The slaughter was repeated at Gujrat, on 14 March, but this time the Sikhs suffered; and after being pursued for a hundred miles, to Rawalpindi, they surrendered. Their young maharaja, Dhuleep Singh, accepted an allowance of £50,000 a year and retired to England, to live as a country gentleman in Norfolk. The Punjab was annexed to British India, and Queen Victoria was given the

maharaja's fabulous diamond, the Koh-i-noor. She was shy of
the trophy, and, in later years, she did not like to wear it in the
presence of princes from India.

*

With the promise of peace, Prince Albert turned back to the
social problems that interested him so much. Late into the night
he sat beneath the green-shaded lamp that he had brought from
Germany, writing the noble thoughts that might cure the ills of
the world. But he also made a remarkable and realistic statement, in a letter to his brother, on 13 May, 1849. He complained
because the 'ultra Tories' abused him for working 'energetic-
ally . . . against their plans'; and then he wrote, 'I am working
at social improvements and I take the chair at public meetings,
etc., etc., which are held for this purpose. The unequal division
of property, and the dangers of poverty and envy arising there-
from, is the principal evil. Means must necessarily be found, not
for diminishing riches (as the communists wish), but to make
facilities for the poor. But there is the rub. I believe this question
will be first solved here in England.'

The Prince was in his thirtieth year, but he had already lost
the vigour that had made Queen Victoria describe him as 'beautiful', only ten years before. He was becoming physically plump,
from too many hours at his desk and not enough in the open
air. Except for the enduring error, in the education of his eldest
son, he was caught up in the web of his own virtues. He frowned
thoughtfully over every cause that came before him. One day, he
noted in a report on workhouses that the greater number of in-
mates were old servants. He realized that men and women in
domestic service should be protected from the caprice of a single
master who might give them a bad reference, so he arranged for
a meeting of responsible people to help all servants; to direct
them to the benefits of annuity schemes and to improve the circumstances of their lives.

A descendant[3] of Prince Albert wrote, almost eighty years

after he died, '. . . my Grandfather's virtues during his lifetime were somewhat overpowering, but have today been reçognised for what they were : a superior, if somewhat heavily Teutonic intelligence combined to an admirable sense of duty, which never allowed him to complain about being misunderstood. But when Death called he gladly followed that call. It is lonely to be over-perfect and unrelentingly virtuous !'

There was one escape from this routine of virtue, in the delight the Queen and the Prince shared in all aspects of the theatre. The Christmas production of *The Merchant of Venice* at Windsor had made them realize that it was their duty, and their pleasure, to encourage actors and their plays. On 6 January, 1849, Queen Victoria wrote to the King of Prussia, 'Chevalier Bunsen has been helping us in an attempt to revive and elevate the English drama which has greatly deteriorated through lack of support of society. We are having a number of performances of classical plays in a small, specially constructed theatre in the Castle. . .'

This interest was not mere patronage of the professional stage. The Queen and the Prince also encouraged their children to read and act plays. Their talents grew, so that, a few years later, on the thirteenth birthday of their eldest son, Princess Victoria 'recited the whole scene of Shylock before the Court', and the Prince of Wales then acted a scene from *Henry IV*, followed by a monologue from Schiller's *William Tell*. Their second son, Prince Alfred, recited the fable of *The Fox and the Crow*. Prince Albert wrote of the performances to his old tutor in Coburg, and added, 'The little ones did their part likewise, and very well too.'[4]

*

On the way to Scotland and Balmoral, in August 1849, Queen Victoria and Prince Albert went to Ireland for the first time. Twenty-eight years had passed since the last royal visit to the 'distressful country', when King George IV had been received

Albert, Prince Consort—from a drawing by Winterhalter.

The Duchess Louise, mother of Prince Albert. From a portrait in the palace in Coburg.

Prince Albert driving his favorites, circa 1843.

Queen Victoria and Prince Albert on a French man o' war during the visit of Louis Philippe to England in 1844.

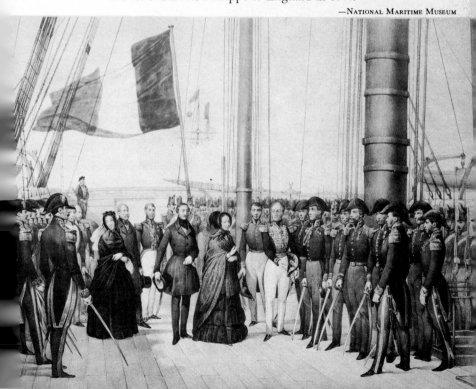

Prince Albert as a young man.

The royal family, with the Prince of Wales,
afloat on Virginia Water.

"The First of May, 1851" by Winterhalter. The Duke of Wellington on his eighty-second birthday, presenting a casket to his grandson, Prince Arthur, with Queen Victoria and Prince Albert looking on. The Crystal Palace is in the background.

The Queen, Prince Albert and the royal children departing
in their railway carriage for Scotland.

The Prince Consort in later life, from a print.

with loud huzzas, although, as Croker recorded, he was 'gayer than it might be proper to tell', and Lady Glengall noted that he was in fact 'dead drunk' and 'could hardly stand'.

For Queen Victoria, who was unreasonably prejudiced against the Irish, the visit was harsh duty. Three years before, on 3 August, 1846, she had admitted in a letter to Lord John Russell that the journey 'must one day or other be undertaken'; but she added, 'As this would not be a journey of pleasure', the expense should not 'fall upon the Civil List'. On 22 December, 1848, Prince Albert had written to the Home Secretary of the 'unhappy country' and its 'state of misery and criminality'. He wrote also of poor-law relief and public grants, and was, as ever, generous with ideas for reform.

It seemed that the Queen and the Prince were both depressed at the prospect of Ireland. The depression vanished as they arrived in the Cove of Cork. The Queen wrote to King Leopold, on 6 August, 'Our visit to Cork was very successful; the Mayor was knighted *on deck* . . . like in times of old.' The reception in Dublin was astonishing, and Lord Clarendon, who was with the Queen and the Prince, wrote to Sir George Grey on 14 August, that even the members of seditious clubs, who had been rebels of 1848, and who had 'threatened broken heads and windows before the Queen came', were now 'the most loyal of her subjects'. Lord Clarendon added that the Irish were not only 'enchanted' by the Queen, but they were also 'pleased with themselves for their own good feelings and behaviour'. They believed that they had 'removed the barrier that hitherto existed between the Sovereign and themselves. . .'

Prince Albert waited until the visit was over and they were in Scotland before he wrote to his brother, on 18 August, 'Our reception in Ireland was a real triumph and a most important proof that the only country in our kingdom which was considered to be unhealthy (at least as regards loyalty) is as healthy as all the other places.' He revealed more of his mind and intentions in a letter to Baron Stockmar, in which he wrote, 'What principally occupies me just now is a plan for the establishment of a free University for Ireland.'

These thoughts came to him at Balmoral, where he wrote, 'Now we are here in our mountain loneliness . . . yesterday . . . I went out shooting for the first time and shot three stags, for which you will envy me.'

Greville, as clerk of the Privy Council, was summonded to Balmoral early in September, and he described the visit with pleasure. He recalled,

> Much as I dislike Courts and all that appertains to them, I am glad to have made this expedition, and to have seen the Queen and Prince in their Highland retreat, where they certainly appear to great advantage. The place is very pretty, the house very small. They live there without any state whatever; they live not merely like private gentlefolks, but like very small gentlefolks; small house, small rooms, small establishment. There are no soldiers, and the whole guard of the Sovereign and the whole Royal Family is a single policeman. . . The Queen is running in and out of the house all day long, and often goes out alone, walks into the cottages, and sits down and chats with the old women. . .
>
> I never before was in society with the Prince, or had any conversation with him. On Thursday morning John Russell and I were sitting together after breakfast, when he came in and sat down with us. . . I was greatly struck with him. I saw at once (what I had always heard) that he is very intelligent and highly cultivated, and moreover that he has a thoughtful mind, and thinks of subjects worth thinking about. He seemed very much at his ease, very gay, pleasant, and without the least stiffness or air of dignity.

Greville admired all that he saw and heard of the Prince, with one exception. He went for a walk with Lord Aberdeen who told him of Prince Albert's 'violent and incorrigible German unionism'. He insisted on 'a new German Empire, with the King of Prussia for its head'. Greville added that he 'saw', by the Prince's conversation at dinner, 'his opinions were just what Aberdeen represented them to be'.

*

Queen Victoria and Prince Albert continued to think of their duties in relation to Europe, while life across the Atlantic and in the British colonies seemed beyond their vision. The Prince allowed a slight change of mind in regard to Germany, which he explained some time later in a letter to his brother. He wrote, on 16 September, 1850, 'I don't like to write of Germany any more. The behaviour of the governments is such that I feel ashamed. . .'

Another thought had already developed in his mind, as early as September 1847, when he wrote to Lord John Russell that England's 'mission, duty and interest' was to put herself 'at the head of the diffusion of civilization and the attainment of liberty'. This noble belief had to wait for an opportunity to express itself.

Among the civil servants in Whitehall was Henry Cole, a remarkable man who was also an artist, a music critic, and a lover of new ideas. He had visited the Paris Exhibition in 1849, and returned with the conviction that Britain should have a bigger and more splendid exhibition that would exalt industry; that would celebrate the quiet, inventive pursuits of craftsmen after a year that had dangerously worshipped the sword.

Prince Albert had been President of the Royal Society of Arts since 1847, so the idea was brought to him. He saw in Cole's plan something of the 'mission, duty and interest' of which he had written to Lord John Russell. There was a realistic reason for such an exhibition: in spite of the dangerous unrest in Britain, her exports had increased during 1848 by ten million pounds. A Royal Commission was set up, and the manufacturers were told that in return for releasing a few of their secrets to the world, they would be making a step towards the 'unity of mankind'.

A succession of deaths disturbed the Prince while he was helping to create the Great Exhibition that was to celebrate his sober and peaceful talents. In December 1849, Queen Adelaide died. She was a sad reminder of the Hanoverian inheritance from which Queen Victoria and Prince Albert had escaped. In

August 1850, Louis Philippe died, at Claremont; but, as Greville wrote from the shore at Brighton, 'hardly more importance attaches to the event than there would be to the death of one of the old bathing-women opposite my window'. In October 1850, the Queen of the Belgians died, leaving 'Uncle Leopold' once more alone.

The loss that devastated Prince Albert was of his secretary and friend, George Anson, who had died in November 1849. They had been together during ten years, so there are few letters to reveal the integrity and affection in their relationship. Prince Albert's honest purposes had always been encouraged by Anson's intelligent sympathy, and the Queen had also been drawn into this pattern of trust. Lady Lyttelton wrote of them both being 'in floods of tears', and of Prince Albert walking about the Palace, during the days after Anson's death, looking 'sad and pale and grave'.

The one happy, family occasion during these months was dismissed with two sentences, in the letter Prince Albert sent his brother, on 1 May, 1850. He wrote, 'Today you receive the news of the birth of a healthy son.' The boy was to become Prince Arthur, Duke of Connaught and Strathearn. His father added to his brief note, 'Victoria was confined at eight o'clock; the child was rather blue, but now is nicely pink.'

On 27 June, 1850, came another alarm. The Queen was leaving Cambridge House in her carriage when a man 'of good family', who had held a commission in the army for five years, stepped forward and struck her across the face with his cane. Prince Albert described him in a letter to Stockmar as 'a dandy, whom you must often have seen in the Park, where he had made himself conspicuous'.

For some days, the Queen's head was 'green and brown from the blow'. During her suffering, news came that Sir Robert Peel had been thrown from his horse. When he died on 2 July, Prince Albert wrote to the Duchess of Kent, then abroad, '. . . blow after blow has fallen on us. . . And now death has snatched from us

Peel, the best of men, our truest friend, the strongest bulwark of the Throne, the greatest statesman of his time.'

The Queen became anxious as she watched her husband's grief. She wrote to King Leopold, 'My poor dear Albert . . . looks so pale and fagged again. He has felt, and feels, Sir Robert's death *dreadfully*. He feels he has lost a second father.' The Queen also appealed to Stockmar, 'Pray, listen to our entreaties to come. . .' She wrote of Prince Albert, '. . . he again wakes so early, and this is a sad distress to me.' The doctor had examined the Prince, and the Queen wrote, 'Clark admits that it is the mind. . . Diet has been of no avail.'

Prince Albert found his escape in work, on the plans for the Great Exhibition and in answering its enemies. Extremists in the Church thought the scheme arrogant and likely to bring wrath from Heaven; some manufacturers complained that the island would be flooded with cheap goods, and that thieves and anarchists would come. There were reports of secret societies formed on the Continent with the plan to assassinate the Queen. Doctors threatened plague, and the arrival of hordes of foreigners with venereal disease. *The Times* abused the Prince for proposing Hyde Park as the site for the exhibition, and reported that aliens were already hiring houses near by, to be used as brothels. The Prince wrote to his brother, on 4 August, 1850, 'Now our Exhibition is to be driven from London; the patrons who are afraid; the Radicals who wish to show their power over the Crown Property. . . We shall probably be defeated and have to give up the whole Exhibition. You see that we do not lie on a bed of roses.'

The gloomy prophets were subdued and the site of Hyde Park was allowed. After other plans had been prepared and committees had argued many months away, Joseph Paxton designed his fabulous palace of glass that would cover eighteen acres.

The Duke of Wellington had said of Paxton, when he was in charge of the estates of the Duke of Devonshire, 'I should have liked that man of yours for one of my generals.' Prince Albert also appreciated Paxton's creative mind and the talents of a man who would dare to plan a building which would require one-third of the glass output of Britain for a year.

Late in August, contractors took over the land and as many as two thousand men were employed in building what was soon called the Crystal Palace, and into which fifteen thousand exhibitors were to bring their creations and their wares, valued at two million pounds. Henry Cole's idea, Joseph Paxton's brave imagination, and Prince Albert's will and diligence, were working together, in harmony and triumph.

*

Lord Palmerston continued to be the chief menace to the peace of both the Queen and Prince Albert, and during this year of preparation for the Great Exhibition they had to pause, many times, to protest against his conduct in the Foreign Office. The first alarm of 1850 came in January when Lord Palmerston ordered a fleet to Pireaus – a hostile demonstration against the Greeks for having deprived a Briton of his land, and because the house of a Portuguese Jew, born in Gibraltar and therefore a British subject, had been pillaged in Athens. The House of Lords condemned Palmerston for his action, but the Commons gave him such a vote of confidence that he enjoyed the glow of a hero. Lord Grey described him as 'the man of the people' and 'the most popular man in the country'.

This personal success for Palmerston, in Westminster, did not please the Queen and the Prince, nor were they pleased with his action in dealing with the draft of the dispatch, sent to the British Minister in Athens. Lord John Russell had made changes in the draft, with which the Queen and the Prince agreed; but Lord Palmerston had ignored their corrections and sent it off as he had written it.

On 17 February, after she had been told of this arrogant gesture, the Queen wrote to the Foreign Secretary, that she 'must remark upon this sort of proceeding', of which this was 'not the first instance', and 'plainly tell Lord Palmerston that this must not happen again'. She admitted his right to state his reasons 'for disagreeing with her views', and her readiness to 'listen to his reasons'; but she added, with fine decision, that she could not 'allow a servant of the Crown and her Minister, to act contrary to her orders, and this without her knowledge'.

A wise, quiet memorandum, of about eleven hundred words, was written by Prince Albert on 3 March, after Lord John Russell had been to Windsor to discuss the question of Palmerston's future with the Queen. It reveals the unhappy conflict, between Palmerston, Lord John, who feared the disruption of the Whig Party if he was dismissed; and the Queen, who distrusted him 'on *personal* grounds' as well as for his policy.

The roots of the Queen's distrust were moral and respectable as well as political. She did not forget the episode at Windsor, early in her reign, when Palmerston had stolen into the bedroom of one of her ladies and might have ravished her, but for her screams. This scandal, which would have been condoned in Georgian times, was unforgivable in the Victorian Court, and the Queen and the Prince found it difficult to discuss Palmerston's future in terms of politics only. The prospect of a man of such 'worthless private character' being in any position of power was alarming to them. Nor were the discussions between Lord John Russell and Lord Palmerston likely to weaken his will: he moulded his own destiny and went his own way, quietly earning the nickname, 'Lord Evergreen,' which he was given when he was older.

Again, in August, the Queen set down her views on Palmerston's duty, in a letter to Lord John Russell. The phrases reveal that her own will was tempered by Prince Albert's quiet wisdom; but the letter, which was shown to Palmerston, made it quite clear that she would no longer endure 'the various neglects' of which she had 'so long and so often to complain'. Then she defined, in numbered paragraphs, exactly what she expected from her Foreign Secretary in the future.

The letter was sent on 12 August, and next day Palmerston

asked for an audience – not with the Queen but with Prince Albert. In time, Palmerston was to respect the Prince's 'eminent qualities', and to say 'how fortunate' it was 'for the country' that the Queen had married him. There is no hint that the Prince ever returned this amiable view of Palmerston, of whom he wrote that he had 'not a grain of moral feeling'. But he set down his sympathetic account of the meeting; of the Foreign Secretary being 'very much agitated', with 'tears in his eyes' that moved the Prince who – as he wrote – had never known him 'otherwise than with a bland smile on his face'. Lord John Russell wrote afterwards that the meeting had 'done a great deal of good'. This seemed momentarily true, for the Prince was able to report that Lord Palmerston had become 'exceedingly attentive and active, writing and explaining to the Queen all that is going on'.

With this stern promise of change, the Queen and the Prince tried to enjoy their holiday at Balmoral. Even there, troubles intruded and the Prince had to write scolding letters to his brother about his debts. But there was one episode that delighted them – a gesture from the Highlanders, 'primitive, true-hearted and without a guile', whom they loved so much. One day, the laird, Forbes of Strathdon, passed by with fifty of his men. They paused by the River Dee and the laird took off one of his shoes and filled it with whisky. Then all the fifty Highlanders drank Queen Victoria's health from the shoe, before they passed on.

There was a more personal prize for Prince Albert when he paused in York, on the way back to London, to speak in praise of Sir Robert Peel. When he arrived at Buckingham Palace, he read in the *Spectator* of his success: 'He has never made a speech in public, on any occasion of mark, without suggesting matter for useful thought . . . there is an individuality about them which stamps their real authorship. . . If he were removed from us, we should miss one of the least obtrusive, but most useful of our public men.'

CHAPTER FOURTEEN

1851-1853

While the Crystal Palace was being built in Hyde Park, Prince Albert was able to enjoy the sight from a window of Buckingham Palace of the great arched roof of the transept, rising one hundred and eight feet, far above the surrounding trees. On 18 February, 1851, he wrote to his brother, 'The goods for the Exhibition are being brought into the building. I am fully occupied with this work. The building itself is truly a work of marvellous art. It will be eleven miles going all round the tables.'

Thackeray was living then in Kensington, and had to pass Hyde Park on his way into London. He doubtless saw the last girders being painted cobalt blue; the scarlet curtains being hung, and the new-fangled gas pipes, laid mile on mile, to light the Crystal Palace at night. Perhaps he was already weaving his pattern of rhymes for his *May-Day Ode*, which was published in *The Times*, and in which he wrote,

> ... A blazing arch of lucid glass
> Leaps like a fountain from the grass
>   To meet the sun!
> A quiet green but few days since,
>   With cattle browsing in the shade:
>   And here are lines of bright arcade
>   In order raised! ...
> Pass underneath the shining arch,
>   'Neath which the leafy elms are green;
>   Ascend unto your throne, O Queen!
>   And take your state.

Prince Albert might have been jubilant, if it were not for the ceaseless troubles of government. The alarm in these months had begun in September 1850, when the Pope appointed an Archbishop of Westminster, and a hierarchy of bishops throughout Queen Victoria's Protestant realm. The country revived the old cry, 'No Popery!', and the Prime Minister wrote on 4 November to the Bishop of Durham of the 'insolent and insidious' action which was 'inconsistent with the Queen's supremacy, with the rights of our bishops and clergy, and with the spiritual independence of the nation'.

While the Crystal Palace was trying to herald a new age of peaceful occupation, the mass of people enjoyed the taste of an old hatred – much to the disgust of Queen Victoria, who wrote privately to her aunt, the Duchess of Gloucester, 'I cannot bear to hear the violent abuse of the Roman Catholic religion, which is so painful and cruel towards the many good and innocent Roman Catholics.'

Prince Albert was more realistic. In January 1851, he wrote cautious memoranda and letters to the Prime Minister, advising, at first, that the Pope be asked to revoke his plan. He then suggested that an agent be sent to Rome to convince the Holy See that Catholics in Britain would suffer from the appointment of bishops – that 'the hostility of the Protestants' had 'been roused to an extraordinary height and that nothing, in the opinion of the Government, would allay it, but the revocation of the late Bull...'

Lord John Russell considered Prince Albert's many suggestions, but he went ahead with his plan to table the Ecclesiastical Titles Bill, to forbid 'the assumption of territorial titles by the priests and bishops of the Roman Catholic Church'. The Bill was introduced when Parliament opened, but its promising career was suddenly interrupted when the government was defeated on an entirely different issue – a proposal to reduce the country franchise. On 22 February, Lord John Russell resigned. The Queen sent for Lord Stanley, to form a new ministry, but he had to refuse, so that Lord John came back into office, with

the Ecclesiastical Titles Bill still unsolved and still the chief subject of the long debates. The Bill, fading in power on the way,
ultimately became law, but so weak that it was soon forgotten.
The political quake was over in time for the opening of the
Great Exhibition, with suitably splendid celebrations.

*

The first day of May 1851 was the proudest in the Prince's
public life. The Queen walked into the Crystal Palace, beside
him, and with their two eldest children. She wore a dress of
pink watered silk, brocaded with silver and diamonds, and a
headdress of feathers and diamonds. She went to her Chair of
State, but it was Prince Albert's victory she was celebrating; his
victory over an apathetic people who disliked foreigners; over
an aristocracy and a hierarchy that resented his moral seriousness, and over the Queen's own early wilfulness and pride. They
walked among the exhibits, followed by the first of the six million subjects who were to see the wonders before the summer
ended. 'God bless my dearest Albert. God bless my dearest
country,' the Queen wrote when the day was over. Then, 'All is
owing to Albert – All to him.'

Three days a week the Queen and the Prince went to Hyde
Park. All else in their lives they had inherited, but they felt that
this was their own creation; a symbol of the Victorian respectability and of the example they wished to set. And all the world
had come to join in the celebration. The Rajah of Travancore
had sent an ivory throne; there were objects made of zebra
wood, terracotta, majolica and lacquer; jewelled weapons from
Madrid, cabinets from Switzerland, chairs made out of coal,
and, from America, Samuel Colt's pistol with a revolving
chamber.

This was not the only surprise from across the Atlantic: there
was also a machine for making ice through the agency of sul-
phuric acid, a model of the floating church that drifted among
the ships on the Delaware, and a colossal organ, crowned by an

eagle, that played endless tunes, while the leaves of the great elm tree moved gently in the breeze that came in from the Park.

Queen Victoria walked the long miles until she was 'quite beaten', and her head was 'bewildered from the myriads of beautiful and wonderful things'. She wrote, 'Albert's name is immortalised.' Her husband was colder in estimating his success; he wrote that the results were 'quite satisfactory'.

*

In September 1845, Greville had described Queen Victoria as being 'naturally inclined to be generous' while Prince Albert was 'fond of money'. Perhaps 'careful of money' would have been a wiser phrase. On 8 October, 1847, Greville wrote again of the Queen and the Prince, 'She acts in everything by his inspiration and never writes a letter that he does not dictate every word of. His knowledge and information are astonishing, and there is not a department of the Government regarding all the details and management of which he is not much better informed and more capable than the Minister at the head of it.'

This was an exaggeration, but there was no doubt that the Prince's diligence was bringing its quiet rewards, in money as well as influence through example. When he married, the estates of the Duchy of Cornwall were still impoverished from King George iv's extravagance. The heir to the throne was to draw his income from these estates when he came of age, and Prince Albert nursed the affairs of the Duchy so carefully that, within eight years, they produced an annual profit of seventy thousand pounds. He had been able to buy Osborne, and was to buy Balmoral also, out of what was saved. He was similarly astute over the profits from the Great Exhibition.

The Crystal Palace fostered industry but it did not assure the peace that was Prince Albert's dream. The ambitious candidates for power, in Europe, were still merely awaiting their opportunities. But the Exhibition had been a surprising business success: soon after it closed, on 15 October, the Royal Commissioners announced that there was a profit of £186,000. It was inevitable, with Prince Albert's influence, that this money should be used to encourage the arts and science, and to nourish the British mind.

In Kensington there were seventy acres of land which were a perfect site for the immense buildings that stand there now – the Victoria and Albert Museum, the Science, Natural History and Geological Museums; the Imperial College of Science and Technology, the Royal Colleges of Art, Music and Organists; the Royal Meteorological and Entomological Societies and others; dominated in the landscape by the Royal Albert Hall, which may be excused for its outward form because of the century of music that has been presented within.

The vast area of museums and colleges is dedicated not merely to the safety of the past. In 1891, the Commissioners in charge of the estate in Kensington introduced annual scholarships, paid for out of their funds; and by 1961, 960 students from Britain and the 'Empire' had benefited from these awards. Of these, ninety-nine had become Fellows of the Royal Society, including two past presidents, and eight had become Nobel Laureates. The violent changes that have come to Britain and her 'Empire' have not interrupted this flow and exchange of scholarship, which continues as the result of the Great Exhibition of 1851 and as a memorial to Prince Albert's imagination.

In 1852, the Crystal Palace was moved to Sydenham, where it served many useful purposes until it was burned down, in 1936. The site in Hyde Park became grassland again, used by the cavalry quartered in Kensington Barracks. This was significant, for Prince Albert's noble intentions were soon to be spoiled by threats of war. But the museums and colleges were built, and eighty years after the closing of the Exhibition, *The Times* paid their creator this tribute :

> Sneers at the Prince Consort are as far behind the times as the faded jokes about aspidistras and anti-macassars . . . the sterling qualities of the man make his fame secure. He was patient and

courteous under an intolerable deal of snubbing and misprision. For all his uninviting sense of duty he was no dullard. He had a clear, sensible mind and worked hard with it.

Four sentences from Prince Albert's letters to his brother reveal his thoughts as the year of the Exhibition closed. On 17 September, he attacked Duke Ernest for saying that 'only the egoist can look back upon his life with self-satisfaction'. This made Prince Albert angry, and he answered, 'I have never yet seen anyone succeeding in overcoming the laws of nature by putting moral duties aside; nor have I seen an egoist who is happy.' On 29 December, he wrote, '. . . I cannot complain of the past year. The Great Exhibition, which caused me so much work and trouble, ended in an astonishingly satisfactory manner.' The last two sentences, written on this last day but one of 1851, concerned Palmerston : the Prince wrote, 'And now the year closes with the, for us, happy circumstance that the man who embittered our whole lives . . . cut his throat himself. Give a rogue a rope and he will hang himself, is an old English saying . . . which has become true again.'

*

Prince Albert's fault was that he wished to manage the affairs and lives of people, in every land and in every walk of life. His virtue was that in this busy pursuit his intentions were always pure and high-minded. He believed in the inherent goodness of human nature, and with this conviction, he went on writing the memoranda in which he defined moral and civil laws for all mankind. It was not likely that he would ever comprehend the dangerous brilliance and despotism of Lord Palmerston, who, late in October 1851, fired the Court and his colleagues into refreshed indignation. This was when Kossuth, the emancipator of Hungary, came to England on his way to America, whither he was to travel in a steam frigate provided by the United States government. Britain was officially friendly with the Emperors of Russia and Austria, whom Kossuth had denounced. The position became delicate when Lord Palmerston decided to receive Kossuth as his guest; even more delicate when the Prime Minister asked him to abandon the plan and he answered that he did not 'choose to be dictated to' as to whom he 'may or may not' receive in his 'own house'.

At a meeting of the Cabinet on 3 November, Palmerston was obliged to agree not to welcome the Hungarian leader, but he received addresses from Kossuth's admirers, in which the Emperors of Russia and Austria were described as 'odious and detestable assassins' and 'merciless tyrants and despots'. These embarrassing addresses were not received in Palmerston's 'own house', but in Downing Street, so that they had official importance.

The 'rope' with which Palmerston was to hang himself, but not unto death, came a month later, on 3 December, after the news of the *coup d'état* in Paris, where Louis Napoleon overthrew the Republic and destroyed the constitution to which he was pledged. The Queen and Prince Albert were as Osborne; they immediately sent a letter to the British Ambassador in Paris, through Lord John Russell, instructing him to 'remain entirely impassive' and take 'no part whatever' in the crisis.

Lord Palmerston ignored this caution and communicated indirectly with the French Minister for Foreign Affairs, expressing his approval of what the President had done. He endorsed this approval in a conversation with Count Walewski, the French Ambassador in London.

Lord John Russell's resentment of the Queen and Prince Albert had changed to respect during the months before these fresh examples of Lord Palmerston's arrogance. On 18 June, 1851, he had written to the Queen that he thought 'the Prince's character very extraordinary for abilities, judgment, information, and a sympathy for all the sorrows and joys of his fellow-creatures'.

The Prime Minister's change of heart no doubt strengthened his decision, at last, to be rid of Lord Palmerston: he informed him that he was 'reluctantly compelled to come to the conclusion that the conduct of foreign affairs' could no longer be left in his hands 'with safety to the country'. Palmerston was offered the small consolation prize of the Lord-Lieutenancy of Ireland, which he naturally declined. He was polite and quiet and he retired to the country to bide his time. In his place, Lord Granville was appointed to the Foreign Office, with the Queen's 'entire approval'.

Palmerston might have retaliated by criticizing the Queen's misuse of 'the proper channels of communication' if he had known of the letter she wrote to King Leopold, on 23 December: 'I have the greatest pleasure in announcing to you a piece of news which I know will give you as much satisfaction and relief as it does to us, and will do to the *whole* of the world. *Lord Palmerston is no longer Foreign Secretary.'*

The Queen's letter to the King of Prussia was similarly indiscreet: she wrote, 'Your Majesty will have wept bitter tears with the rest of Europe on hearing of Lord Palmerston's retirement from my Cabinet!' She added that she hoped 'the public' would understand that 'England's national policy was not correctly expressed' in Lord Palmerston's 'interpretation of it'.

Greville wrote '*Palmerston is out* . . . I nearly dropped off my chair.' The Austrian Chancellor celebrated the event with a ball, and the Prussians conjured up a doggerel rhyme to express their pleasure. But Prince Albert was not so optimistic: when he wrote to his brother on 22 January, 1852, he made a list of the troubles with which the New Year began, including 'the campaign we must still have with Palmerston, that we get the better of him and that he disappear *for ever* from our Foreign Office'.

*

Fear of invasion is instinct in the English, living on their 'fortress built by Nature for herself', and they have looked across the Channel and the North Sea in a state of anxious suspicion since the Roman conquest. In almost every century since then, the fear has stirred and the coast has been armed against attack. Early in 1852 the old dread of France was reawakened, as Louis Napoleon, adventurous – but in smaller measure than his uncle – clutched the prizes of power that were to lead, late in the year, to his assuming the Imperial title, as Napoleon III. Prince Albert was one of the first to try to awaken the country to the duty and necessity of vigorous defence. On 27 January, he wrote to Prince William of Prussia of Louis Napoleon's 'arbitrary tyranny' and of the 'public' being 'occupied and bothered by the idea of a possible French invasion'.

Greville had once accused Prince Albert of being 'full of ambition'; but if this was true, his ambitions were not for power. They were inspired by his immaculate sense of what was right and what was wrong. In April 1850, when the Duke of Wellington had proposed that the Prince should succeed him as Commander-in-Chief, he had refused, in a long, thoughtful letter, in which two sentences were significant. He wrote that the husband of a female sovereign should 'entirely sink his *own individual* existence in that of his wife', and that, if he undertook 'the responsibility', he would 'not be satisfied to leave the business and real work in the hands of another'.

There was no personal ambition in the way Prince Albert tried to make the government realize what Louis Napoleon's extravagant designs might lead to. He studied the records of Britain's defences and was appalled. He wrote to Lord John Russell, 'This is the third time during the Queen's reign that an apprehension of war and consequent panic have seized the public mind of this country.' He urged the Prime Minister to send him statements 'showing the whole of our means at present available, both naval and military'. On 3 February, 1852, the Queen wrote to King Leopold, 'Albert grows daily fonder and fonder of politics and business, and is so wonderfully *fit* for both – such perspicacity and such *courage* – and I grow daily to dislike them both more and more. We women are not *made* for governing – and if we are good women, we must *dislike* these masculine occupations. . .'

Prince Albert's fondness for politics and business was now centred on increasing the country's defences, and his interference was not resented by the Prime Minister, who wrote to him on 16 February, 'I have seen the Duke of Wellington this morning and have given him the Depôt plan. It may be useful if your Royal Highness will see him from time to time in relation to the Army. On the one hand, your Royal Highness's authority may overcome the indisposition to change which he naturally entertains; and on the other, his vast experience may be of great use to your Royal Highness in regard to the future...'

Four days later, on 20 February, Lord Palmerston had what he described as his 'tit-for-tat with John Russell', when the government was defeated on his amendment to the Militia Bill. Russell resigned, but he took his fall with the generous remark, 'It's all fair. I dealt him a blow, and he has given me one in return.'

The fear of what Louis Napoleon might do was diverted for some months into fear of what the new 'Protectionist' Tory ministry might do, with Lord Derby (previously Lord Stanley) as Prime Minister, and Benjamin Disraeli as Chancellor of the Exchequer and Leader of the Commons. In time, Disraeli was to lead the Tories along the broader path of Conservatism, and to receive from the Queen the affectionate trust she had given to Lord Melbourne; but in 1852 she was apprehensive; she wrote to King Leopold of the 'not *very* pleasant events' that had brought Lord Derby and his 'very sorry Cabinet' to power.

Prince Albert was also dejected : he wrote to his brother, on 16 March, 'Here an inefficient Ministry is dragging on its existence. . . The Opposition is totally disorganized. Lord John Russell has lost all power over his party.' But he added, 'In spite of this, prosperity in the country is unusually great and especially the lower classes are very well off. Circumstances have never been so fortunate for them...'

*

The Queen was at Osborne for her thirty-third birthday, on 24 May. Prince Albert planned extensions to the gardens and he wrote to his brother, 'The lime-blossoms and oranges remind me terribly of Gotha.' He pressed flower petals in his Prayer Book and yielded to sentimentality, of which he believed the English incapable. Some years later he wrote, 'Sentimentality is a plant that cannot grow in England . . . an Englishman, when he finds that he is being sentimental, becomes frightened as at the thought of having a dangerous illness, and he shoots himself.'

Life at Osborne was mostly their own. The Queen and the Prince spent their evenings quietly: he read the *Mémoires de St Simon* aloud, and they sang duets. When he was alone, Prince Albert read the diaries of Samuel Pepys.

The Court was at Balmoral for Prince Albert's thirty-third birthday, on 26 August, when he wrote to his brother, 'Our birthdays are beginning to make us rather old. I wonder whether you have the same feeling? It may come to me because I see youth growing up around me. I can hardly believe that in five years I may have a married daughter and in six years I might be a grandfather. . . Your shooting in Hungary must have been very interesting. I began my season today by missing three stags which were in the thicket quite near to the house. . . Next summer we intend to build, the estate being ours now. In two years the house will be ready. This one will be pulled down, as it is in a bad place as there is no view. . .'

The Queen and Prince Albert were still at Balmoral when a Highlander hurried to them with the news that, on 14 September, the old Duke of Wellington had died peacefully in his armchair at Walmer Castle. 'The whole world has suffered a loss,' wrote the Prince; 'we especially have lost a good friend.'

When the King of Prussia wrote to the Queen of the death of the Duke, she answered with a letter of political hope. She wrote, 'May the future find the European powers who acted in concert at the last victory of Wellington and Blücher as united and valiant as before, should there be any fresh threats against the general peace from the side of France! On our side, nothing will be left undone to maintain friendly relations, but we believe that to achieve success in this line, a degree of armament is necessary.'

Prince Albert's thoughts were similar, but more realistic. He had once written, 'The poor soldiers always do their duty in the most brilliant manner; but as soon as matters come again into the hands of politicians and diplomats, everything is again spoiled and confused.' On 2 November, 1852, the Prince wrote to his brother, '*L'Empire* will soon be called out and Paris and then all Europe may expect a shock. We are cleaning our old rusty cannons and we are building fortifications. We have 80,000 men ready and we are improving our weapons. As regards the latter, I shall be much obliged if you could procure me a Prussian needle gun. I should think you could get one from Erfurt and send it to me direct. This would save much time.'

For a few months, the Prince was able to enjoy the encouragement of Benjamin Disraeli, whose reports each day were as clear in thought as they were flowery in language. He apologized once for 'a somewhat crude note', but he was certain that the Queen would prefer 'a genuine report' to 'a more artificial and prepared statement'. Prince Albert was not deceived by the Chancellor of the Exchequer's extravagant phrases, but he was pleased when Disraeli wrote that he was ready to 'provide for the defence of the country'.

It seemed that the year 1852 might close calmly. On 9 October, Louis Napoleon had said, at Bordeaux, 'Certain minds seem to entertain a dread of war; certain persons say the Empire is only war. But I say, the Empire is Peace, for France desires it.' But the relief from fear of France was spoiled by anxiety at home. On 3 December, Mr Disraeli introduced his budget with a brilliant speech that lasted five and a quarter hours. The debate that followed lasted four long nights, ending with a speech by Mr Gladstone, of a different kind of brilliance, that helped to sway the vote against the government. The 'unable ministry' which had distressed the Queen and the Prince so much was defeated, and within a few hours Lord Derby arrived at Osborne to hand his resignation to the Queen.

The aim of both Queen Victoria and Prince Albert was to bring the leading Whigs and the followers of Sir Robert Peel together, with Lord Aberdeen as Prime Minister. This was achieved and there was confidence once more in the Palace. The Queen wrote of Aberdeen as being 'brilliant and strong'; of the new 'Liberal' government being 'the realization of the country's and our most ardent wishes', and that it deserved 'success'. Prince Albert wrote to his brother, 'At last Aberdeen succeeded in obtaining a union between the Peelites, Whigs and Radicals, which gave us a Ministry of extraordinary talent, method and experience. Even Palmerston belongs to it, and if he is in a department in which he has to work like a horse, he cannot do any mischief. . . If peace is maintained it will be through the voice of England. But if England has nothing behind her, she will not be listened to.'

Two months later, on 26 February, 1853, Prince Albert wrote one of the few letters to his brother in which he revealed interest in the world beyond Europe. He referred first to the 'fortifications' in English ports, and the increase and 'drilling' of the militia; and he wrote, 'This year we shall have 85,000 men. All this guarantees peace.' Then, 'The Indian empire has an addition in Pegu, but the war with the King of Ava is still going on, and that with the Burmese also. At the Cape it is dying off, so we shall soon have some regiments free and be able to draw them back.' Then he anticipated the next tragedy of war: he wrote, 'The most threatening place in Europe is at present Turkey.'

CHAPTER FIFTEEN

1853-1855

Queen Victoria's early fear, that Prince Albert might 'thwart' her, had long been forgotten. Her letters reveal her obedience to his mind, and a womanly reaction to events that were purely political to him. When she learned that Napoleon III was to marry Eugénie de Montijo, she wrote to the King of Prussia, '*Le grand évènement du jour* is the incredible marriage of the Emperor Nap. In France it is being very badly received. The future bride is beautiful, clever, very *coquette*, passionate and wild. What do they say about it in Germany?'

In the same letter, dated 24 January, 1853, the Queen wrote, '. . . our already so numerous family is going to have an addition in the early spring. But, as always, I am going on very well, and I am doing everything as usual.' On 7 April, Prince Albert wrote to his brother, 'The telegraph has already spoken and I hope you know already that you have become an uncle for the eighth time. . . Victoria and the little boy are very well.' The child was christened Leopold,[1] because this was 'the dearest name' to the Queen 'after Albert'. They added Duncan because, she wrote, it was 'a compliment to dear Scotland'.

The eldest of the eight children, Princess Victoria, was in her thirteenth year, and already revealing the intellectual promise denied to the Prince of Wales. Baron Stockmar wrote, 'I think her to be exceptionally gifted, in some things even to the point of genius.' It was natural for her to write 'a short compendium of Roman history', while her brother looked out of the window at the fields on which he was not allowed to play. He was in his twelfth year, still isolated from the friends and games for which he craved. His father took him to speech-days at both Eton and Harrow, and when he went for afternoon drives he saw boys of his own age playing cricket or football, but always at a distance. Slowly, the public became aware of the prince who was to be king : they had seen him at the opening of the Great Exhibition, wearing a kilt; and on 15 November, 1852, he had stood with his mother and father on the balcony of Buckingham Palace to watch the funeral procession of the Duke of Wellington, who had been a hero to the Prince of Wales for as long as he could remember.

For Prince Albert, the duties of being father of a large family seemed less absorbing than his plans for defending London and arming the country. One of his schemes which Lord Aberdeen, the Liberal Prime Minister, accepted, was for a training camp on Chobham Common, and later – an innovation in military history – the building of a permanent training camp at Aldershot, where soldiers could be prepared for actual battle. In June 1853, troops marched on to Chobham Common and 'established themselves in a line of tents extending over upwards of two miles'. The Prince wrote of each move in the preparation for the war that was to come so soon – but against the Russians, not the French. He visited the camp several times and once he slept in a tent, so that he could take part in the manoeuvres like a real soldier. He caught a severe cold during this rehearsal for warfare, but he could not be discouraged.

Queen Victoria also went to see the troops in their tents, and she used the curious phrase, 'our dear camp', to describe them. She sent photographs of Chobham Common to the King of Prussia, and she wrote to King Leopold, on 10 August, 'When I think that this camp, and all our large fleet, are without doubt the result of Albert's assidious and increasing representations to the late and present Governments, without which I fully believe very little would have been done, one may be proud and thankful; but, as usual, he is so modest that he allows no praise.'

On 11 August there was a review at Spithead. Prince Albert described the day to Stockmar: he had been to see 'the finest fleet perhaps that England ever fitted out . . . forty ships of war of all kinds, all moved by steam-power but three'. The *Duke of Wellington*, with 131 guns, went without sails, propelled only by the screw, at eleven miles an hour. He added, 'I must rejoice to see that achieved which I have struggled so long and hard to effect. . . I still suffer a good deal from rheumatism in the right shoulder, which makes even writing difficult.'

＊

When the Queen and Prince Albert left for their summer holiday in Scotland, the country seemed safe and prosperous. The new castle at Balmoral was 'up one storey', and the children were well and happy. All the reports before they left London had been of strength and confidence. Gladstone's first budget had shown a surplus of almost two and a half million pounds, and there were signs that Britain was accepting moral and humane responsibilities, as well as seeking for territory and wealth. She was leading the world in the campaign against slavery, and there was a movement to lessen 'Jewish disabilities'. Even Lord Palmerston, at the Home Office, was fitting into the pattern of creative improvement. Instead of tantalizing diplomats and alarming the Court, he was putting down 'smoke nuisances', purifying the water in the Thames, and improving the drains in London.

Queen Victoria enjoyed the illusion of escape at Balmoral, but Prince Albert was not deceived. In the months since he had written to his brother that Turkey was the 'most threatening place in Europe', an obscure but old dispute between France, Russia and the Porte over the guardianship of the Christian shrines at Jerusalem, had become a dangerous conflict, when Russia demanded the right to protect the Greek Church throughout the Turkish dominions. Behind this apparently high moral purpose of the Russians it seemed that there might be a sinister design, linked with the dream of Peter the Great, to extend their empire and power to the Mediterranean and through Afghanistan into India.

When the Porte rejected this demand – on the advice of Lord Stratford, the British Ambassador at Constantinople – the Russian army occupied the two Danubian principalities of the Sultan (the modern Roumania), and France and Britain ordered their fleets to the Dardanelles. But there was still hope that the diplomats would move carefully and avoid actual battle.

The Court was at Balmoral on 5 October, when Prince Albert sent an urgent letter to Baron Stockmar: 'Come soon if you can... The Turks have declared war; what will the four Powers do? . . . We cannot look on and see the Porte destroyed by Russia; active assistance is European war...'

Six days later, Queen Victoria wrote to Lord Clarendon, the Foreign Secretary, 'It appears that we have taken on ourselves, in conjunction with France, all the risks of European war.'

The pattern of power, and fear, had changed quickly: the French – the possible enemies of a few months before – had become Britain's allies. But the two governments withheld 'active assistance' to the Porte until 22 October, when their fleets moved to the Bosphorus, with orders to pass into the Black Sea at the first sign of the Russian fleet coming out of Sebastopol, their base in the Crimea. Thus encouraged, the Turks crossed the Danube on 28 October and attacked the Russian army occupying the principalities; and on 30 November, the Russian navy retaliated by destroying the Turkish fleet at Sinope. Even then, there were attempts to limit the conflict: early in the new year, when the combined British and French fleets entered the Black Sea, they were ordered merely to 'invite' the Russian ships to return to Sebastopol. But diplomacy was no longer effective: the Tsar was too angry at the presence of the Allied fleets to be pacified, and the British people had developed a violent urge to fight in defence of the Turks.

In Whitehall, the prospect of war was confused by a further political battle. Lord Palmerston considered that as Britain had already sent a fleet to support the Turks, it was her duty to fight for them 'at all hazards', to 'maintain the integrity of the Ottoman Empire'. Lord Aberdeen still hoped for peace; he had written to the Queen, 'No doubt it may be very agreeable to humiliate the Emperor of Russia; but . . . it is paying a little too dear for this pleasure, to check the progress and prosperity of this happy country, and to cover Europe with confusion, misery, and blood.' The division in the Cabinet was aggravated by the feud between Palmerston and Lord John Russell. On 16 December, Palmerston resigned : he said later that this was because of a domestic issue – his 'dislike' of Lord John's 'plan of reform' – and he wrote to Lord Lansdowne that he did 'not choose to be dragged through the dirt by John Russell'.

This distinctly political crisis, in which the Queen and Prince Albert had no part, led to a strange and bitterly unjust scandal. London newspapers charged the Prince with having forced Palmerston's resignation and with harbouring Russian sympathies. The 'massacre' of the Turkish fleet at Sinope did not seem to interest them so much as the dishonest pleasure of accusing Prince Albert of being the evil 'influence behind the throne'; of his being the 'friend of Russia', and – because of Prussia's neutrality in the dispute – of his working 'for the Coburgs and against England'. His alleged infamy became a shrieking song in the streets; groups of people sang,

> We'll send him home and make him groan,
> Oh Al! you've played the devil then;
> The German lad has acted sad,
> And turned tail with the Russians.

The malicious scandal gathered its noisy force until it was said that Prince Albert was a traitor; that he had been impeached for high treason, arrested, and committed to the Tower of London. Thousands of Londoners surged under the Tower walls, waiting to see him brought in as a prisoner.

Prince Albert endured this injustice with extraordinary calm. He wrote to Baron Stockmar, on 7 January, 1854, 'We are all

well in health, except for catarrh on my part. Morally, in this
new year, as in the old, we have many torments. The attacks
upon me continue with uninterrupted violence. . . There is no
kind of treason to the country of which they say I have not been
guilty. All this must be born tranquilly until the meeting of
Parliament on the 31st, when Aberdeen and John Russell are
prepared to undertake my defence.'

On 24 January he wrote again to Stockmar, a letter² of
almost two thousand words. In the first sentence he complained,
'. . . we might fancy we were living in a madhouse. . . One main
element is the hostility and settled bitterness of the old High
Tory or Protectionist Party against me on account of my friendship with the late Sir Robert Peel, and my success with the Exhibition. This has shown itself in the clearest and strongest way.
The stupidity of the Lord Mayor in wishing to erect a monu-
ment to me brought matters to a climax. . .'

The Prince then described the reasons for the 'animosity'
against himself and the Court, for his 'interference' in politics,
and because of his 'confidential intercourse' with the Commander-in-Chief, Lord Hardinge, 'in all military matters'. He
explained the calumnies he suffered and then wrote of their
effect on 'that important substratum of the people . . . slow of
thought and uneducated', who had never troubled to consider
'the position of the husband of a Queen Regnant'. He wrote,

When I first came over here, I was met by this want of knowledge and unwillingness to give a thought to the position of this
luckless personage.

As I kept quiet and caused no scandal, and all went well, no
one has troubled himself about me and my doings; and anyone who
wished to pay me a compliment at a public dinner or meeting, ex-
tolled my 'wise abstinence from interfering in political matters'.
Now, when the present journalistic controversies have brought to
light the fact that I have for years taken an active interest in all
political matters, the public, instead of feeling surprise at my
modesty and my tact in not thrusting myself forward, fancied
itself betrayed, because it felt it had been self-deceived.

Later in the letter the Prince wrote, 'I may say with pride, that
not the veriest tittle of a reproach can be brought against me
with truth. . . One word more about the credulity of the public.
You will scarcely credit, that my being committed to the Tower
was believed all over the country – nay, even "that the Queen
had been arrested!"

'. . . It was anything but pleasant to me amidst it all, that so
many people could look upon me "as a rogue and traitor", and
I shall not be at ease, until I see the debate in Parliament well
over. . .

'Victoria has taken the whole affair greatly to heart and was
excessively indignant at the attacks. . . Since yesterday I have
been quite miserable. . .'

Another letter, from Prince Albert to his brother, found
eighty years afterwards in Coburg, confirms the honesty of his
intentions. He wrote, on 6 February, 1854, 'The naked position
is this; we and France are determined not to allow Russia to
destroy and conquer Turkey.'

Lord Palmerston had withdrawn his resignation and rejoined
the government after only ten days, but the abuse of Prince
Albert went on, and it was not until 29 January that Greville
was able to write, 'The attacks on the Prince are subsiding.'
Greville had spoken to Lord John Russell of the rule that the
Prince should be present when the Queen interviewed her ministers, and he wrote in his diary, on the same day, 'Lord John
said that he found it established when he came back, and he saw
no objection to it. He told me last night that the Queen had
talked to him about the present clamour, which of course annoyed her, and she said, if she had had the Prince to talk to and
employ in explaining matters at the time of the Bedchamber
quarrel* with Peel, that affair would not have happened. Lord
John said he thought she must have been advised by somebody
to act as she did, to which she replied with great candour and
naïveté, "No, it was entirely my own foolishness." '

Greville added, 'This is the first time I have heard of her

* *See* pp. 38–39.

acknowledging that it was "foolishness", and is an avowal creditable to her sense.'

Two days later, Parliament met and Prince Albert's name was cleared. Compliments came, to dispel abuse. Lord Aberdeen had written that it was 'an inestimable blessing' that the Queen possessed 'so zealous and so disinterested an adviser'. This was the spirit of the Prince's vindication. He wrote to his brother, '. . . you will have been glad to see that the first debate scattered all the stupid accusations against me to the four winds. The feelings are at present exceedingly good.' To Stockmar he wrote, on 2 February, '. . . My political status and activity, which up to this time have been silently assumed, have now been asserted in Parliament and vindicated without a dissentient voice.'

*

The Queen and Prince Albert were at Windsor Castle when news came of the 'vindication'. They were able to enjoy a spell of quiet with their family. The Prince wrote to his brother, on 6 February, 'We skate a great deal and this gives the children, especially, great pleasure. They are now studying a French comedy which is to be performed in a few days.'

On the 10th, the anniversary of the wedding of the Queen and Prince Albert, the 'French comedy' was supported by a surprise. The children also gave a representation of the Four Seasons. Princess Alice entered as Spring, 'scattering flowers and reciting verses'. Then came their eldest daughter, 'as Summer, with Prince Arthur stretched upon the sheaves as if tired with the heat and harvest work'. Prince Alfred was crowned with vine leaves and he wore the skin of a panther. Then came the Prince of Wales, against a bitter winter scene covered with icicles, with Princess Louise at hand, 'muffled and charming' and 'busy keeping up a fire'. Then all the Seasons gathered upon the stage, with Princess Helena veiled in white and holding a long cross, while she pronounced a blessing upon her parents.

The scene was described by Baroness Bunsen, who wrote at

the end, of Prince Leopold being carried in by his nurse. He looked at them all with his 'big eyes, stretching out his arms to be taken' by his father.

The sentimental entertainment was no more than a furtive escape for Prince Albert. The Court returned to London and he continued his letters, written sometimes from seven o'clock in the morning until late at night, under the green-shaded lamp of duty.

On 23 February, four days before Britain and France sent an ultimatum to St Petersburg, the Prince wrote to his brother, 'Our division of 12,000 men and 30 cannon has left for Malta. . . Our principal activity is directed to the treaties and boundaries of 1815, to see that they are kept up. We therefore demand a declaration from everyone who joins us – a declaration that we ourselves give, that we do not intend to acquire any possessions or territorial extensions by the war, nor to accept them. If this declaration is given by all parties, this war will distinguish itself from all former wars in history, by the unselfishness of the allies.'

On 23 March, four days after the Emperor of Russia had rejected the ultimatum, Prince Albert wrote again, 'Our preparations for the war are progressing twice as fast as the French. The fleet will be exceedingly fine, perhaps a little too strong for the shallow sea. The 25,000 men for Constantinople are organised; 10,000 of them have already arrived at Malta; the artillery has left and the cavalry is to go through France, and, at the wish of the Emperor, to march through Paris!' He added, 'Who would have thought a year ago that such things might happen!'

Five days after this letter was written, France and Britain declared war on Russia and the 'Crimea' became a cruel and ill-planned reality, beyond the help of political argument. On 3 April, Prince Albert wrote to his brother, 'I hope you found our declaration of war dignified. . .'

There was only one more voice of personal scandal – a rumoured threat that the Emperor of Russia was to publish the letters Prince Albert had written to him. The Prince told his brother, 'My correspondence with him refers only to the announcements of the births of our children, so it is as uninteresting as it is innocent!'

Seventeen days later, on 24 April, he wrote, 'The London people are very military and of course understand everything better than the Government. How, at 1,000 miles distance, a war is to be led successfully by the Government, the Press and the usual gossip in the clubs, is still to be proved. . .' On 16 May, he wrote again, 'The English are remarkably interested in the war against a power whose constitution and foreign policies they detest. . . The fact that £10,000,000 of *new* taxes are to be raised is a proof of our seriousness. . . Our calamity is our prosperity. We cannot get soldiers, mariners, *ships*!! Commerce, industry and emigration are so enormous. Ships are being built in great numbers, but they are at once taken in use. . . The war will not be ended quickly if the Germans do not take part. But the victor in the long run will be the one with the biggest purse. . .'

Queen Victoria forgot her early plea that she was only a woman and that her place was in the family circle: later, in October 1894, she wrote to Princess Augusta of Prussia, 'I assure you that I regret exceedingly not to be a man and to be able to fight in the war. My heart bleeds for the many fallen, but I consider that there is no finer death for a man than on the battlefield.'

This heroic boast seemed to inspire her. On 2 March she had got up early in the morning to see the Scots Fusilier Guards march past Buckingham Palace, on their way to the Crimea. She went in her yacht and led the fleet as it sailed towards the 'blood-red blossom of war'. She sent endless letters to her ministers, but in these it is Prince Albert's quiet practical mind that is revealed, asking the questions she set down at his dictation. On 3 July, after 5,000 additional soldiers had been ordered to sail, she wrote, '. . . the Queen feels very uneasy at the very defenceless state in which the country will be left . . . we never can forsee what may not suddenly spring up at any moment . . .

which may require a force to be in readiness for any particular purpose.' Then the questions:

> What store of muskets are there *here*?
>
> When will the new ones be ready?
>
> What is the force of Artillery left in the country in men and horses?
>
> What amount of troops are there in the country, of Infantry (deducting the 5,000 men under orders for the East), and of Cavalry, and where are they stationed?
>
> How much Militia has been and will be embodied?
>
> What is the Naval Force at home?
>
> How much serviceable ammunition is there both of Artillery and small arms in the country?

Prince Albert had written, hopefully, to his brother on 16 May, 'If only we could take Sebastopol!' This victory was far away, and he was to write fifty volumes of letters and memoranda before the battles were over. He complained, on 21 June, '. . . We have much trouble with the Ministry. Aberdeen still lives in 1814, Lord John in 1830, Palmerston in 1848.'

*

Early in September 1854, the Prince wrote three of his few letters to the Queen, while he was away in Boulogne, where he went to meet Napoleon III. In the first letter he described the journey across the Channel, in the *Victoria and Albert*. He wrote, 'I sit in the cabin at my table (yours is there empty), and wish you on paper a loving good-morning. The night was superb . . . we travellers sat upon deck till half-past eleven, in the glorious moonlight. It was close upon twelve when I got to bed in the cabin, which had a very blank and desolate look. . .

'The Emperor met me on the quay, and brought me here in his carriage to an hotel at the back of the town near the railway station. . .'

Prince Albert described his host as 'very nervous', but 'kindly and cordial' and 'much gayer than he is generally represented'.

The Prince had 'two long talks with the Emperor in which he spoke very sensibly about the war and the *question du jour*'. In his letter to the Queen he wrote, 'People here are far from sanguine about the results of the expedition to the Crimea . . . nevertheless, so far as the Emperor is concerned, determined to consider the war and our alliance as the one thing paramount, to which all other considerations must give place.'

Next day, the Prince wrote, 'The Emperor thaws more and more. . . He told me one of the deepest impressions ever made upon him was when . . . he arrived in London shortly after King William's death, and saw you at the age of eighteen going to open Parliament for the first time.'

When he returned to England, the Prince described Napoleon III as 'quiet and indolent from constitution', and his education as being 'very deficient' on subjects of the 'first necessity to him'. The Emperor admitted Prince Albert's superiority of mind when he said, after their meeting, that he had 'never met with a person possessing such various and profound knowledge', and that he had 'never learned so much in a short time'. He was 'grateful', and he thought the Prince had 'one of the highest intelligences' of his time, and was 'struck beyond measure with the depth and justice of his views'.

*

Between 13 and 18 September, the Allied armies landed in the Crimea, unopposed, on a beach thirty miles north of Sebastopol; and on the 20th they were encouraged by their first victory over the Russians, on the banks of the Alma. But the incompetence of the French commander, and the reluctant obedience of Lord Raglan to his plan, threw all their advantages away. Instead of making an immediate attack from the north on the great Russian naval base, they hesitated long enough for the enemy to increase their strength, with both men and fortifications; and the Allies were obliged to make a flank march to the harbours

- Kamiesh and Balaclava - to the west and south of Sebastopol.

The story of the long siege that followed - a full-scale war within an area smaller than the Isle of Wight - is told in hundreds of books. It is part of every English schoolboy's history - the wasted heroism of the Light Brigade at Balaclava on 25 October, and the curious behaviour of Lord Cardigan; and in November, the battle of Inkerman in which the infantrymen were the heroes. But November in the Crimea was the beginning of the cruel winter, and there was little hope of further action until the spring.

The people at home were nearer to the story, day by day, because, for the first time, there were war correspondents with the British army, and they sent back truthful reports of the degradation the soldiers endured in the bitter weather that was Russia's ally; reports of the dying men, diseased and neglected, muttering, 'Sebastopol - has it fallen? - would that I had been in at the last.'

No longer would the story of war depend on the cautious dispatches of commanding officers, and the illusions of regiments, with their silver trophies, recalling old battles over the table in the mess. The war correspondents made the Crimea immediate and real to the British public, they emphasized the tragic distance between those who make wars and those who are compelled to fight them. The reports in the London press, of the horrors the soldiers had to endure, were a fresh menace to the dilatory politicians. Readers of the newspapers sometimes knew the truth on the same day as the ministers in Whitehall: they sometimes learned facts of which the government seemed unaware, or wished to hide. It was an appeal from William Howard Russell, war correspondent for *The Times*, that inspired Florence Nightingale to 'go forth and minister to the sick and suffering soldiers of the East in the hospitals of Scutari'.

Prince Albert also read the newspapers, and on 11 November - six days after the battle of Inkerman - he wrote to the Prime Minister,

This morning's account of the losses in the Crimea etc., the want of progress in the seige with an advancing adverse season and the army of the enemy increasing, must make every Englishman anxious for his gallant brothers in the field, and the honour of his country.

The Government will never be forgiven, and ought never to be forgiven, if it did not strain every nerve to avert the calamity of seeing Lord Raglan succumb for want of means. . . The time has come for vigorous measures and the feeling of the country is up to support them, if Goverment will bring them boldly forward.

He asked the Prime Minister to come and stay that night in Windsor Castle, with the Secretary of State for War, so that they could 'talk these matters over'.

The Prince, no doubt remembering the King's German Legion that had fought with the British in the Napoleonic wars, urged Lord Aberdeen to employ mercenaries. But the Tories and the Radicals opposed him; they made the curious protest that it would be 'looked upon as ingratitude' to the British soldiers already in the battlefields. Prince Albert wrote to his brother, 'They say that it is a foreign idea and that it must have come from me. For this reason I must keep away from it and I must by no means appear to be the patron of the German Legion, against the English Army.'

It seemed that at least some of the will to govern came from the Palace, for Lord Aberdeen yielded and the Prince was able to write, 'We saw 3,408 men at Shorncliffe and were highly pleased with their bearing and spirit'. The Legion was made up of both Germans and Swiss. Prince Albert wrote, 'The English uniform suited the German faces rather strangely, but they were decidedly better made and put on with great neatness. . .'

In February 1855, Lord Aberdeen's ministry was defeated after J. A. Roebuck, a radical backbencher, had moved for a committee to enquire into the condition of the army in the Crimea. In Parliament and outside, there were demands for sweeping changes in government and for dynamic war leadership. The new Prime Minister was to be Lord Palmerston, then seventy years old. Queen Victoria and Prince Albert had to acknowledge the great wave of public feeling in his favour and to conquer their old prejudice against him; and this they seemed to do, for Lord Palmerston wrote to his brother, 'I have no reason to complain of the least want of cordiality or confidence on the part of the Court.'

Lord Palmerston's audacity, so alarming in peace, was essential to the ruthless conduct of war. The mass of people responded to his leadership and to his immediate intention to strengthen the army. He quickly disproved Disraeli's accusation that he was 'an imposter, utterly exhausted . . . now an old painted pantaloon'. The new Prime Minister soon justified the vigour of his mind in the vigour of his administration. His methods had not changed: one of his first actions was to write a personal letter to Napoleon III and thus cause the Court 'some uneasiness'. Prince Albert wrote that this 'sort of private correspondence' was 'novel and unconstitutional', but he came to realize that Palmerston's nature was as unchangeable as his own.

Queen Victoria was consoled as she read reports of Florence Nightingale and her 'capable and devoted nurses', who had been engaged in their realistic and kindly task since November. And there came, with the spring – early in March – the encouraging news that the Tsar, Nicholas I, the villain of the piece in the public mind, had died, and that his son, Alexander II, ruled the enemy in his place. One of Florence Nightingale's nurses wrote of the British soldiers raising themselves in their beds to cry, 'Nicholas is dead. . . Thank God. . . All blessings be with you for bringing us such blessed news. . . If he died by poison we should have peace. . . He has been the death of thousands.'

CHAPTER SIXTEEN

1855

In April 1855, while the Allied armies waited in the Crimea, recovering from the disasters of winter, burying their dead, but also welcoming the reinforcements that arrived for the battles of the coming summer, the Anglo-French alliance was encouraged by the visit of the Emperor and Empress to England.

The scene was Windsor Castle, where Queen Victoria and Napoleon III might have talked of the myths of power and allegiance, if they were so inclined. The Tsar Nicholas I had been a guest there eleven years before; now he was their dead enemy. King Louis Philippe had stayed there, in October of the same year, and he had died in England, as an exile, in August 1850. His widow had been to the Castle only three days before the Emperor arrived. She had come and gone in an ordinary coach, and her state was now so humble – 'poor and unthought of', as Queen Victoria recalled – as Napoleon III's had been during his own exile in England, before he returned to France, and power, in 1848.

Such figures in the dark, cynical arches of Anglo-French history, going back to William the Conqueror, who built the first wooden fortress on the hill above the Thames, cast no shadow on the amiable and immediate behaviour of Queen Victoria, Prince Albert and Napoleon III.

Greville wrote of the Emperor, 'Everybody is struck with his mean and diminutive figure and vulgar appearance'. But the Queen was pleased with him: she thought him 'civil, amiable, and well-bred in his manners'. When she walked with him and Prince Albert in the Park, she was content to listen as they talked of the strength of armies and the intricacies of campaigns. It was the Prince's voice, not hers, that spoke with authority for the government and the country.

On 17 April, there was a review of troops in Windsor Park, which the Queen described as 'beautiful and exciting', with the Emperor bowing from his seat on 'a very fiery, beautiful chestnut'. That evening, Queen Victoria danced with him in a quadrille, in the Waterloo Chamber. Next day, after a Council of War, she invested him with the Order of the Garter. The nephew of the terrible Napoleon Bonaparte was now her 'nearest and most intimate ally'.

The Queen wrote to Princess Augusta of Prussia, on 23 April, of the Emperor being 'remarkable . . . dignified, decorous, tactful and unbelievably calm', and of the Empress as 'a very charming, lovable creature, also extremely tactful, yet natural in her manner'. Then, realistically, she added, 'The fact that our political interests are the same, that we are both in the same boat, naturally contributed to the success of the visit.'

There do not seem to be any personal letters from Prince Albert describing his days with Napoleon III; but, after their serious conversations on the entanglements of alliance, he went back to his desk and wrote the gist of what was said into a memorandum for Lord Palmerston. Nor is there any record of his writing to Stockmar: it was a letter from the Queen that inspired the old adviser to answer, on 22 April, that the splendour of the Emperor's reception would 'for his whole life' prevent him 'from sinning against England'.

*

The success of the Emperor's visit had interrupted Queen Victoria's task of caring for the wounded soldiers being brought home from the Crimea. While Prince Albert conferred with the ministers and framed his reports for the War Office, the Queen visited hospitals and complained when the windows were so high that the men, turning in their beds, could not look out and see the English spring. She protested also because some of them were brought home in hulks, and because, at Chatham, they had to eat and sleep in the same room. She wrote of her 'dear, brave noble heroes', and of her wish to present them with medals, not only for the pleasure it would give them, but also because it would 'no doubt have a very beneficial effect on re-cruiting'. She wrote to King Leopold of her own pleasure when the soldiers refused to hand their medals back for their names to be engraved on them, 'for fear that they should not receive the identical ones put into their hands by me'.

*

In July, plans were being made for a return visit to the Emperor of the French, but there were new alarms before the Queen and the Prince could leave England. First, there was an outbreak of scarlet fever in the royal household, with four of the children among the victims. Prince Albert described his family problems in an undated letter to his brother. He wrote from Osborne, 'Our scarlet fever patients are convalescents now and fortunately Vicky and the two elder boys . . . and what is the chief thing, Victoria, were spared. All these small quarantines totally disturbed our family life.'

The Prince then wrote of the plans to visit France, 'Your enquiry considering our journey to Paris confirms a rumour which came to our ears, namely that you intend to surprise us in Paris by appearing there. I consider it my duty not to leave you in any doubt, that you would not do us a favour by being present. Our visit is to be a *strictly English visit* to the Emperor and the *French people*, not an assembly of the Coburg House at the Bonaparte Court. The people would not see any reason for your presence and only *lie all the more about it.*'

Duke Ernest was apparently subdued by his brother's protest and he remained in Coburg when Queen Victoria and Prince

Albert crossed to France on 18 August, with their two eldest children. No English sovereign had driven through the streets of Paris since Henry VI went there for his coronation, in 1422. But there was no sense of history in the pleasure of the French people in greeting Queen Victoria and the Prince. The visit co-incided with exciting news by telegraph from the Crimea: an attack by the Russian field army against 37,000 French and Sardinian troops on the heights above the Chernaya river had been repulsed with heavy loss to the enemy; and it was now certain that Sebastopol must soon fall to the Allies. The people of Paris therefore had a realistic reason for being elated, on the day that their Emperor drove past with his guests from England.

There had been a delay on the way, and the procession through the city did not begin until almost dusk, but the Parisians were still waiting, and they cried '*Vive la Reine d' Angleterre*' so eagerly that she bowed and smiled. A spectator noticed that her smile increased when the people cried, '*Vive le Prince Albert.*' The veteran Marshal Magnan, who had known Paris for fifty years, said he had 'never seen such a scene as this, not even when Napoleon returned from Austerlitz'.

With his usual calm, the Prince wrote to Stockmar from the Emperor's summer palace at St Cloud, 'We are all well. The Emperor in high spirits . . . the nation flattered and friendly.' The Queen had wondered, a few months before, whether Napoleon III had 'strong *moral* sense of right and *wrong*'. This doubt seemed to pass as she talked to him, begging him to speak out if he had any grievances or complaints and assuring him that by doing so, 'all misunderstandings and complications would be avoided'.

Among the Parisians who might have seen the monarchs driving through the streets was Anatole France, then eleven years old. In time he was to write, 'War is not an art, and chance alone decides the fate of the battles. When two generals come face to face, both stupid, one of them must of necessity be victorious.' This might have been the mood of the conversation between the Emperor, the Queen, and Prince Albert, for they talked of the errors of the French generals, and the Queen and the Prince listened while Napoleon III spoke 'very openly and frankly of the defects' in the British generals, in return.

Prince Albert celebrated his thirty-sixth birthday at St Cloud. The Queen wrote, 'May God ever bless and protect him for many, many years to come, and may we ever be together to our lives' end.' Among the presents she had brought him, from England, were some 'pretty Crimean studs', with a blank on one of the buttons, waiting for the name *Sebastopol*.

The Emperor composed special music for Prince Albert's birthday, and when they stepped on to the balcony of the palace, three hundred drummers announced the dawn of his thirty-seventh year. All seemed trust, laced with manners and reason. The Queen wrote of her host, 'I should not fear saying anything to him.' And the Prince of Wales, then almost fourteen years old, knelt beside the tomb of Napoleon I, in the heart of the city which he was to love so much when he grew up.

When the Queen returned to England, she spoke of Napoleon III as her 'personal friend'. She wrote, 'Albert . . . is naturally much calmer and particularly much less taken by people; much less under *personal* influence than I am.' But he had admitted to her that it was 'extraordinary' how 'very much attached' one became to the Emperor.

＊

There were cautious watchers of the enthusiasm. One of the Duchess of Kent's little court, Lady Augusta Bruce, who had lived in France many years, dined with the Queen and the Prince soon after their return, and she wrote to her sister, 'She feels the cordiality immensely, and the idea of cementing a lasting union is, I see, one which kindles her enthusiasm and delights her. Then I think she is *quite* charmed with the Emperor; feels that she has never met on equal terms anyone like him.' Lady Augusta wrote also of Prince Albert, that he said 'less than he thinks and feels, invariably'. She added that she was slightly alarmed by the Queen's 'laudation of French', and she hoped that 'dear Louis Napoleon' would live up to the Queen's faith in him and end 'by putting a little sense' into his people.

Greville wrote, on 21 August, of the 'fine and animated' scene of the Queen's arrival in Paris, but also of the solemn questions of war and finance that seemed to be overlooked during the exchange of royal visits. The Chancellor of the Exchequer, Sir George Cornewall Lewis, who 'had been all along against the war, and thought it ought to have been prevented', told Greville that the House of Commons had only one 'fear', and this was 'lest the war should not be conducted with sufficient vigour'. Sir George thought the 'rage for war' was 'as violent as ever', and that it had 'little or no effect on trade', which was 'steady and flourishing'. But he believed also that unless 'some great successes' came to 'infuse fresh animation into the public mind', the civilians would 'begin to tire of the contest' and to reflect that it was 'being carried on at an enormous cost for no rational object whatever, and merely from motives of pride and vanity and a false notion of honour.'

The 'great success' came eighteen days later, on 8 September, while the Court was at Balmoral, enjoying their first summer holiday in the new castle which, within, reflected a confusion of tastes and emotion. Prince Albert's memories of German castles were influenced by his new love, for Scotland. The carpets were of tartan, to celebrate the Queen's descent from the Stuarts; even some of the linoleum was tartan, also the poplins and the silk. The walls were lively with trophies of the chase. Lady Augusta Bruce, whose own ancestral home was in Scotland, thought that Prince Albert's decorations were 'all highly characteristic and appropriate, but not equally *flatteux* to the eye.'

The news of the fall of Sebastopol reached Balmoral on 10 September. The Queen wrote to King Leopold next day, 'We . . . were sitting quietly round our table after dinner . . . to my grief we have not *one* soldier, no band, nothing here to make any sort of demonstration.'

This was not quite true. On the top of Craig Gowan, a hill within sight of Balmoral Castle, was a wood pile that had been waiting a year for news of victory. Prince Albert hurried from the dining-table, took a torch from a Highlander, and set the beacon alight. The Queen watched the blaze from a window; she could see her husband outlined against the flames, while the Highlanders climbed the hill towards him. They joined in what the Prince described in a letter to Stockmar as 'a veritable witch's dance, supported by whisky.'

After watching the delightful scene, Queen Victoria wrote in her journal that they were all 'in great ecstasy'. Prince Albert described the celebration as 'wild and exciting beyond anything'. The middle-aged, solemn man caught some echo of the boy who had pretended to be a Saxon knight at Rosenau, thirty years before.

This hour at Craig Gowan was one of the few scenes of jubilation in which Prince Albert had danced his pleasure since he came to England. There was reason for him to enjoy 'inward refreshment' in the years of the Crimean war, for his sane and imaginative ideas had done much to lessen the fundamental error of the campaign. Just as he had been the first to suggest the training grounds of Chobham Common and Aldershot, and to revive the concept of the foreign legion, so he had continued his letters to the ministers, each with its fresh idea, all through the war. These ideas were accepted, even by Lord Palmerston, once the 'old sinner' and now so 'proud', as Lord Clarendon noted, of 'having overcome the repugnance of the Court'. This theme,[1] of Prince Albert's informed interest and ideas, had already led to many innovations during the war : he had recommended plans as immense as the reorganization of the army in the Crimea, and as detailed as the increase in the size of the drill ground at Colchester; as far-seeing as the establishment of reserves for the garrisons in Malta and Gibraltar, and as human as the award of the Victoria Cross, which he devised early in 1855 – a decoration for sailors and soldiers of every rank, entirely for their personal valour.

Prince Albert's letters revealed his increasing judgment, especially one that he wrote to Stockmar on 13 September, 1855.[2] The space of his knowledge, and his discernment of the military pattern, give the narrative some of the wisdom one would expect to find in the quiet recollection of good history; not in a hasty report, written from brief telegrams, in the remote valley of Balmoral.

*

The fall of Sebastopol made the Court and the country seem certain of final victory, and the Queen wrote more of her family and less of war. When she walked on the moors with Prince Albert, there were at least seven of their children old enough to scamper among the heather. Queen Victoria was still too conscious of her royal duty towards her children to allow her maternal emotions much play. One day when Prince Leopold was naughty, the Queen suggested that a beating would be good for him. The Duchess of Kent pleaded that it would make her sad to hear him cry. 'Not when you have eight, Mama,' answered the Queen. She added, '. . . that wears off. You could not go through that each time one of the eight cried.'

In a letter written the next year, on 6 October, to Princess Augusta of Prussia, the Queen confessed her own hardness as a mother. She wrote, from Balmoral, 'I see the children much less, and even here, where Albert is often away all day long, I find no special pleasure or compensation in the company of the elder children. . . And only exceptionally do I find the rather intimate intercourse with them either agreeable or easy. You will not understand this, but it is caused by various factors. Firstly, I only feel properly *à mon aise* and quite happy when Albert is with me; secondly I am used to carrying on my many affairs quite alone; and then I have grown up all alone, accustomed to the society of adult (and never with younger) people – lastly, I cannot get used to the fact that Vicky is almost grown up. To me she seems the same child, who has to be kept in order and therefore must not become too intimate.'

Princess Victoria's marriage was being planned even before she had been confirmed. She had continued to develop the thoughtful virtues her parents would have welcomed in their eldest son. She would never have been found, in later years, as her brother was, bored by the memorials of Egypt and sitting at the base of a pyramid reading *East Lynne*. On every occasion, the daughter proved her superiority: even when they gave drawings to be sold for the Patriotic Fund, hers, entitled 'The Battlefield', brought 250 guineas. The Prince of Wales had drawn a figure, 'The Knight', and it was sold for only 55 guineas. Prince Albert taught his daughter to sit at his desk and help him with his work, when she was only fourteen.

The Princess had been ten and a half years old when she first met Prince Frederick William of Prussia, at the opening of the Crystal Palace. Ambition, with a leavening of romance, decided their future, and, after an exchange of official letters, the Prince came to stay at Balmoral during the summer holidays in 1855. He was almost twenty-four years old; tall, broad-shouldered and painstaking, and he walked in awe of Prince Albert's wisdom. On the afternoon of 29 September, they were all out riding when Frederick William spurred his horse forward in the narrow track so that he was riding next to the Princess. He leaned down and picked a sprig of white heather. As he placed it in her hand he confessed his love for her. When they returned to Balmoral the child was so confused by her emotions that there was 'an abundance of tears'.

Prince Albert wrote to his brother the same day, 'The marriage cannot be thought of before she is 17, in November 1857. You, too, will be convinced of the importance of this event and you will rejoice with us. . . There is one thing I must beg you to do. Do not speak about our secret to anybody; it is to be kept *strictly secret*. Of course, all the world will talk about it. But as long as we ourselves say nothing, it will not matter.'

Melancholy was already marking the Prince for her own:

even in this letter concerning his daughter's future happiness, he added a sentence or two of complaint about the 'dreadful attack of rheumatism' in his right shoulder, which caused 'so much pain and sleepness nights' and made it 'totally impossible' to 'get about'. In three weeks he had not shot more than 'one and a half stags ! ! !'

In another, undated letter, Prince Albert wrote to Duke Ernest, 'The intended is more and more in love every day. Victoria is quite impatient about it, as she cannot imagine that the child can arouse such feelings. Vicky is very reasonable. She will go well prepared into the labyrinth of Berlin.'

The 'secret' was not kept: on 3 October, *The Times* made a violent attack on the proposed alliance with one of the 'paltry German dynasties', and vilified the King of Prussia as 'the degenerate successor of Frederick the Great'. The writer prophesied the day when the Prussian royal family would be stripped of all their pomp and the Princess would be sent back to England, 'an exile and a fugitive'. The Queen and the Prince turned from the 'infamous' pages of *The Times* to enjoy Lord Palmerston's assurance that the marriage would 'be an event of outstanding importance for England, and Europe'.

Prince Albert wrote to his old tutor of Prince Frederick William as 'a truly good young man', and of his daughter, 'She has many things to learn . . . both from books and in the world, into which she is already beginning to go.'

For an hour each day the Princess sat with her father, listening obediently to his lessons; and when she was alone she translated sober books from German into English. On 8 April of the following year, when the Princess was fifteen years and five months old, her mother wrote to Princess Augusta, 'Vicky is to make her first appearance at a drawing-room the day after tomorrow, wearing feathers and train! She will be dressed quite simply in white . . . her gown to be trimmed with cornflowers. She will wear a wreath of the same flowers on her head.'

CHAPTER SEVENTEEN

1855-1858

The 'secret' betrothal of the Princess Royal was a planned but graceful interlude during the Crimean war. The Russians were still clinging to the heights north of Sebastopol, and another winter of misery seemed inevitable. When the Court returned to London from Balmoral, Prince Albert found the government and the people as eager as ever for conquest. On 19 November, 1855, he wrote to his brother, 'England is thoroughly sound in spite of the streetboy character of the Press, and the so-called political people. As regards our army, I can only say that we began the war in the Crimea with 25,000 men and 35 cannons, and after the loss of our whole army in the winter, we now have 51,000 men and 94 cannons, and 4,000 cavalry who are going out next spring in best health and spirits.'

The fear of war seemed to stimulate those who were not fighting it : the dockyards and arsenals were working as never before, but there were still grumbles of discontent in the Crimea. On 10 November, Sir James Simpson, who had reluctantly succeeded to the British command five months before on the death of Lord Raglan, suddenly resigned. He was described as a 'good man', but not equal to his task. Lord Palmerston wrote to Prince Albert, 'To find any officer against whom nothing can be said implies the choice either of such men as Wellington or Napoleon, or of men who have never been employed at all; and that of itself would be an absolute disqualification.'

Prince Albert suggested that the army in the Crimea should

be divided into two corps, each under the command of a senior officer of high position, and subject to the general control of the Commander-in-Chief. The plan was accepted and Lord Palmerston wrote again to the Prince, 'I and all the other members of the Cabinet feel greatly obliged to Your Royal Highness for having suggested an arrangement which had not occurred to any of us.'

The Prince's diary and letters reveal no pleasure over such praise; only the melancholy grumbling which was to spoil these last years of his life. Rheumatism was creeping deeper into his body and crippling him. He wrote, 'I have endured frightful torture. I continue to suffer terribly.'

*

Early in the New Year, 1856, when peace came near, the Queen signed the Royal Warrant instituting the Victoria Cross. It was her idea that the motto on the Cross – devised by her husband – should be 'For Valour'. She wrote to the Secretary of State for War that this 'would be better' than 'For the Brave', which 'would lead to the inference that only those are deemed brave who have got the Victoria Cross'. As the horror of the war slowly faded and the dead were being counted, the Queen read reports of the robust work of Florence Nightingale and her nurses, going where she had wished to go – to the burning edge of battle. She wrote, 'Dear Miss Nightingale . . . I need hardly repeat to you how warm my admiration is for your services, which are fully equal to those of my dear and brave soldiers.'

The Queen saw the ending of the war with grateful delight, while Prince Albert moaned over his pain and his tasks. On 19 February he wrote to his brother of the cry in Paris for 'Peace! Peace!' And then, 'We are awfully overwhelmed with work, and soon there will not be enough room in the same country for the Monarchy and *The Times*. The first wishes to do good; the latter is satisfied with doing mischief. . . The nation remains admirably sound, strong and progressive. The people bear the sacrifices of the war without grumbling. They love their Queen and adore her, and her army and navy. The workmen all over the country save one penny every Saturday for the Patriotic Fund, for the widows and orphans of the soldiers and sailors. I have the administration of the Fund and we have already got one and a half million pounds sterling. The colonies have behaved exceedingly well during the whole affair.'

An armistice was agreed on 26 February and the peace treaty was signed on 30 March. Six days later Prince Albert wrote to Duke Ernest, 'Vicky's confirmation, and the peace made in Paris, open our mouths and allow us to inform all our relations of a fact which they probably imagined, without having permission. Vicky and Fritz Wilhelm of Prussia are an engaged pair...'

Prince Albert then wrote, 'I am now satisfied with the peace. Our allies would certainly not have continued the war... The French come begging to our camps, where there is plenty. This does not appear in the newspapers. Exactly for this reason, it is true.'

The London crowds were also 'satisfied with the peace'. They forgot that they had hurried to the Tower little more than two years before, hoping to see the Queen and Prince Albert being brought in as traitors and prisoners. Now they spent their leisure waiting outside the railings of Buckingham Palace, watching the Queen and the Prince drive out – to Chatham, where they solaced the wounded, and to Aldershot, to review eighteen thousand soldiers. The Queen wore the uniform of a Field-Marshal and she rode past the troops on a chestnut charger. The short, lively woman, for whom the feelings of the mass of people had varied from blame to devotion, was now the symbol of victory. The soldiers flung their helmets and shakos towards the sky, and the dragoons waved their glittering sabres in the sunlight. The parade ground rang with the cry, 'God Save the Queen'.

There are no private letters from Prince Albert to his brother, to Stockmar or his old tutor, to reveal his thoughts during this spring of celebration. He had seen the Crystal Palace rise from the calm lawns of Hyde Park, to prove his belief in peace and industry; he had seen Aldershot grow as a strong preparation for war. He had been responsible for both these utterly different approaches to the future. He had seen the campaigns in the Crimea refreshed by his memoranda, and the army and navy strengthened through his foresight. If only he had been blessed with a sense of humour he might have smiled within, as he saw the Queen bestow the Order of the Garter on Lord Palmerston. He wrote, on 12 May, 1856, to his brother, 'In the last weeks we have had really too much to do.' He was to escape, with the Queen and their children, to Osborne. He wrote of the gardens he had made there, 'Nature is still rather behind.' Then he described the complications of bringing up his sons: 'There will be an alteration in our family life, as we have engaged an intelligent engineer officer as tutor for Alfred. The brothers are to be separated as the differences in their ages and capacities are disturbing in their education. Alfred is to live in the Royal Lodge at Windsor. . . Bertie will remain here, at Osborne, when we go to Balmoral.'

Strangers liked the Prince of Wales, who was then fourteen and a half years old. They wrote of his 'youthful simplicity' and of his 'frank, open countenance'. But these were not the merits Prince Albert sought in his eldest son, who continued to displease him in all things. He was delighted when the American Minister spoke of the Princess Royal's 'excellent head', after sitting next to her at dinner, but depressed when he read his son's essasys, because they were 'bald, ungrammatical, and badly penned'.

As a reward for doing three weeks of concentrated study, the Prince of Wales was allowed to go on a walking tour in Dorset, but with adult guardians and no one of his own age. He tried to escape attention under the name of Baron Renfrew, but the incognito collapsed and there were such cheerful demonstrations from the villagers that it was thought wise to interrupt the holiday and take him home. Next time, boys of his own age were added to the party for a tramp through the Lake District. For him, this was a success: encouraged by the mischief of his contemporaries, the Prince chased a flock of sheep into a lake. The female owner threatened to chastise him and he was so pleased that he did a water-colour drawing of the episode in his sketch-book.

In the summer and autumn of 1857, the Prince of Wales went to Europe without his parents, for the first time, but with a formidable entourage – his tutor Gibbs, an instructor, also Prince Albert's private secretary and his equerry. This solemn company was leavened by four of the boys from Eton, with whom he had shared the Sunday afternoons at Windsor. They travelled by way of Liège, Namur and Aix-la-Chapelle, to Königswinter, a few miles from Bonn, where Prince Albert had discussed 'juridical principles' and 'philosophical doctrines' twenty years before. There was faint hope that the Prince of Wales would absorb any shade of his father's example, but he was kept at Königswinter with his friends for a month of sober studies. While he was there the Prince met Prince Metternich, then aged eighty-four. He was shy in the presence of the old man whose word had once been law in Europe for more than thirty years: there was a fearful gap between the splendid old statesman and the Prince who was to be King. Metternich wrote afterwards, '*Le jeune prince plaisait à tout le monde,*' but added, '*Il avait l'air embarrassé et très triste.*'

The Prince of Wales was allowed a brief holiday in Switzerland, with a timid attempt at climbing over the glacier at the foot of Mont Blanc: then, after the four months abroad, he returned to England to be prepared for his confirmation. He viewed this so solemnly that he asked to be allowed to take the sacrament of his own accord but this was forbidden. The Queen and Prince Albert attended Holy Communion only at Christmas and Easter, and there was no reason why their son should not do the same.

As an escape from his literary studies, which bored him so much, the Prince of Wales had set his heart on a military career. But whilst Prince Albert approved of his son's formal association with the army, at his seventeenth birthday, he insisted that this move should be preceded by more learning, and eventually an examination in military and other subjects. So he made an experiment : he removed his son from the social temptations of the Court and arranged for him to have a temporary and separate establishment. White Lodge, in Richmond Park, was chosen, but the distance did not lessen the control of the boy's thoughts and habits. He had already been given an allowance to buy clothes, during his visit to Europe, but the gesture had been announced in a letter from his father with the warning that he must never wear 'anything *extravagant or slang*', and that he was to avoid 'foolish and worthless persons'.

Similar restrictions were continued in the small establishment in Richmond Park, where the tutors and equerries were all men of Prince Albert's choice; men who were bound to obey the letters of advice sent day after day, all out of touch with the needs and tendencies of the pupil. He was warned against 'Satirical or bantering expressions . . . lounging ways, such as lolling in arm chairs or sofas', and to remember that 'A *practical joke* should never be permitted'. This was sad advice for a Prince who was to lead a society in which moralising was an embarrassment and practical jokes were the essence of social delight.

A letter Prince Albert wrote to his brother two years before, on 14 November, 1856, reveals the humourless melancholy into which he had fallen. He wrote, 'Man is a beast of burden and he is only happy if he has to drag his burden and if he has little free will. My experience teaches me every day to understand the truth of this, more and more.'

There was no better occasion for imposing such alarming thoughts on the Prince of Wales than when he began his eighteenth year. On the morning of 9 November, 1858, a letter was delivered to the Prince, signed by both his parents. A few sentences from the long document are enough to prove that it lacked the joy one would expect in a birthday letter. The young Prince was told,

> Life is composed of duties, and in the due, punctual and cheerful performance of them the true Christian, true soldier, and true gentleman is recognised.
> You will in future have rooms allotted to your sole use, in order to give you an opportunity of learning how to occupy yourself unaided by others. . . Your personal allowance will be increased; but it is expected that you will carefully order your expenditure. . . You will try to emancipate yourself as much as possible from the thraldom of abject dependence for your daily wants on your servants. The more you can do for yourself and the less you need their help, the greater will be your independence and real comfort.

Then came the enumeration of duties, according to the Church Catechism, and a reminder that the 'first and principal' precept of all was 'that you should love your neighbour as yourself and do unto men as you would they should do unto you'.

Greville wrote of the letter as one of 'the most admirable . . . ever penned'. But he added that when the Prince brought it to the Dean of Windsor, he was 'in floods of tears'.

*

The Queen and Prince Albert had a different problem in planning the life of their second son, Prince Alfred. His dream was a sailor's life, and he was already working diligently under the care of the 'intelligent engineer officer'. He was the only member of the family who seemed constantly aware of a world beyond Britain and Europe. He was to be the first Prince to visit South Africa, Australia and New Zealand, and he already treasured maps which he studied, in search of these countries.

Duke Ernest was anxious : with no heir of his own it was now almost certain that Prince Alfred would inherit the duchies of Coburg and Gotha. Would the habits of a sailor, with all the world in his hands, make the Prince unwilling to accept the little space of Coburg for his life? There was a further problem for Queen Victoria and Prince Albert: if the Prince of Wales died, Prince Alfred would be heir to the throne, so there were 'almost endless reasons why Alfred's education must not be for Coburg alone'.

There is an undated letter written by Prince Albert to his brother, some time in the spring of 1857, that tells the story of the young Prince who had 'hardly any knowledge' of his 'original Saxon ancestors' and who wished 'to enter the navy'. His father wrote, 'This is a passion which we, as his parents, believe not to have the right to subdue.' He added, with curious disregard for his domination of his eldest son, 'It is certainly not right to break the spontaneous wish of a young spirit.' He described Prince Alfred: 'He has a great inclination for natural history and mechanics'; but it was 'his love for the Blue Jackets' that always turned up 'with greater force'. Then, 'An example of his perseverance is his violin, which he learned to play secretly, in his free time, wishing to surprise us.'

Prince Albert then referred to the fact that Prince Alfred was second in succession to his mother's throne, and the difficulties that might arise if they were to make 'a German of him' and his elder brother were to die. However, it was agreed that Prince Alfred should visit Coburg early in April, on his way home from Geneva, where he was going to 'perfect himself in French'. Prince Albert wrote later, 'If you will only give him a room, he will not disturb you in the least.'

In another letter, to his old tutor, Prince Albert described his second son, who was then almost thirteen years old: 'You will see no likeness to me in him, but you will find him a dear, sensible lad, full of intelligence and keen to learn ... I wish I could take him round myself and show him all the beloved spots ... you will understand my feelings. But I must be content with imagining it.'

Prince Alfred went to Gotha, and to Coburg, where he walked in the garden at Rosenau and stood at the window of the room in which his father was born. He returned to England in time for his mother's birthday, 'full of joy and freshness'. His father was so delighted that 'all the plagues and serious business' of his desk were necessary to bring him back to reality. His soul was 'lost in the dear memories'. But his weary body did not respond to this sad happiness. He wrote to his step-mother, 'I get on pretty well, in spite of a weak stomach with which I came into this world, and which I shall take with me to the grave.'

CHAPTER EIGHTEEN

1857-1858

When the Anglo-French alliance was threatened in April 1857 by overtures of friendship between Russia and France, Prince Albert was asked by Lord Palmerston and Lord Clarendon, the Foreign Secretary, to write Napoleon III a letter of friendly advice. When the ministers read the long letter, before it was sent, they thought it 'most excellent', and Lord Clarendon wrote to the Prince that it would 'open the Emperor's eyes to the consequences of his adulation of Russia'.

This new proof, that his wisdom and good intentions were increasingly appreciated by the ministers, and that he was even allowed to speak for England, did not seem to impress the Prince. But he was rewarded in August when Napoleon III came to stay at Osborne. They walked together in the gardens and their conversations were such that the Emperor wrote afterwards, 'One goes away from him . . . more disposed to do good.'

Except for his stubborn inability to comprehend his eldest son, there seemed to be no fault in Prince Albert. He was in advance of his time in realizing the responsibilities that are inherent in privilege, and he still glanced to the left in his thinking. Perhaps this is why, after seventeen years in England, he remained prejudiced against most of the old nobility and the 'landed gentry'. As late as November 1857, Lord Carlingford wrote in his diary,[1] 'Prince Albert thinks poorly of the English aristocracy as ignorant & bigoted; knows they don't like him; he likes the professional classes.'

The Prince's sense of responsibility went beyond the 'professional classes', to many causes where the workers and the poor were concerned. One example of this followed his appointment as Master of Trinity House, when he showed his sympathy for the ballast-heavers, whose conditions of labour were humiliating. The story is told in their own memorial, sent to Queen Victoria after Prince Albert died. They wrote, 'Before he came to our rescue, we could only get work through a body of riverside publicans and middlemen, who made us drink before they would give us a job. . . The consequence was that we were in a pitiable state; this truck-drinking system was ruining us body and soul, and our families too. . . We got no help till we sent our appeal to your late Royal Consort. . . He at once listened to us . . . he could put himself down from the throne he shared to the wretched home of us poor men. . . At once our wrongs were redressed and the system that had ruined us swept away.'

The ballast-heavers were the first Britons to call the Prince, 'Albert the Good'.

*

On 3 March, 1857, Lord Palmerston accepted Disraeli's challenge to dissolve Parliament and hold a general election, after the government had been defeated over their handling of a remote and belligerent dispute with China. The same day, Prince Albert wrote to his brother, 'We are in terrible political trouble. Victoria does not feel well. She is in her last month and hardly able to do what is expected of her.'

The reason for Queen Victoria's indisposition was that her ninth and last child, Princess Beatrice, was soon to be born, on 14 April. Prince Albert repeated his concern to Lord Palmerston, to whom he wrote that the Queen felt herself 'physically quite unable to go through the anxiety' of another ministerial crisis at this time.

The elections were to return the Liberals to power with an even greater majority; but more troubles were in store, and, for

Prince Albert, there was a personal sadness later in March when Stockmar came to England for the last time. He was seventy years old and, he said, 'no longer equal' to his tasks. He would say good-bye 'forever'.

There is no letter from Prince Albert to describe this break with all his past; the loss of the company and encouragement of the old Baron, who had helped to form his character, and to guide him, since he was a boy; who had said, all those years ago, 'I seem to be here to care more for others than for myself.' He departed, but there was the consolation of one more prize for his pupil before the year ended.

In May 1856, Queen Victoria had written a long memorandum, recalling the 'bad grace' of several members of the royal family in refusing to give precedence to Prince Albert, in the first year of their marriage. Several times since then, he had been humiliated on great occasions, in the presence of European royalty. The Queen wrote, 'While last year the Emperor of the French treated the Prince as a Royal personage, his uncle declined to come to Paris avowedly because he would not give precedence to the Prince; and on the Rhine in 1845 the King of Prussia could not give the place to the Queen's husband which common civility required, because of the presence of an Archduke, the third son of an uncle of the then reigning Emperor of Austria...'

Queen Victoria wished to free her husband from this entanglement of precedence; she wrote that she had 'a right to claim' that her husband should be 'an Englishman, bearing an English title, and enjoying a legal position which she has not to defend with a wife's anxiety...'

There was one curious meaning in the word 'anxiety', which Prince Albert explained in a letter to his brother, on 29 September, 1857, when the honour he deserved was granted to him, after the cautious deliberations of the ministers. He wrote, 'I am to have the title, "Prince Consort of the United Kingdom of Great Britain and Ireland". This ought to have been done, as you thought yourself, at our wedding.' Then, 'What pressed the question is the fact that our children, who are all princes of the country and of the house, are growing up. If their father is not a prince of the country, wicked people might later on succeed in bringing up the Prince of Wales against his father, and tell him that he should not allow a *foreign* prince to take a place before him...'

*

The Prince Consort turned from his belated honour to bigger spaces of anxiety. The distant war with China was to lead to the capture of Canton, by British and French forces, on 29 December, 1857, and six months later to the peace treaty of Tientsin. But the nearer and more alarming danger had come in May 1857, with news of the mutiny among the Indian regiments at Meerut. This arrived while Queen Victoria was still giving medals to the survivors of the Crimea, so the thoughts and perils of war merely travelled from one land to another. English officers, women and children were being massacred in India and the rebels had retreated to Delhi to gather more supporters. By the following July, 30,000 native troops were to desert from the army in northern India.

Ignoring the recent lessons of the Crimea, the government had already reduced its forces and Lord Clarendon had to admit, 'We are utterly defenceless.' Once more the will to fight seemed to come from the Queen and the Prince. On 29 June, 1857 – three days after she had given the first Victoria Crosses to her heroes, in Hyde Park – the Queen complained to Lord Panmure, the Secretary for War, 'The Empire has nearly doubled itself within the last twenty years, and the Queen's troops have been kept at the old establishment.' She then set down her views of what should be done to strengthen her forces, in phrases that sound like the Prince dictating, and she ended her letter with the reprimand, 'If we had not reduced in such a hurry this spring, we should now have all the men wanted.'

Queen Victoria's will to fight did not diminish her care for the soldiers who had returned from the Crimea. She thought it would be 'cruel and unfair to the gallant men' to send them to war again in India. She wrote to Princess Augusta of Prussia, 'I am sure of your sympathy about India. . . It is far worse than the last campaign; that at least was a glorious, honourable war. . .'

At the end of August the Court went to Balmoral. Prince Albert wrote to his brother, on 4 September, 'It is becoming more beautiful every day. . . I have been out stalking only twice.' He wrote also, 'We succeeded in bringing a little more military spirit into the Ministry which was overtired by endless speeches regarding India. . . We have an army of 80,000 armed men against us and the few Europeans are totally cut off from the forts and arsenals, where the Indian regiments are. It is impossible to speak of the horrors that happen there. The heroism of the English and their full confidence in God is admirable.'

More realistic reasons for confidence were already changing the fortunes of the British army in India. On 11 July, Lord Palmerston had sent for Sir Colin Campbell and offered him the command-in-chief. When he asked the old soldier how soon he could sail, Campbell had answered, 'Tomorrow.' He arrived in India in August to find that the tide of fortune had already turned; Delhi and Cawnpore had been rescued and, with troops that had been intended for China, Campbell advanced to Lucknow, which, after reverses and slaughter, was finally compelled to surrender in March of the following year.

There were three episodes, more private and revealing, in the lives of the Queen and the Prince before they resumed their tasks at Windsor. On 29 September, Prince Albert was able to announce to his brother that he was 'Prince Consort' at last. Then, on 5 October, Florence Nightingale came to stay. The fierce will-power that had intimidated the nurses at Scutari relaxed in the quiet of the Highlands. Lady Augusta Bruce wrote of her as 'modest, retiring and fearful of notice'. She pleaded for the wounded soldiers, still in the English hospitals. There was one man who had lost both his arms and who had become the

Queen's own charge. The wretched man had turned to the brandy bottle for solace, and when the Prince Consort was told this, he said the soldier was 'incorrigible'. But the Queen, always patient with tipplers, said she would *never* give him up. Florence Nightingale turned to her and smiled her thanks.

The third episode came soon before the Court left Balmoral. It may have reminded the Queen that other monarchs bore more terrible and lonely burdens than she had to endure. The King of Prussia's mind broke under the weight of his duties, and on 23 October his brother, Prince William – the husband of Queen Victoria's friend – assumed the regency. The Queen had written to Princess Augusta ten days before, when the change was threatened, 'Please accept our warmest and heartfelt sympathy, but we beg you not to look too gloomily and despondently towards the future.' Then the challenging sentence, from the woman who had never known fear, 'Why should you be so afraid?'

*

After he returned from Balmoral, the Prince Consort found a new interest to suit his studious mind. The time had come for the British government to frame measures for transferring control of the dominions of the East India Company to the Crown. News came of the temporary relief of Lucknow, and of the beleaguered city blessing the name of Colin Campbell; but news also of the bitterness between Britons and the natives in India being more sullen than ever before.

The Prince Consort seemed aware, with a sudden sense of history, that the Muslims and Hindus were alienated for ever from Christian ethics and thinking. He had written to the Prince of Prussia, on 27 July, 1857, 'The Indians are not a people capable of conquering independence for themselves, to say nothing of maintaining it. Since the days of Bacchus and Nimrod, India has constantly been overrun and conquered by new races – the Assyrians and Persians, the Greeks under Alexander, the

Hiungnu, Tartars, Arabians, and others, down to the most recent times. The conquerors have brought under the yoke and oppressed the races whom they found in possession, but have neither rooted them out nor absorbed them; thus they remain intermingled, but without national coherence.'

The remote, enduring conflict in India was overshadowed in January 1858 when there was an attempt to assassinate Napoleon III, by conspirators who had hatched their plot in England – members of the Carbonari Society, who succeeded in injuring the Emperor and killing or wounding sixty people who were near him. The grenades were examined and proved to have been made in England. The amiable walks and trust, shared by the Emperor and the Prince Consort in the garden at Osborne five months before, were forgotten: French officers tried to incite their ruler to take revenge; to invade England since it harboured and encouraged their enemies. Mass hysteria became violent on both sides of the Channel; twenty thousand Londoners gathered in Hyde Park and shouted, 'Down with the French.'

The Emperor persisted in his friendliness, but the harm done to the relationship between England and France was to endure for a long time. The immediate crisis was in Parliament, where Lord Palmerston, under pressure from the French Foreign Minister, introduced a Conspiracy Bill which aimed at treating conspirators as felons. The strength of the government had already been strained by the measure to transfer the control of India to the Crown. The Conspiracy Bill broke Lord Palmerston's power: his ministry was defeated and Lord Derby took office – much against his own wish since his followers were in a minority – with Disraeli as Chancellor of the Exchequer and leader of the House of Commons. The Conservatives inherited a heavy burden of tasks in India, where the mutiny continued and Sir Colin Campbell was still struggling to retake Lucknow; in China, where the British were still fighting to increase their commerce; and at home, with the aftermath of the attack on the

Emperor of the French and, nearer to the political scene, the question of parliamentary reform.

On 26 February, 1858, the Prince Consort wrote, '. . . Today the seals, offices and all business of the old Government are to be given over to the new. . . We intend to rest at Osborne. . . I have not yet got rid of the cold which I caught at the review at Woolwich. Victoria has suffered rather from rheumatism. The new Ministry, with a minority of 123 votes in the House of Commons, and 10 in the House of Lords, has now to decide about the Conspiracy Bill, the India Bill and the long promised Reform Bill.' He complained later, 'A Tory Ministry, with a Radical programme, carrying out Republican measures, with a Conservative minority, against Liberal opposition, is a considerable difficulty for a constitutional monarch.'

●

There was one prospect of happiness during this dark beginning of 1858, in the marriage, on 25 January, of Princess Victoria to Prince Frederick William, in the Chapel Royal – where the Queen had been married to Prince Albert eighteen years before. The prospect had been menaced by leading Prussians who objected to their prince being married in a foreign land, but this passing trouble had inspired Queen Victoria to fine indignation. She had written to the British Ambassador in Berlin, '. . . the assumption of its being *too much* for a Prince Royal of Prussia to *come* over to marry *the Princess Royal of Great Britain* IN England is too *absurd* . . . it is not *every* day that one marries the eldest daughter of the Queen of England.'

The Queen described 24 January as 'Poor dear Vicky's last unmarried day'. She had been to see the rooms prepared for her daughter's honeymoon, and she wrote, 'It quite agitated me to look at them. Poor, poor child.'

Before the wedding they all paused to be daguerreotyped, but the Queen 'trembled so' that her likeness came out 'indistinct'. There was one sign of private happiness that had flowered during the years. At her own marriage, in February 1840, the Queen had been estranged from her mother; but this time, she was delighted to see the old Duchess of Kent, 'looking so handsome in violet velvet trimmed with ermine, and white silk and violet.'

The Queen wrote also of the bridegroom looking 'pale and much agitated', and of the bride, 'our darling Flower', with 'such an innocent, confident, and serious expression'.

When the wedding was over, all returned to Buckingham Palace. The Queen described this scene also, in her journal. 'On arriving . . . we went with the young couple to the celebrated window at which they stepped out and showed themselves, we and the Prince and Princess [of Prussia] standing with them.' She could not know that eighty-seven years later, her greatgrandson would step out of the same window, to share, with his subjects, the second victory of British arms over the German people.

Eighteen years before, Queen Victoria and Prince Albert had driven to Windsor for their honeymoon in an old travelling coach. In 1858, the bride and bridegroom made the same journey by train; and from the station to the Castle they were drawn up the hill in their carriage by a team of boys from Eton.

*

At one of the dinner parties before the wedding, the Queen had written of the 'gay and pretty dances . . all the Princes dancing'. But she noted that the Prince Consort 'did not waltz'. When the two days of honeymoon were over, the Queen and the Prince joined the bride and bridegroom, for more parties; but still he did not waltz. His daughter, who reflected his own qualities, and limitations, was leaving him and he would be more alone. The adoration of his wife and her obedience to his superior mind did not fill all his needs. Nor could the confidence of ministers satisfy him entirely: he remained on the lonely height of royalty where they could never intrude. His daughter shared both heart and mind with him upon that height, and their parting was terrible for both of them.

Before she left England with her husband, the Princess Royal clung to her mother and cried, 'I think it will kill me to take leave of dear Papa.' The Prince Consort went with them to the ship at Gravesend. Snow was falling, and they shivered beside the river as they waited on the wharf. The decorations sagged, and young girls who had come to scatter flowers before them had to paddle through the slush.

The Princess boarded the ship with her husband, but she quickly went below, not daring to come on deck to wave to her father. He waited until the ship faded out of sight; then he returned to Buckingham Palace, where he wrote to his daughter next day, 'My heart was very full when . . . you leaned your forehead on my breast to give free vent to your tears. I am not of a demonstrative nature, and therefore you can hardly know how dear you have always been to me.'

CHAPTER NINETEEN

1858-1859

Lord Canning, the Governor-General of India, had written to Lord Granville, on 11 December, 1857 – in the spirit that earned him the name 'Clemency Canning': 'As long as I have breath in my body, I will pursue no other policy than that I have been following; I will not govern in anger. Justice, and that as stern and inflexible as law and might can make it, I will deal out. But I will never allow an angry or undiscriminating act or word to proceed from the Government of India, as long as I am responsible for it.' Then the proud sentence, 'I don't care two straws for the abuse of the papers, British or Indian.'

This good purpose was in tune with the Prince Consort's thinking, and with his influence on the leaders of the Conservative ministry – Lord Derby, the Prime Minister, Disraeli, the Chancellor of the Exchequer, and Lord Malmesbury, the Foreign Secretary. The first task they shared was the framing of the Bill for the Better Government of India, providing for the transfer of the entire administration from the Company to the Crown – with a Viceroy in place of the Governor-General, a Council of India in place of the Board of Control, and a Secretary of State in place of the President of the Board. The draft of the Bill was sent to the Queen and the Prince, and all but one of the changes they suggested were made.

Late in June 1858, when Disraeli informed the Queen that the Bill had been read a second time without a division, he ended his letter with a flash of romantic phrasing such as she was to enjoy so much during the later years of her reign. He wrote, 'It is, the Chancellor of the Exchequer really thinks, a wise and well-digested measure, ripe with the experience of the last five months of discussion; but it is only the ante-chamber of an imperial palace; and your Majesty would do well to deign to consider the steps which are now necessary to influence the opinions and affect the imagination of the Indian populations. The name of your Majesty ought to be impressed upon their native life. . .' He was tempting her towards the Imperial Crown he was to hand to her eighteen years later.

•

When the Princess Royal went with her husband to her new life in Prussia, it seemed that she took her father's heart with her. His relationship with the Queen had settled into an unselfish habit; the reports of their eldest son still made him petulant. When the London 'season' began later in the year, and the Prince of Wales was on one more visit to Germany and Switzerland with a staff of improving seniors, the Prince Consort thought it would be best for his son to stay away from the gaiety. He wrote to his brother in Coburg, '. . . as long as he is neither fish nor flesh, as the old saying is, it would not be good for him.'

Prince Alfred was also travelling in a world beyond his father's experience : before the year ended he was away with the bluejackets, to Malta, Tunis and Algiers. His father wrote, 'The sea and his service seem to do him much good.'

The warm, lonely letters were to the Prince's daughter : he wrote, 'If you have succeeded in winning people's hearts by friendliness, simplicity and courtesy, the secret lay in this : that you were not thinking of yourself. Hold fast this mystic power; it is a spark from Heaven.' Then came wise caution, based on his own experience in England : 'The public, just because it was rapturous and enthusiastic, will now become minutely critical and take you to pieces automatically. This is to be kept in view.'

The Prince endangered his daughter's success in her new

country with too much advice, and by a visit too soon after her marriage. She surprised the correct Prussian society by gathering musicians about her, as her father had done when he first came to England; and she drove out with only two horses when four were the least her position demanded. Her husband was with her, obedient and conventional, but the mind and voice to which she listened were those of her father.

The Prince Consort was drawn back into Germany by his daughter's letters and by the sentimentality into which he escaped from duty. Thirteen years had passed since he had been to his childhood haunts in Coburg, and he decided to return there, alone. There were to be no receptions nor, he wrote to his brother, 'visits from other Princes'. He went in May 1858, but the old ghosts eluded him : he wrote to the Queen, 'I have become an utter stranger here.' He picked flowers and sent them to her, in a box : he looked through the tunnel of trees towards the fortress on the hill – the shrine of his history; he walked in the fields, but a new generation of farmers had grown up to till them, and they did not recognize him. He returned to Schloss Ehrenburg to see the shells he had collected when he was young; still in tidy lines, as he had arranged them. He had ordered his life as meticulously as he had arranged the shells, and the prize seemed to be increasing despondency. 'I have eaten nothing all day,' he wrote to the Queen; then he gathered cowslips in a field and sent them to her with a note, 'Make tea of them, in honour of me, and let Bertie have some.'

In August, the Prince Consort went to Germany again, to Prussia; this time with the Queen. Their first grandchild was to be born early in the following year. 'This will give to the coming grey hairs in my whiskers a certain significance,' wrote the Prince.

On 12 August, while they were still travelling, a telegram arrived for the Prince : he brought it to the Queen and said, *'Mein armer Cart ist gestorben!'* Cart had been his servant from childhood; he had sharpened the Prince's wooden sword when he pretended to be a Saxon knight. The Queen and her husband shared a devotion to servants that was affectionate, always tolerant, and strangely personal. She comprehended the Prince's despair, and wrote in her diary, 'I turn sick now in writing it. . . I burst into tears. All day long the tears would rush every moment to my eyes. . . Cart was with Albert from his seventh year. . . He was the only link my loved one had about him which connected him with his childhood, and the only one with whom he could talk over old times. . . Albert felt the loss so much, and we had to choke our grief down all day.'

The Queen and the Prince continued their journey – through Hanover, where they might have thought of the dark, selfish conception of monarchy they had inherited and of the refreshed and different example they were setting; then on to Brandenburg, where they found their 'darling child' waiting for them on the platform, with a nosegay in her hand. They went on to Potsdam and then drove out to Babelsberg Castle, where they were to stay; where the Princess had tried to make the rooms as English as possible, with flowering creepers about the screens and lamps and pictures. After dinner, the Queen wrote in her journal that her daughter seemed 'low and nervous'. She added, 'God knows, I felt the same,' and she regretted that she would not be able to be 'with her at that very critical moment, when every mother goes to her child'. The Prince Consort was less demonstrative: he wrote to his brother, 'We found Vicky very well, although her state is rather too much for a young person of only seventeen years.' He added, 'We are living a very retired life here at Babelsberg.' But this did not mean that they could escape from the Minister for Foreign Affairs, who was with them to hand over the papers that arrived each day from Whitehall.

In one of the dispatch boxes was the draft for the Proclamation for India. The changes that the Queen and the Prince Consort made to the document are interesting in the light of the century that has passed since then. In a letter on 15 August the Queen set down her objections to the draft: she wrote to the Prime Minister, 'The Queen would be glad if Lord Derby would write it himself in his excellent language, bearing in mind that it is a female Sovereign who speaks to more than 100,000,000 of Eastern people on assuming the direct Government over them after a bloody civil war... Such a document should breathe feelings of generosity, benevolence, and religious feeling, pointing out the privileges which the Indians will receive in being placed on an equality with the subjects of the British Crown, and the prosperity following in the train of civilisation.'

The draft Proclamation was altered by Lord Derby, in 'strict harmony with the Queen's wishes'; and when she returned to England with the Prince, they dealt with the fate of India, not as a new possession but as an extension of personal obligation and duty. The Prince drew up a report on the reorganization of the Indian army, and his ideas were confirmed by Lord Clyde (Sir Colin Campbell) and other officers who had served in the sub-continent. The Queen was equally eager about the affairs of her new dominion : she insisted that her ministers should advise her of all moves and problems affecting the government of the country. She could not anticipate the sour ingratitude of history that led to such acts as the Pakistanis removing her statue from beneath its canopy in Lahore and consigning it to a cellar, when they broke free of both Britain and India, in 1947.

•

When their visit to Germany was over and the royal yacht brought the Queen and the Prince Consort back to Osborne, Prince Alfred was waiting for them on the wharf, wearing his midshipman's uniform. He had passed his examinations, solving all the mathematical problems 'almost without a fault', and doing all his translations without a dictionary. The Prince Consort was so proud that he sent his son's papers to the Prime Minister. Lord Derby's reply must have pleased the father : he was 'grateful', he wrote, that 'Her Majesty's Ministers had to pass no such examination . . . it would increase the difficulty of forming an Administration.'

These reports on Prince Alfred were in contrast to those from

White Lodge, where the Prince of Wales resisted learning the mathematics and fundamental principles that his younger brother enjoyed. On the rare evenings when the Prince dined out, the people he met liked him. Disraeli, who had once described the young man's talk as 'chitter chatter', sat next to him one night, some time later, and changed his mind: he found him 'intelligent, informed and with a singularly sweet manner'. These virtues must have been subdued within the Prince's little court, for his new governor, Colonel Robert Bruce, complained that his pupil was still 'prone to listlessness and frivolous disputes'.

There was another 'pupil' who was responding, more obediently, to the example set by the Prince Consort. He was Prince William of Prussia – father-in-law of the beloved Princess Victoria – whose regency in the place of his demented brother was made permanent on 7 October, 1858. Here was a rewarding field for spreading the gospel of constitutional monarchy. Stockmar rose from the quiet of retirement in Coburg and hurried to Berlin, to instil his liberal theories into the Regent, and the Prince Consort sent him many pages of advice – though Prince William was old enough to be his father. The spirit of this advice was revealed in one sentence, in a letter dated 22 December, 1858. The Prince Consort wrote, 'The Regent's position is that of moderator, and your readiness to use it everywhere with firmness will be of essential service to the general weal.' He congratulated Prince William on his choice of new ministers, and he wrote to Stockmar, 'What an excellent turn all matters have taken in Berlin. Indeed one cannot sufficiently praise the Prince.'

The relationship with France was less encouraging, towards the end of 1858. During an impromptu family trip to Normandy, in the *Victoria and Albert*, in August of the previous year – ten days after Napoleon III's visit to Osborne – the Prince Consort had been alarmed when he saw the new defences and docks being built at Cherbourg, the old fortress that looks across the Channel to Southampton Water. Though they enjoyed their brief holiday, Queen Victoria and the Prince were careful to notice these preparations, and the Queen wrote in her journal, 'It makes me very unhappy to see what is done here, and how well protected the works are, for the forts and the break-water (which is treble the size of the Plymouth one) are extremely well defended . . . there are at least 8,000 workmen employed, and already millions have been spent.'

In January 1859, the Prince Consort was to write, to Lord Malmesbury, that Napoleon III had been 'born and bred a conspirator'; that it was too late for the Emperor to 'get out of this turn of mind, scheming himself and suspicious of others'. The Prince had foreseen the danger during the private visit to Cherbourg in 1857: he had written to Stockmar of his 'grave cause for reflection', and he had awakened the fears of the ministers with his reports. He was alarmed again when he was to go to Europe with the Queen in the summer of 1858: he had written to his brother, on 10 July, '. . . we are pressed by the Emperor . . . to go to Cherbourg. As the festivities there, in reality, include a glorification of the army and navy against England, we do not intend to take part in them. We shall leave before they begin. . .'

The Queen and the Prince Consort met Napoleon III at Cherbourg on their way to Germany, and the Prince wrote afterwards, 'I am conscious of a change in the Emperor.' Perhaps the change was in his manner, because of an intrigue he could not disclose: only a few days before he had secretly agreed to support Cavour in his fight to free the Italian States from Austrian domination. Napoleon III was to be given Nice and Savoy as prizes for his trouble. The scheming went on: in his New Year letter to Queen Victoria, the Emperor announced the betrothal of Prince Napoleon, son of Jerome Bonaparte, to Princess Clothilde, daughter of Victor Emmanuel II, King of Sardinia – the monarch whose ambition was eventually to unite all Italy under his crown.

Napoleon III's intentions were no longer secret. His plan to help expel the Austrians from Italy and gather some of the spoils for himself was now openly declared.

At the end of 1858 the Prince Consort was able to watch some of the improvements in English life that he had enjoyed so much; the cleansing of the once foul waters of the Thames, the completion of the new Chelsea Bridge, and the opening of Battersea Park as a pleasure ground for the poor. In a broader world of good, he was able to comprehend America a little more clearly, since the first cable had been completed across the Atlantic, on 16 August. Thus, slowly, with the exchange of greetings between the Queen and President Buchanan, over the 'wondrous wire', there began a new relationship that would ultimately strengthen Britain in her ancient quarrels with Europe. But the image of the relationship was still faint in 1858; and in the first weeks of the new year, the Prince Consort was more concerned by the organized risings that had already begun throughout northern Italy, and the clear threat – as he wrote to Stockmar on 2 January, 1859 – that there would 'certainly' be 'war in the spring'.

*

In the letter in which he prophesied war, the Prince Consort complained, 'I am weary and out of heart.' On the same day, the pattern of the dark future was suggested in the birth of his first grandson, Prince William of Prussia – the Kaiser of contemporary history. While Queen Victoria was writing that she was 'proud and happy' because her daughter had presented an heir to the Prussian throne, the Prince of Wales, who was to be the enemy of the child when he grew up, was preparing to visit Rome, and to be received by the Pope – the first time an English prince had made such a gesture since the Reformation. But the gesture was laced with caution: Colonel Bruce was to be with the young Prince in case his spontaneous tongue ran wild. As the Queen wrote to King Leopold, after the audience, '. . . it would never have done to have let Bertie go alone, as they might hereafter have pretended, God knows! what Bertie had said. . .'

Queen Victoria had been wise. On 10 February, the Prince of Wales, with Colonel Bruce beside him, was received by Pius ix, and the conversation remained merely polite until near the end, when His Holiness broached the subject of reviving the Roman Catholic heirarchy in England. As Sir Sidney Lee recalls, in his biography of the Prince, 'At this point Bruce's patience gave way, and, contravening the calls of etiquette . . . he contrived to bring the interview to a hurried close.'

The Prince's stay in Rome was planned also for the improvement of his mind. He went to the tombs of Shelley and Keats, and he met Robert Browning, who thought him 'a gentle, refined boy'. But the pleasures ended suddenly on 19 April, when the Austrians sent an ultimatum to Turin, demanding the disarmament of Sardinia. The demand was rejected on the 28th; and when the Austrian army crossed the Ticino and invaded Piedmont on the 29th, the first French troops had already landed at Genoa. On 3 May, Napoleon III formally declared war against Austria. Nine days later, England proclaimed her neutrality.

The Prince of Wales was hurried from Rome to Gibraltar, in a British ship, and he spent the next two months travelling in Spain, Morocco and Portugal, with his governor and his tutors.

*

On 10 February the Prince Consort had written to his brother, 'The Emperor Napoleon seems determined to provoke, and much, including much fine German, blood will flow. When or how we may be dragged into the whirlpool I cannot calculate, but I am sure that in the long run we shall be unable to escape it. May God forgive the man who wantonly between sleep and waking is bringing so much unhappiness into the world.'

The Prince had tried to turn his mind to peaceful occupations, and he had written to his daughter of the South Kensington Musuem with its two new galleries; of the pictures to be hung there, and of the prospect of another Exhibition 'like that of 1851'. But the war in Italy overshadowed these quiet plans and thoughts, and the Prince's letters described instead the advance of the French and their victories at Palestro, Magenta and Malegnano, and the bloody battle at Solferino, on 24 June.

The rival emperors of Austria and France were suddenly chastened by an alarm from Prussia. Six of her army corps were mobilized and she threatened to come in on Austria's side. This preparation was all the more dangerous because of the extravagant attitude of some of the press: the *Allgemeine Zeitung* urged the Prussians to take advantage of the absence of the French army and march on Paris. The Prince Consort wrote more pages of wise advice to the Regent of Prussia, but they could not influence the fearful situation in which the rulers were caught. The Emperor of Austria preferred to lose his power in Italy rather than recognize Prussia as an equal, and Napoleon III was not prepared to fight both; so an armistice was agreed, on 6 July, and the preliminaries of peace were signed at Villafranca on 12 July.

On 11 August, after the envoys of the rival powers had met in Zürich to draft a treaty, the Prince Consort wrote to the Regent of Prussia 'May Heaven direct for the best! We need its help in every part of Europe. If only it would shed upon our leading statesmen a ray of its Holy Spirit, we should be living through a less difficult and unpleasant period.'

Such pure thinking could not guide the actions of ambitious men. Napoleon III had returned to Paris with the gilt look of a conqueror. Nice and Savoy were to be his ultimate prizes, and he had made Victor Emmanuel master of Italy's destinies. The poison that had stimulated, and destroyed, the first Napoleon was in his blood also. The neighbouring countries were agitated, and the English became conscious once more of the ancient perils of the Channel. Their sovereign revealed the nation's anxiety in her Speech from the Throne at the opening of Parliament. She asked for one million pounds to convert her Navy to steam power. The mass of people revived their inherent fear of their historical enemy: the volunteer movement spread so quickly that by the following summer one hundred and thirty thousand men had been enrolled. On 23 June, 1860, eighteen thousand of them marched past Queen Victoria as she stood on a dais in Hyde Park.

The Prince Consort's concern for England's safety increased his private melancholia. He wrote to his daughter in Prussia, on 24 August, 1859, of his failing health and energies, and of his belief that 'worry over political affairs' was 'chiefly to blame for it'.

*

The 'political affairs' that worried the Prince had begun many months before, on 28 February, 1859, when Disraeli had introduced his Reform Bill to the Commons. The debate that followed inspired many fine orations that were reported to the Queen, in Disraeli's fine phrases. He wrote, 'A night of immense power and excitement. Two of the greatest speeches ever delivered in Parliament.' In one letter he described Lord Palmerston as 'infinitely audacious'. This audacity helped to force the Conservative government into an election, which Lord Derby and his supporters could not survive. He was obliged to place his resignation in the Queen's hands, and on 12 June Lord Palmerston became Prime Minister again, at the age of seventy-four – almost twice as old as the Prince Consort in years, almost half as old in spirit. Lord John Russell agreed to serve under him as Foreign Secretary and W. E. Gladstone was appointed Chancellor of the Exchequer. It was an impressive government, looking back both to the Whig past and the Liberal future.

It was characteristic of the Prince at this time, when the Italian war was still being fought, and the 'ill-devised' Bill for parliamentary reform was harassing the politicians, that he sat quietly beneath his green-shaded lamp and wrote an immense report on the organization of the various civilian bodies into a permanent and co-ordinated means of defence. He named the report, 'Instructions to Lord-Lieutenants', and sent it to the Secretary for War. The orders he enumerated and described were so complete that they were adopted by the Cabinet and issued immediately.

Six days after Lord Palmerston assumed power, the Prince
Consort wrote, with great perception, to his brother, 'The English Government is a popular one and the constitution is becoming more and more democratic. People *do not calculate*. As
masses, they cannot calculate. They *feel* only, and are therefore
not led by interests nor state – or public law, principles or deduc-
tions, but only by feeling. If you prefer the word, by *instincts*.
To the last belong the feeling for right, the wish for freedom
and principally for self-preservation. . . Since 1817, the English
have been endeavouring to obtain a wider development of freedom and individual purpose, at home, and the same for all
Europe. . . Since 1830, democracy has been getting the upper
hand in England. And the French are following. . .'

*

In May 1859 there had been private distress for the Queen and
the Prince Consort, when the Duchess of Kent was so ill that
she could not join in her daughter's birthday celebrations. The
tranquil old lady, now aged seventy-two, who had been the innocent cause of so much torment more than twenty years before,
was loved by all who knew her. She had recovered enough by
25 May for the Queen to write to King Leopold, 'Thank God!
today I feel another being, for we know she is in a satisfactory
state. . . But I am thoroughly shaken and upset. . . I hardly
myself knew how much I loved her, or how my whole existence
was bound up in her, till I saw looming in the distance the
fearful possibility of what I will not mention.'
    It seemed that the year 1859 would end with a semblance of
peace and quiet. On 9 September, soon after his fortieth birthday, when the Court was already on holiday at Balmoral, the
Prince Consort wrote to his brother, '. . . on the 14th I am going
to Aberdeen, to preside at the meeting of the British Association for the Advancement of Science, where I am to give the
opening speech. For weeks I have been trying to arrange something popular about science, which is not to be tedious. . . On

the 22nd, all the scientists are to come here to take part in a Highland fête, with atheletic games. But they are not expected to take an active part.

This quotation is from the only letter that survives of those the Prince wrote to his brother during the summer holiday at Balmoral. He went to Aberdeen, without the Queen, and during almost an hour he made one of his most brilliant speeches, fascinating an audience of 2,500 scholars with a definition of fundamental principles, of which he was now master. While he was away, the Queen wrote to King Leopold, 'Albert left me yesterday for his great undertaking at Aberdeen, which, I have heard by telepgraph, went off extremely well. He returns to my joy this evening again. I feel so lost without him.'

The Prince returned to Balmoral to enjoy reports of his success; then, in October, the Court moved back to Windsor Castle, where one of the first tasks was to prepare for the admission of the Prince of Wales as an undergraduate to Oxford University. While Prince Alfred was serving happily with his ship in the Mediterranean, the Prince of Wales kept to his books, showing a little more 'zeal and good will' in his studies. The real source of happiness for the Prince Consort came with the arrival of his eldest daughter and her husband, at Windsor, in time to celebrate the Prince of Wales's eighteenth birthday on 9 November. But the 'dear visit' was soon over, and on 3 December the Princess returned to Berlin. Her father wrote to her a few days later, 'Thus do the waves close in and run on their way...'

The theme of complaint was continued in the Prince Consort's letter to Stockmar at the end of the year: he wrote, 'We are quite well, all except my stomach, which is in a state truly pitiable, and is responsible for my waking early in the morning, and being unable to sleep again – "a shocking bore" as the popular phrase here says.'

CHAPTER TWENTY

1859-1860

Before he went to Oxford, in October 1859, the Prince of Wales stayed in Edinburgh for three months, to study applied science in addition to all his accustomed subjects. This would prepare his mind for the changes that the Prince Consort already anticipated, in the pattern of Britain's future. Sir Sidney Lee[1] describes the habits of these months, when the young Prince studied 'scientific principles . . . theoretically and experimentally'; when he also visited iron and gas works, cotton mills and textile factories, 'in order to familiarize himself with industrial processes.'

Sir James Clark, the Court physician, had warned the Edinburgh professor in charge of this span of the Prince's studies that he would find his pupil 'very backward for his age'. The professor did not agree; he thought 'the Prince's powers of application' were 'underrated' and that both his 'disposition and capacity promised well.'

Thus improved, with some knowledge of science and industry, the Prince of Wales was admitted to Oxford. The Prince Consort wished his son to belong 'to the whole University' and not to one 'particular college'. But the Dean of Christ Church said that this would be difficult in the pattern of Oxford and, although the Prince Consort went there with the hope of persuading him, no concession was made, except that the Prince was allowed to have his own house outside the college, with Colonel Bruce still watching over him.

While he was at Oxford the Prince was the living symbol of

a history that failed to stir his imagination; otherwise he might have been nourished by the example of the only other heir to the throne who had studied at the university. This prince, afterwards Henry v, who went to Oxford in 1398, was wild and reckless in his youth, but, after he was crowned, was blessed with every virtue and courage a king should have. There was a portrait of him in Queen's College, where he had been a student. If the Prince of Wales could have comprehended the splendid story he might have enjoyed some secret refreshment from it; but this was not in his mind, or his nature. All he could do was try to respect his father's opinion that 'the only use of Oxford is that it is a place of study'.

Half a century later, the Prince of Wales's grandsons were to mix in the heart of university life: one, afterwards King Edward viii, was to become a familiar figure walking through the cloisters of Magdalen, with a banjo under his arm; and at Cambridge, his brother, afterwards King George vi, was fined for smoking in the street. But this age of freedom for princes had not yet come. The Prince Consort approved of his son joining 'convivial meetings' at dinner, but only with 'the most distinguished men of the place'. This pompous demand was increased by Colonel Bruce's watchful care. But there was a humanity in the pattern of the Prince's life at Oxford that defeated some of his father's unhappy strictures. The professors and tutors were used to the frailties of the young and some of them asked the Prince to dinners where he was allowed to smoke in private and thus encourage a habit that endured. The Dean of his college thought him the 'nicest fellow possible, so simple, naïf, ingenuous, and modest, and moreover with extremely good wits; possessing also the royal faculty of never forgetting a face.'

*

The New Year letter written by the Prince Consort to his daughter in Prussia, on 4 January, 1860, was a solemn reminder of hopes 'which God will surely suffer to be fulfilled'. He wrote

of 'this suffering and difficult world', and of the moral laws
that were 'the end and aim of all education and culture,' as he
and his daughter had 'long ago discovered and reasoned out together'. Queen Victoria heralded the beginning of 1860 more
simply : she wrote to King Leopold, 'I never remember spend-
ing a pleasanter New Year's Day, surrounded by our children
and dear Mama.'

When the peaceful holiday ended the Queen and the Prince
returned to their worries over the security of the country. It was
true that the financiers, industrialists and farmers were prosperous, and the growing strength of the militia and the defences
lessened the fear of what Napoleon III might do next. Even
though the Emperor of the French encouraged the commercial
treaty with England that was signed at the end of January, his
ambitions and his interference in Italy still alarmed the nation.
But this popular fear, which increased when Nice and Savoy
were ceded to France, in March, did not justify any offensive
action. The British government had remained aloof from the
struggle against Austria, and sought to remain aloof from the
strife that still beset the Italian states; and *The Times* echoed
responsible opinion in the comment 'We wish well to Italy, but
we do not go to war for an idea.'

The leaders, including the Prince Consort, contributed only
advice and memoranda to the troubles in Europe, and Disraeli
pleased many people when he said, in January, 'What is the
moral that I draw from these conflicting opinions? It is that
Italy is at the present moment in a state far beyond the management and settlements of Courts, Cabinets and Congresses. . . I
say that what is going on in Italy can only be solved by the will,
the energy, the sentiment, and thought of the population
themselves.'

In February, Disraeli's rival, W. E. Gladstone, the Chancellor
of the Exchequer, also made a brilliant speech, on the less engaging subject of the Budget. To pay for the increased defences
of the country the tax assessment was to be raised from sixpence-
halfpenny to sevenpence on all incomes over £100, and from

ninepence to tenpence on incomes over £150. Gladstone's ora-
tion, described by Sir Edward Bulwer Lytton as 'among the
monuments of English eloquence', reconciled the House and the
country to accept the new burden. The Prince Consort was
equally pleased : he wrote to his brother on 17 March, 'Gladstone is now the real leader of the House of Commons, and
works with an energy and vigour altogether incredible.'

*

On 10 February, 1860, the Prince Consort wrote to Stockmar,
'I cannot let this day come to a close without writing you a line.
It is twenty (!!!) years to-day since we plighted our troth in St
James's. I see you still standing in the pew not far from the
chancel, as the negotiator of the marriage treaty. . . We have
gone through much since then, and striven after much that is
good; if we have not always succeeded, the will at least was
good, and we cannot be sufficiently grateful to heaven for many
a blessing and many a success !' Queen Victoria wrote a postscript
to the letter : 'One little word I must add on this blessed day !
Words cannot express my gratitude and my happiness. I wish I
could think I *had made* one as happy as he has made me. But
this is not for want of *love and devotion*. Few possess as
much. . .'
   Still, with their different natures, the Queen and the Prince
Consort saw their children in different ways. The Prince had
written to his eldest daughter, on 25 January, on the second
anniversary of her marriage, 'In love consists the inward tie; in
love is the fundamental principle of happiness.' The Queen did
not see her daughter in this idealistic light, and she set a dangerous 'Victorian' example of firm and intolerant control of a
parent over children. Her attempts to direct her daughter's life
in Prussia had distressed the Princess so much that she had
sought Stockmar's help and advice. This was back in December
1858, when the old Baron was in Berlin, where he talked the
subject over with Lord Clarendon. As Greville recorded, on the

12th, Stockmar said to Lord Clarendon, 'I want to talk to you on a very important matter and to invoke your aid.' He then spoke of the Princess : 'Her mother is behaving abominably to her . . . she is worried and frightened to death.' The Queen still wished 'to exercise the same authority and control over her that She did before her marriage', and she was writing 'constant letters full of anger and reproaches' that made her daughter 'seriously ill'.

Greville's record is strangely dramatic : he wrote that in Stockmar's opinion the Prince Consort 'could do nothing', as the Queen was 'so excitable' that he 'lived in perpetual terror of bringing on the hereditary malady'.[2]

When Lord Clarendon returned to England from Berlin he spoke boldly of the Princess's grief to her father, who said, as Stockmar had said before, that he had 'always been embarrassed by the alarm he felt lest the Q's mind should be excited by any opposition to her will'.

Apparently the Prince Consort dared to speak to his wife of the harm her letters of admonition could do, but the Queen continued to jeopardize her daughter's affection. Late in October 1860, when the Princess came from Prussia to stay with her parents, Lady Augusta Bruce wrote that 'The Q' found the Germans 'rather pompous' and that she 'pitched into' the Princess 'for showing symptoms'.

*

Late in the spring of 1860, when the Prince of Wales was still at Oxford, it was decided that he should spend part of his next holidays in Coburg. The Prince Consort asked his brother to have 'no ceremonies whatever' and to receive him 'as a member of the family'. On 6 April he wrote of his son, 'He likes to ride. He would also be happy if he could shoot a mountain-cock, if one is to be had. He likes going to the theatre and we have nothing against his going on Sunday, *but he must go to church in the morning.*'

On 27 April the Prince Consort wrote again, after his son

returned from Coburg, 'He came home well and merry. . . He has a strange nature. He has no interest for things, but all the more for persons. This trait in his character, which is often found in the Royal family, has made the family so popular. But it also arouses the dangerous inclination for what they here call "small talk".'

His second son, Prince Alfred, was increasing his conquest of the seas; he was to go as far as South Africa before the year ended. His father was pleased because 'prejudice' had no chance in the Prince's mind 'against straight-forward logic'.

The future of his second daughter, Princess Alice, then seventeen years old, was also promised, in June, when Prince Louis of Hesse came to stay at Windsor for the Ascot races. The Prince Consort wrote to his brother on 31 July, 'As we spoke about Alice's future while you were here, I wish to let you know that we have had offers from Darmstadt, which we have accepted in a friendly manner for the present. Young Prince Louis seemed to take a fancy to Alice while he was here and he seems to have lighted a flame in her, too . . . we think it better to let the two young people become better acquainted with each other before binding themselves. For this purpose the young man is to pay a visit here in the course of the winter.'

While these calculated patterns for the future of their grown children were being devised, the Queen and the Prince Consort still enjoyed the different, innocent surprises of their youngest child, Princess Beatrice, who would run in from the garden and ask the old Duchess of Kent to play the piano, so that she could sing in what Lady Augusta Bruce described as a 'most husky pot-house voice'.

*

One of the pleasures for the Queen and the Prince Consort was their escape, three or four times each year, to Osborne, their own quiet English house. The extravagant decorations of the rooms were in strange contrast to many of the pictures the Prince

bought and kept near him. Osborne, like Balmoral, Buckingham Palace and Windsor Castle, was becoming a memorial to
the curious conflict, or difference, that can estrange taste from
knowledge. The new furniture and paraphernalia were almost
alien to the scholarly wishes and discrimination that the Prince
had first revealed when he was a student, buying early German
wood carvings, and drawings by Dürer and Van Dyck, from a
dealer in Cologne.

This predilection for sculpture and pictures continued and
grew during all his years in England. With the Queen he had
learned etching and lithography, but he never pretended to be
more than a patron of the arts. Many years later, Lady Bloomfield recalled that he had said to her at dinner, 'I consider that
persons in our position of life can never be distinguished artists.
It takes the study of a whole life to become that, and we have
too many other duties to perform to give the time necessary to
any one particular branch of art. Our business is not so much to
create, as to learn to appreciate and understand the works of
others, and we can never do this till we have realized the difficulties to be overcome. Acting on this principle myself, I have
always tried to learn oil-painting, water-colours, etching, lithography, &c. &c., and in music I learnt thorough-bass, the piano-
forte, organ and singing – not, of course, with a view of doing
anything worth looking at or hearing, but simply to enable me
to judge and appreciate the work of others.'[3]

The Prince Consort proved the sincerity of this in the company he chose. In *Victorian Patrons of the Arts*,[4] Mr Frank
Davis recalls, 'The evidence from artists themselves bears witness
to his knowledge of the technical side of painting. Frith, in his
autobiography, notes how surprised he was by the Prince's intimate knowledge, as the painter puts it, "of what I may call the
conduct of a picture". Speaking of "Derby Day", Frith continues: "He told me why I had done certain things and how, if
a certain change had been made, my object would have been
assisted. How the masses of light and shade might still be more
evenly balanced, and how some parts of the picture might

receive still more completion. – I put many of the Prince's suggestions to the proof after the close of the exhibition, and I improved my pictures in every instance." '

The Prince Consort's private rooms at Osborne were hung with twenty-six early paintings; among them Duccio's 'Crucifixion', which he had bought when he was twenty-seven. Many of his pictures are now in the National Gallery, and they include the beautiful 'Portrait of a Woman of the Hofer Family', of the Swabian School, and 'A Girl Waiting', of the Netherlandish School. Mr Davis describes the Prince in his book as 'conscientious, hard working and sensitive', as a man of 'high seriousness', and as one of the 'four remarkable persons' of the Victorian era to whom the British owe 'an immense debt as collectors of works of art for the nation'. Two of the others were Charles Eastlake, Director of the National Gallery for ten years until his death in 1855, and the vigorous Henry Cole, who had been the Prince's 'right hand man in promoting the Great Exhibition of 1851'. They were his friends; not the rich private collectors in their mansions.

At the end of his tribute, published in 1963, Mr Davis wrote that the Prince Consort, 'by precept and example, set a standard of connoisseurship unknown before his day in official circles'.

*

On 15 March, 1860, Lord John Russell, then Foreign Secretary, again revealed his trust in the Prince Consort's judgment : he wrote, 'I confess I should esteem it as a great favour if your Royal Highness, who is so well acquainted with Germany, would furnish me with some clue to our future policy in regard to that country.' Within three days the Prince produced a letter of two thousand words, dipping wisely into history, and then describing the policy in which he believed – that salvation for the minor states of Germany could come only from Prussia. He wrote that the Prussians had 'no fixed view' as to how this task would be accomplished; and added, 'Without interfering with the Federal Constitution, and the external form of Germany, which is recognised by Europe, she ought to proceed by treaties with the separate States to effect that union. . .' He thought also that the minor States should feel secure against being 'absorbed into Prussia'.

In a letter to his daughter, written about the same time, the Prince wrote, 'Prussia's position is a weak one, and will continue to be so, as long as she does not morally dominate Germany.' He added, '. . . to be herself German is the secret to bring this about.'

There was one more proof of the Prince's wisdom, during the spring and early summer. On 1 March, Lord John Russell had placed his measure for further parliamentary Reform before the House of Commons. It was an anniversary dear to him : in the same month in 1831, when the Prince Consort was a boy of eleven, Lord John had introduced his first Reform Bill with a speech that established his popularity and his fame. But the reforms that were still dear to him were no longer in the mind of the government or of the people. The Prince Consort had written, during the previous year, that Britons 'wanted in fact no reform, but a Bill to stop the question of reform'. This proved true : Lord John's Bill was withdrawn on 11 June, 'almost in silence'. He wrote of his defeat, 'The apathy of the country is undeniable, nor is it a transient humour. It seems rather a confirmed habit of mind. Four Reform Bills have been introduced of late years. . . For not one of them has there been the least enthusiasm.'

*

On 24 May, 1860, Queen Victoria celebrated her forty-first birthday at Osborne. She wrote to Princess Augusta of Prussia, 'Where could I point to another woman who after twenty years of such marital felicity still possesses it? My dearly beloved Albert shows me not only as much affection and kindness as ever, but as much love and tenderness as on the first day of our marriage. How can I ever repay him for it?'

The day had been beautiful, and it had ended with music on the terrace. The Queen wrote of the 'dancing and merriment', and of her pleasure because 'Dear Mama was able to join in everything'.

Queen Victoria's own robust health and freedom from deep analysis prevented her from comprehending natures different from her own. She might have been perplexed and alarmed if she had known that, the day before the birthday celebrations, her husband had written to their daughter in Prussia of being 'tortured' by his duties. He wrote of the world of 'miserable men', and of the 'treadmill of never-ending business'. The Prince Consort likened himself to the donkey at Carisbrooke nearby, and wrote that the wretched animal was his 'true counterpart', adding, 'He, too, would rather munch thistles in the Castle Moat, than turn round in the wheel at the Castle Well; and small are the thanks he gets for his labours.'

CHAPTER TWENTY-ONE

1860

The year 1860 saw the beginning of a change in Britain's attitude towards the new world; the beginning also of a change in the thoughts of Queen Victoria, the Prince Consort, and their sons. Except for his wise interest in the fate of India, in 1858, the Prince had continued to think across the Channel, into Europe. He was like the average responsible Briton in this; most of them, remembering the example of the American colonies, assumed that Canada, Australia and New Zealand would also ripen into freedom and fall from the parent tree. Even among families whose sons had emigrated to these lands, the bonds became thinner when the older generation died and new generations were maturing on the colonial earth. But the sons and daughters born in the new countries remained in love with Britain, and the monarchy endured as the symbol of their beliefs. The first surprising proof of this had come when Canada equipped a regiment of infantry and sent them to the Crimea, to fight as soldiers of the Queen.

After the Crimean war, the Canadians had asked Queen Victoria to visit them, but she had pleaded that the risks and fatigues of such a journey would be too much. The Canadians then asked if one of the Queen's sons might be sent to be their Governor. This also was refused because the sons were too young and uncertain for such a lonely responsibility. But the Queen and the Prince Consort agreed that in July 1860, the Prince of Wales should go to Canada, to open the great railway bridge across the

St Lawrence, and then lay the foundation stone of the new Parliament House in Ottawa.

On 29 February, the Prince Consort wrote to his brother, '. . . During the summer vacation he [Bertie] is to go to Canada to inaugurate the large bridge over the St Lawrence River, in Victoria's name. The colonies urgently invited *us* to come. He is to represent England, and the Canadians wish to show the Americans how happy, free and yet monarchical it is possible to be.'

The next surprise was a letter from the Democratic President of the United States, James Buchanan, inviting the Prince of Wales to cross the border from Canada and be a guest in his country. The corporation of New York added their gesture: they also wished to be hosts to the Prince during his journey.

There were undercurrents of anxiety over what seemed a simple and amiable plan for the Prince's visit. Was the President as forthright as he seemed? Was the annexation of Canada a possible plan in his mind? The Americans had proved that territorial aggrandizement was inherent in states, no matter where they found the illusion of freedom : they had already annexed California in the west and Texas in the south. Why not Canada in the north?

Other possible sources of discontent menaced the visit. The British campaign against slavery stung and antagonized many Americans who still profited from the trade. And there was the enormous Irish population in the Eastern States, still out of love with their former oppressors in England. In Canada, there was the enduring conflict between Protestants and Catholics, which had lost none of its zest through being transplanted into a new land. The Prince of Wales was to travel among many angry people, and it was fortunate that he was still young and free from both suspicion and prejudice. The compensation for his intellectual limitations was simpleness of heart : apart from occasional gusts of impatient temper, the Prince was usually willing to like everybody he met.

For some weeks the plans for the North American visit were

so new and engrossing to the Queen and the Prince Consort that affairs in Europe took second place. Even the revolution in Sicily, and Garibaldi's landing at Marsala, in the name of Victor Emmanuel – nourishing signs of Italian unity – did not stimulate the Prince Consort's indefatigable pen so much as the careful instructions that were to curb his son's freedom during the remarkable journey. There were also orders to be written for Prince Alfred, who was already on his way to Cape Town, where he was to open the new breakwater.

These far-flung enterprises seemed suddenly to fascinate the Prince Consort. 'What a charming picture is here of the progress and expansion of the British race', he wrote to Stockmar, for whom a bridge over the St Lawrence and a breakwater in Cape Town were beyond the old horizons of power.

On 9 July, 1860, the Prince of Wales sailed for Canada, having written to his mother, 'I will do my best.' His governor, now General Bruce, went as chief censor of his actions and words; also the Duke of Newcastle, the Colonial Secretary, to write speeches and direct the policy of the tour. Two journalists were included in the party; one to write for *The Times* and one to draw pictures for the *Illustrated London News*.

The conquest began in Newfoundland where the Prince first landed – a very young English colonel in uniform, wearing the ribbon of the Order of the Garter. The wife of the Archdeacon of St John's wrote back to England, 'It was a most politic step to have sent him on this tour. His appearance is very much in his favour, and his youth . . . there is scarcely a man or woman who can speak of him without tears. The rough fishermen and their wives are quite wild about him. . . Their most frequent exclamation is, "God bless his pretty face and send him a good wife." '

A prince was still the symbol of something the colonists missed in their sturdy pursuit of freedom, and for them, as he passed by, he had a romantic and heroic look. But neither his father nor General Bruce had seemed to consider the value of the Prince's own young charm in the adventure : the Prince Consort wrote to remind him that his success was because of his mother,

though he told Stockmar in a letter, 'Bertie is generally pronounced the most perfect product of nature.' General Bruce
watched his pupils's innocent progress, and he wrote, 'H.R.H.
acquitted himself admirably, and seems pleased with everything,
himself included.'

In Nova Scotia the Prince turned from the acclamation one
day to see the ruins of the house in which his grandfather, the
Duke of Kent, had lived with Madame de St Laurent, seventy
years before.[1] It was still called 'The Duke of Kent's Lodge'.
The Prince wrote to his mother, 'There is nothing remaining of
it, except a rotunda in which the band used to play.' He picked
a sprig of sweet briar as he walked in the forsaken garden and
sent it to the Queen as a memento of her father, because he
'thought' she 'might like it'.

He continued his journey through eastern Canada, enjoying
his success as much as the people enjoyed the sight of him. He
turned from the ceremonies in the evening to read constant reports from home; of big sums of money being voted for defences; of his father's plans for his second Great Exhibition; of
the celebrations for King Leopold's thirty-ninth year on the Bel-
gian throne, and of the growing strength in Italy of Victor
Emmanuel, whom the Prince had liked when they met in 1856
because the King had boasted that he could cut off the head of
an ox with one blow from his sword. The distances between
Europe and Canada seemed to lessen on 31 July, when news
arrived of the birth of the Prince's niece, in Berlin. He wrote to
his mother, 'Your telegram reached me in seven days.' It was
'the quickest time ever known'.

*

During June and July 1860, the terrible massacres of Christians
in Syria horrified the powers; but England was also suspicious
when Napoleon III sent troops to protect the martyrs. The
Court and the government remembered how the champions

of persecuted minorities had often gathered prizes as well as
honour for their generosity, so the Emperor was once more sus-
pect. He was 'hurt' by the obvious mistrust in Britain and he
wrote to his ambassador in London, hoping that 'a conversation
in perfect frankness' with Lord Palmerston would 'remedy the
existing evil'. He added, 'Since the peace of Villafranca I have
had but one thought; one object – to inaugurate a new era of
peace.'

The Prince Consort was among those who remained suspicious of the Emperor. On 7 August, he stood beside the Queen
when she reviewed 22,000 volunteers in Edinburgh, with
200,000 civilians looking on from the 'fine mountain of Arthur's
Seat'. The Prince wrote to Stockmar that the review was 'mag-
nificent', adding that the French were 'out of humour' because
of the demonstration.

From Edinburgh the Court went to the peace of Balmoral,
where the Queen and the Prince made one great expedition.
They climbed the highest mountain in Scotland, with two of
their daughters. On the way, there was a conversation between
the Queen and John Brown, the gillie, which should be remembered, for it gives the beginning of a reason for the sympathetic
and unusual friendship between the monarch and her servant,
after the Prince Consort's death.

The Prince Consort had gone on ahead with John Grant, the
other Scottish servant of whom they were both so fond. The
Queen and John Brown were following when they overheard
the Prince 'talking so gaily with Grant'. The Queen wrote the
story in her journal that evening. 'Brown observed to me, in
simple Highland phrase, "It's very pleasant to walk with a
person who is always content." ' They had talked then of the
Prince's good temper when he was out shooting, and Brown
said, 'Everyone on the estate says there never was so kind a
master.'

*

The quiet daily habits of life at Balmoral allowed the news that came from the outside world to seem less terrible. The intrigues of Napoleon III, Garibaldi's victories on the Italian mainland, and another distant conflict with China, continued to concern the Queen and the Prince Consort; but there was more personal interest for them in following their eldest son's exciting progress through Canada. Even there, the Prince of Wales came on old conflicts that alarmed his parents. He went to Quebec, where, for the first time, he conferred the honour of knighthood on two of his mother's colonial subjects; he went to the Heights of Abraham, and in the evening he danced every one of the twenty-two dances at the Mayor's ball. He moved on to Montreal, where he drove home the last rivet in the bridge over the St Lawrence; then he went on to Ottawa and laid the cornerstone of the new Parlaiment House, planned as a symbol of the union of Upper and Lower Canada. But the symbol lost its charm and meaning after the Prince passed up the river into Lake Ontario. There, in Kingston, the Orangemen, clinging to an old and faded anger, planned to welcome the Prince, not as Queen Victoria's son and heir but as the descendant of King William III, their patron saint. The Duke of Newcastle had been warned that the street decorations were mostly in orange, with portraits of William III hanging in the arches, so he ordered the Prince's ship to sail on. But a similar demonstration met them in Toronto, where the Orangemen had hung a big transparency of William III from a triumphal arch. The mayor apologized, and a deputation came from Kingston to repent their clumsy manners.

If there were faults in the progress, neither the Prince of Wales nor his staff could be blamed. The Prince was born to please and be pleased, as was proved when he came to Niagara Falls, where Blondin was waiting to entertain him. The famous acrobat crossed the rapids on a tightrope, first with a wheel-barrow, and then on stilts. Then he offered to wheel the Prince across the tightrope, from Canada into the United States. The Prince was willing, but the Duke of Newcastle and General

Bruce thought it better not, so the heir to the throne entered the robust new country, graciously, on his feet.

Queen Victoria and the Prince Consort had devised a plan almost as curious as Blondin's. They had ordered that their son should drop his royal titles and prerogatives and enter the United States with the name of Baron Renfrew, and that he should be treated as a private person on an educational tour. The Americans ignored the foolish incognito: they offered dalliance to alleviate duty, to which the Prince succumbed, and the name Baron Renfrew was forgotten all the way.

*

Two days after the Prince of Wales crossed into the United States, Queen Victoria and the Prince Consort, with Princess Alice, left for what was to be their last visit together to Coburg. Their journey began with grief, for the Prince's step-mother died while they were on the way. The little court was already in mourning: even young Prince William, who had been brought from Prussia for the occasion, had black bows all over his white dress. He was 'so good', and the Queen was 'so happy' to see her grandson for the first time.

When the Queen and the Prince walked 'across the fields, along a pretty little stream', they came to Rosenau, but they did not go inside to tempt the ghosts. The Queen was delighted with everything she saw; the 'carts always drawn by oxen, the peasant women working in the fields, with their coloured handkerchiefs and aprons, fearfully laden with those heavy baskets.' She sat with her sketch book and enjoyed her modest talent in water colours, with 'the air like a warm summer's day, and listening to the tinkling of the cowbells'.

For the Prince Consort there was plenty to encourage his lament for the past. He saw 'Dear old Stockmar . . . looking quite himself, though a little weak'; he attended the funeral of his step-mother, and he saw the sarcophagus of his own mother –

all drawing his thoughts back to times the Queen could never share. Then came the threat of a tragedy.

One day the Queen was walking with Princess Alice, 'going along merrily', when a messenger arrived and told them that the Prince Consort had been forced to jump from his carriage when the horses bolted along the highway. He suffered only a cut on one of his legs and a scratched nose, but the Queen was terrified when she saw him, lying on his valet's bed with a lint compress on his face. She wrote, 'Oh, God! What did I not feel! I could only, and do only, allow the feelings of gratitude, not those of horror at what might have happened, to fill my mind. . .'

When they returned to England the Queen proved her gratitude by giving a sum of money, to be paid each year in Coburg, to 'a certain number of young men and women of exemplary character belonging to the humble ranks of life'. They were to be taught trades, provided with tools, and given dowries when they married.

*

When the Queen and the Prince Consort were back in England, the Prince of Wales was still moving from city to city in the United States, but in remarkable circumstances. The elections of 1860 and the victory of Abraham Lincoln were in the air, so the Prince had to compete for the limelight. He went from Detroit to Chicago, and then to St Louis where the Duke of Newcastle noted that there was 'none of the cheering and noisy enthusiasm of the loyal Canadians', but 'great curiosity . . . and great courtesy'. In Harrisburg, at the Governor's request, the Prince sat in the chair used by John Hancock when he signed the Declaration of Independence. And on 3 October, the Prince arrived at the White House, where he was depressed to find that dancing was forbidden, 'even on the carpet'. Two days later he made the pilgrimage to Mount Vernon, and *The Times* correspondent wrote :

Before this humble tomb the Prince, the President, and all the party stood uncovered. It is easy moralising on this visit, for there is something grandly suggestive of historical retribution in the reverential awe of the Prince of Wales, the great-grandson of George III, standing bareheaded at the foot of the coffin of Washington. For a few moments the party stood mute and motionless, and the Prince then proceeded to plant a chestnut by the side of the tomb. It seemed, when the Royal youth closed in the earth around the little germ, that he was burying the last faint trace of discord between us and our great brethren of the West.

The American newspapers repeated these noble intentions, which were to be threatened, almost disastrously, in the following year. The *Daily Tribune* announced the hopes of all good and patient men :

It was not a figure of the over-excited mind that he was the bearer of the olive branch of peace and real good will whose present courtesies fortokened the closer planning of the interest of England and those of the States, and the fond union of their common energies in the cause of justice for all people under heaven.

Such pompous phrases were for journalists to weave and for politicians to tear to pieces. Five months after the Prince of Wales sailed for England the Civil War began, and it was only because of the Prince Consort's wisdom that Britain was not drawn into the conflict.

With the threat of war across the Atlantic, and continued fighting in Italy to emphasize the virtues of domestic peace, the Queen and the Prince Consort welcomed their sons home from their journeys. Prince Alfred arrived back from South Africa with the gratifying compliment of the Governor, Sir George Grey, that he was 'a noble young fellow, full of life and fun'; and the Prince of Wales, destined for more serious tasks, returned from America to be a student once more at Oxford, where he paused to write to his mother, 'I have been attending my lectures very regularly this week.'

*

The Prince Consort still used the phrase 'vortex of society' to describe the perils from which his eldest son should be protected, although he had already travelled so far, and met so many people. But the tone of behaviour had changed considerably during the twenty-four years since Prince Albert arrived, a sleepy young pedant, to stay in Kensington Palace. Victorian ethics had emerged to correct, or deny, the dissoluteness for which Queen Victoria's uncles had set the example, and London society was learning to revere respectability. The new morality had been declared in the Queen's protest to the Lord Chamberlain over the candid reports of divorces in the press; some of them 'so scandalous' that it was 'almost impossible for a paper to be trusted in the hands of a young lady or boy'. They were more dangerous than the 'worst French novels'.

The Queen was as strict with her younger children as she was with her daughter in Prussia. When Prince Louis of Hesse formally asked for Princess Alice's hand, the Queen wrote to King Leopold, 'I shall not let her marry as long as I can reasonably delay her doing so.' She relented in time to announce the betrothal when she opened Parliament in February 1861; but she still insisted that Prince Louis should spend the greater part of the year in England, so that the young couple would be obliged to live her life rather than their own.

*

As the greyness of the English winter came, the Prince Consort was sick and desolate. He could not sleep; his gums were swollen and the nerves in his cheeks were inflamed. The Queen watched him, anxiously and with fear. The only considerable error in all the twenty years of his life in England – his treatment of his eldest son – was the natural result of the severe code that he had made for himself. The code was killing him, with the help of criticism and frequent doubt of his motives. Even at this late hour, *The Times* criticized him, and suspected him of plotting in his constant correspondence with his daughter in Prussia. He

wrote to her on 6 December, 1860, 'I was too miserable yesterday
to be able to hold my pen.' When he was well enough to write,
he resumed his urgent letters to the ministers. He wrote to Lord
John Russell, 'It is a perfect disgrace to the country, and particularly to our Admiralty, that we can do no more than hobble
after the French.' He wrote also to the Admiralty, pleased because 'a further supply of iron-clad ships' was being built. But
numerical equality with France was not enough. He wrote, 'Our
Foreign ports will require defence and support as well. . . We
must at the same time always presume that a co-operation of
Russia with France against us is not unlikely. . . The number
we ought to possess is therefore very great indeed.'

Christmas was near – the coldest for fifty years. The Prince
Consort had written to his daughter in Prussia, 'How wisely is it
ordained that in general we do not know our destiny and end;
but for this no one would wish to live.' In return, the Princess
sent him a long memorandum, *On the Law of Ministerial Responsibility*, which she had written following the celebration of
her twentieth birthday.

The Court was at Windsor and on Christmas Day the Queen
withdrew to write to King Leopold – to tell him that it was 'a
really true winter's day, with twenty-two degrees of frost', but
that there was 'much enjoyment in skating'. Affairs in Italy
were still 'in a sadly complicated state', and despite Garibaldi's
continued successes in the name of King Victor Emmanuel, the
Queen could 'not in the least see the end of it all'. But there was
'most satisfactory' news from China, where an act of gross
treachery and brutality towards a party of European envoys had
been punished with the utmost severity by an Anglo-French
expeditionary force. The treaty of Tientsin was ratified at last,
and the way was open for still more British trade in the East.

On 26 December, the Prince Consort also withdrew from the
festivities at Windsor to write to his eldest daughter. 'Again
have we missed you greatly at our Christmas table . . .' he wrote.
'Oh! if you, with Fritz and the children, were only with us.'
Then came a long, grave sentence: 'Prejudice walking to and

fro in flesh and blood is my horror, and, alas, a phenomenon so common; and people plume themselves so much upon their prejudices, as signs of decision of character and greatness of mind, nay, of true patriotism; and all the while they are simply the product of narrowness of intellect, and narrowness of heart.'

The Prince Consort looked out of the window and saw the snow thick and silent on the ground, and the rooks flying in the black skeletons of the chestnuts. He thought of Stockmar, and wrote to him, 'The poor birds miss your kind and sympathetic hand, which used to scatter bread-crumbs for them in the days that are gone.'

Every prospect seemed to depress him and he wrote of the plans that would separate his children still further from him – the coming marriage of his second daughter; the visit of Prince Alfred to the West Indies, and the strange decision to take the Prince of Wales from Oxford and send him to Cambridge, for further education.

CHAPTER TWENTY-TWO

1861

During the first months of 1861 the Prince Consort complained continuously, 'I am tired, I am tired.' The world marched on with its old evils – the renewed intrigues of Russia with the goal of the Dardanelles and the distant mirage of Afghanistan and India; the tireless ambition of Victor Emmanuel, soon to be declared King of Italy; the friendly surface and doubtful depths of Napoleon III; and then, the growing antagonism between the northern and southern states of America. The older troubles were the immediate concern of the Foreign Office and the armed services. The new fear, from across the Atlantic, made the Lancashire and Cheshire spinners anxious because war in America would cut off their supplies of cotton, on which they depended for their livelihood.

The Prince Consort wrote endless memoranda on all these problems, with occasional flashes of wise insight such as come to sick men. On 2 January, the demented King of Prussia died and his brother, Prince William, succeeded to the throne, with Queen Victoria's friend, Augusta, as his queen. The Prince Consort wrote to his daughter, now Crown Princess of Prussia, 'In seeing and observing the approach of death, as you have been called upon to do, you have become older in experience than myself. I have never seen anyone die.'

On 24 January, the Prince complained to Stockmar, 'I reproach myself for writing to you so seldom nowadays; but the work increases daily, and I am often fairly puzzled how to get through it.' There were the fortifications at Portsmouth and Gosport to inspect; the plans for the second Great Exhibition to complete; the possible actions of King Victor Emmanuel and the French occupation of Syria to watch, and the building of more armour-plated ships to be encouraged. He wrote in the secret pages of his diary, on 17 February, 'My sufferings are frightful;' and four days later he wrote again to Stockmar, 'Sleepness nights and pain have pulled me down.' He was not yet forty-two years old, but he wrote with the mind of a weary and disillusioned man.

There was one example of courage near the Prince that might have encouraged him. The Duchess of Kent, almost seventy-five years old, was ill and in constant pain, but she had still played old tunes on the piano, with her bandaged hands, until an operation in February made it no longer possible. She died on 16 March. The Queen wrote of the previous day, 'I knelt before her, kissed her dear hand and placed it next my cheek; but, though she opened her eyes, she did not, I think, know me. . . At four I went down again. All still – nothing to be heard but the heavy breathing, and the striking, at every quarter, of the old repeater, a large watch in a tortoise shell case, which had belonged to my poor father. . .'

Lady Augusta Bruce was in the room when the Prince Consort endured his first sight of death. She wrote afterwards, 'The poor Prince burst into tears, and raising the Queen, led her away. . . I never saw such tenderness, such gentleness, such tact as His – oh! He is one in millions – well might She love Him as She did. I was so struck with his appreciation of Her. It was so true, and for One who is supposed to place intellect and reasoning powers above all, so remarkable.'

Even this private grief brought its public cruelty. A rumour spread through Britain and far into Europe that the Queen had lost her reason. The gossip continued for several months: on 18 June, the Prince Consort wrote to his brother, 'I cannot understand how these horrid, vile rumours about her mental state could arise. People here and on the Continent are much occupied with these rumours. They have annoyed me tremendously, as I know what the consequences might be. She herself is perfectly unaware of this scandal.'

*

On 15 April the Prince Consort had written to Baron Stockmar, 'Home politics have quite gone to sleep.' He was at Osborne with the Queen, sharing his time between the gardens which he had designed; in reminding Prussia that she 'must first be morally master of Germany' before she could 'lift up her head in Europe', and – a most unusual indulgence – in reading some novels. They included George Eliot's *Mill on the Floss* and *The Woman in White*, by Wilkie Collins, which he thought most interesting and exciting.'

The Queen spent hours in sorting her mother's papers, among which she found 'little books' with accounts of her own 'baby-hood'. She wrote to King Leopold, on 9 April, 'They show such unbounded tenderness.' The Prince Consort wrote to Stockmar of the Queen's increased understanding of her mother during the closing years; of how she watched over her with affection she had once withheld. He appreciated 'the influence of this on her character'.

*

The Prince of Wales was studying at Trinity College, Cambridge, and living in his own house, with General Bruce doing his best to curb his pupil's zest for pleasure. He hunted, and he played tennis; and he went to plays and farces produced by the Dramatic Club. But the Prince Consort went to see him now and then to watch over his behaviour.

In May the Prince Consort sent a petulant letter to his brother, who had ignored him for two months. He wrote, on 11 May, 'You must have a very easy conscience if you say that you need

not bother so much, as I am no longer interested in Germany.'
On 18 June he wrote of an epidemic of measles which brought
the three youngest children to their beds, and also of the plan
to send the Prince of Wales to Ireland during the holidays from
Cambridge. He was to go into camp with the Second Battalion
of the Grenadier Guards at The Curragh. He would 'begin on
the lowest step of the ladder . . . to make every step as long as it
is considered necessary to learn it thoroughly, but not a day
longer.' This would be an 'incentive for him to get on', as it
would 'lie in his own hands to make progress'.

Even with the Grenadiers the Prince of Wales was not left
alone. At the end of August his mother and father crossed to
Ireland and hemmed their son in with official occasions, and a
review, of which the Queen wrote, 'We drove up to where the
troops were assembled. . . Then we drove down the line. As we
approached the Cavalry, they began to play one of dearest
Mama's marches, which they did again in marching past. This
entirely upset me, and the tears would have flowed freely, had I
not checked them by a violent effort. But I felt sad the whole
day, except when we came to Bertie, who looked very well.'

The Prince of Wales, who was not yet twenty, had already
begun to sow his wild oats, with the help of brother officers who
smuggled an actress, Nellie Clifden, into his quarters for his
pleasure.[1] The Queen and the Prince Consort did not learn
about their son's folly until many weeks later, when he was back
at Cambridge, but they had long been anxious to avoid such behaviour by committing him to an early marriage. With the help
of King Leopold and Stockmar, they had written a list of seven
likely princesses, with the sixteen year old Alexandra of Denmark as the fifth most eligible. The compliment that moved
her up to the first place came from the Crown Princess of
Prussia, who was 'quite enchanted' when they met at Strelitz.
She wrote of her as the 'most fascinating creature in the world'.

The plan had led to an angry exchange. The Prince Consort
had written to his brother on 21 July,

I received your protest against a marriage between Bertie and a
Danish Princess. . . Your position, your relationship and your
friendship give you a right to think of Bertie's welfare and the
political unions for his future. But what annoys me is that you
spoke to a third person about such delicate and secret affairs, and
that you sent me a memorandum which was written by a
secretary. . .

We took care not to let Bertie know about the existence of
Princess Alexandra, but we told him of all other possibilities. We
find it rather strange that just *you* should tell him about this one
Princess and warn him not to marry her. . . It was wrong to do so
behind our backs. . . Now he has heard from all sides about the
beauty of the Princess and he has seen photographs of her in the
rooms of [her great aunt] the Duchess of Cambridge, at Kew, and
they confirmed what he had heard. We explained the political
difficulties such a marriage would bring with it, as well as we could.
He understood, as well as a young man of his age and his capacities
is able to understand them. But as we practically have public opinion
against us, and as we should also have our Ministers, people and the
Press against us, we were anxious to find another lady suitable for
Bertie. (It is his wish to marry soon and it is in his interests, morally,
socially and politically.) But we find there is really no other Princess he could marry. The Princess of Meiningen and the daughter of
Prince Albrecht, he had the opportunity of seeing when he was in
Berlin, but they did not please him. Vicky has racked her brain, too,
to help to find someone, but in vain. The daughter of Prince Fried-
rich of the Netherlands is too ugly. There are positively no other
Princesses except the sister of Louis . . . this would connect us for a
second time with Darmstadt. All this made clear to us that Princess
Alexandra is the only one to be chosen.

But now we must see that this marriage is not looked upon as a
triumph for Denmark over us and Prussia, and that it came about
without the Danes knowing about it, without the knowledge of our
Ministers and the Cambridges, but quite alone, through the media-
tion of our Prussian children . . . if you wish to found a happy
future for Bertie we have no other choice. . . I do not know if it is
prudent to let you know all this. . .

The background to the first meeting between the Prince of
Wales and the Danish Princess was solemn : it was in the cathe-
dral at Speyer, on 24 September. They met again at Heidelberg,
and the Prince Consort wrote on 4 October, 'We hear nothing

but excellent accounts of the Princess Alexandra; the young people seem to have taken a warm liking to one another.' This was confirmed when the Prince of Wales came home : his father wrote to Stockmar of his being 'greatly pleased'.

*

When the Prince Consort had opened the Royal Horticultural Gardens on 5 June, he was accompanied by five of his younger children, wearing deep mourning for their grandmother. The sombreness was increased by the Prince's own 'pallid and some-what worn look'. In the evening he presided at a meeting of the Society of Arts, to listen to plans for the next Great Exhibition. Affairs at home were sad but tranquil, and the real alarms still came from Europe and America. The death of Cavour was fol-lowed by rumours that the King of Italy would cede Sardinia to France. And there were more arguments over the plans for the unification of Germany. But the disaster that menaced the heart and pocket of Britain was the American Civil War, which had begun with the bombardment of Fort Sumter, in Charles-ton, on the morning of 12 April. The first peril to Britain was the threat to the Canadian frontier, and later in the year rein-forcements were sent to help protect the colony. The second peril was the fall in supplies of cotton for the mills in the North of England, and for this there was no protection. The govern-ment failed to find sufficient cotton from India and other sources, and, during the entire war, Lancashire suffered terrible depression and privation.

In October, the Court moved to Windsor, and after news came of the coronation of the King of Prussia, on the 18th, the Prince Consort was able to feel confident that his daughter had profited from his years of affectionate instruction. Lord Claren-don had 'a very long conversation' with the Crown Princess in Berlin, and he reported to the Queen that he was 'more than ever astonished' at her '*statesmanlike* and comprehensive views ... of the policy of Prussia'. He wrote that he was 'not at all astonished, but very pleased to find how thoroughly appreciated and beloved' she was 'by all classes'. He added that 'Every member of the Royal family' had 'spoken of her . . . in terms of admiration'.

The Prince was grateful, and he turned back to the last of his tasks. Gratitude was inherent in him – a virtue rare among princes; but he quickly succumbed to his melancholia. It was about this time that he confessed to the Queen, 'I do not cling to life. You do; but I set no store by it. If I knew that those I love were well cared for, I should be quite ready to die tomorrow. . . I am sure, if I had a severe illness, I should give up at once; I should not struggle for life. I have no tenacity for life.'

The severe illness came soon after. It was encouraged by grief over a fatal outbreak of typhoid fever in the Portuguese royal family – the Prince's kinsmen. On 6 November, young Prince Ferdinand died in Lisbon. His brother, King Pedro v – then aged twenty-four – had also caught the disease, and the Prince Consort, who loved him as a son, was alarmed for his safety. During this spell of anxiety the Queen and the Prince enjoyed their last happy family occasion, when the Prince of Wales came to Windsor to celebrate his twentieth birthday. At his father's suggestion he led his mother into the dining-room. The Queen wrote in her journal, 'I pray God, to assist our efforts to make him turn out well. . .'

On 10 November the Prince Consort went up to London to look into the affairs of the Duchy of Cornwall and to preside at a meeting of the governors of Wellington College. When he returned to Windsor Castle he learned that King Pedro's condition was worse, and two days later came the news of his death. The Prince was stricken with grief and he wrote to Stockmar, on the 14th, 'With us you will have bewailed the sad calamity in Portugal. You knew my love for Pedro . . . and you will therefore be able to imagine my distress. . . I am fearfully in want of a true friend and counsellor, and that *you* are the friend and counsellor I want, you will readily understand.'

The death of his young cousin preyed on the Prince Consort's

mind, and he was unable to sleep. On the 22nd he drove down
to Sandhurst to see the new buildings for the Staff College and
the Royal Military College. The day was cold and dark and he
had to inspect the cadets in what he described as 'terrific rain'.
Two days later, a Sunday, he walked down to Frogmore with
the Queen, to see the Duchess of Kent's mausoleum. That night
the Prince complained in his diary, 'Am full of rheumatic pains,
and feel thoroughly unwell. Have scarcely closed my eyes for
the last fortnight.'

There was one, last distress for the Prince. A few days after
the Prince of Wales's twentieth birthday, his parents at last
heard what had been gossip in the London clubs for some time,
of his escapade with the actress in Ireland. Every belief and
trust in the Prince Consort was offended. He and the Queen
had created their own image of domestic virtue, without any
example from her ancestors or from his family in Coburg. Now
there was the terrible fear that their eldest son was to revive
the loose habits of the Hanoverians, which were horrible to the
Prince Consort. He wrote to his son, then back at Cambridge,
'with a heavy heart' upon the subject that had caused him the
'greatest pain' he had 'yet felt in this life'. He urged him in a
further letter to 'fight a valiant fight', and stressed the necessity
for 'an early marriage'; and he wrote, 'You *must* not, you *dare*
not be lost. The consequences for this country, and for the
world, would be too dreadful.'[2]

The Prince Consort travelled to Cambridge on 25 November,
to walk and talk with his son – and to forgive him. It was another cold and stormy day, and he wrote in his diary that he was
'still greatly out of sorts'. He returned to Windsor the next
morning, feeling 'very uncomfortable from pains in the back
and legs'. The doctors diagnosed his illness as influenza.

On 27 November, the Prince was still moving from room to
room in his dressing-gown, and the red dispatch boxes from
Whitehall were being brought to him as usual. Next day came
news of the boarding of the British mail streamer *Trent*, on her
way from Havana to England, by an armed guard from the

San Jacinto, a man-of-war belonging to the Federal government of the United States. A round shot, followed by a shell, had been fired across the bows of the *Trent*, which was obliged to stop. The *San Jacinto* then showed her colours for the first time, and a Federal officer, with an armed guard of marines, boarded the *Trent* and took off four passengers – two envoys of the Confederate States, and their secretaries, bound for the courts of Britain and France.

This violation of neutrality and international law horrified the British Parliament. Eight thousand troops were sent immediately to Canada, and on 29 November the Prime Minister, Lord Palmerston, wrote to the Queen after a meeting of the Cabinet: they had decided to demand that the Confederate envoys should be 'set free and restored to British Protection', and that if this were refused, Lord Lyons, the British Ambassador, 'should retire from the United States'. *The Times* later recalled that 'Britain nearly went to war with America' because there was 'not a telegraph across the Atlantic' – as the first cable, laid in 1858, had broken down after a few weeks. But perhaps, in the event, it was fortunate that there could not be quick transmission of the British government's anger, and that the Prince Consort was able to make his wise changes to the vital dispatch.

The draft of the dispatch, hastily written by the Foreign Secretary, now Earl Russell, arrived at Windsor Castle in the evening of 30 November. The Prince sat up late to study it and he rose early next morning to add his suggestions. The last of the thousands of pages of memoranda he had written during the years grew beneath his feverish hands. He thought Lord Russell's language extravagant and defiant, so he wrote his own draft for the dispatch,* adding a note in the Queen's name: 'She should have liked to have seen the expression of a hope, that the American Capt. did not act under instructions or, if he did, that he misapprenhended them', and that 'H.M's. Govt. are

---

* See pages 224 and 225 for quotations from the original and amended drafts.

RELEVANT PARAGRAPHS OF THE CABINET'S DRAFT SUBMITTED TO THE QUEEN

Her Majesty's Government having taken these facts into consideration have arrived at the conclusion that the conduct of the Commander of the *San Jacinto* was not justifiable by International Law. Certain individuals have been taken from on board a ship of a Neutral Power, which was pursuing a lawful and innocent voyage. Her Majesty's Government are unwilling to imagine that the United States Government will not of their own accord be anxious to afford ample reparation for this act of violence committed by an officer of the United States's Navy against a Neutral and friendly Nation.

The reparation which Her Majesty's Government expect and with which they would be satisfied would be:

1. The liberation of the four gentlemen captured, and their delivery to Your Lordship [the British Ambassador in Washington] with a view of their being again placed under British protection.
2. An apology for the insult offered to the British flag.

RELEVANT PARAGRAPHS OF AMENDED DRAFT
RETURNED BY THE PRINCE CONSORT

It thus appears that certain individuals have been forcibly taken from on board a British vessel, the ship of a Neutral Power, while such vessel was pursuing a lawful and innocent voyage, an act of violence which was an affront to the British flag and a violation of International Law.

Her Majesty's Government, bearing in mind the friendly relations which have long subsisted between Great Britain and the United States, are willing to believe that the United States Naval Officer who committed this aggression was not acting in compliance with any authority from his Government or that if he conceived himself to be so authorised, he greatly misunderstood the instructions which he had received.

For the Government of the United States must be fully aware that the British Government could not allow such an affront to the National Honour to pass without full reparation, and her Majesty's Government are unwilling to believe that it would be the deliberate intention of the Government of the United States unnecessarily to force into discussion between the two Governments a question of so grave a character, and with regard to which the whole British Nation would be sure to entertain such unanimity of feeling.

Her Majesty's Government therefore trust that when this matter shall have been brought under the consideration of the Government of the United States, that Government will of its own accord offer to the British Government such redress as alone would satisfy the British Nation, namely: the liberation of the Four Gentlemen and their delivery to Your Lordship in order that they may again be placed under British protection, and a suitable apology for the aggression which has been committed.

unwilling to believe that the u.s. Gt. intended wantonly to put an insult upon this country...'

The Prince Consort handed the papers to the Queen at eight o'clock in the morning of 1 December, saying, 'I am so weak, I have scarcely been able to hold the pen.' The drafts were returned to Whitehall and the dispatch was altered to conform to the Prince's suggestions, which Lord Palmerston considered 'excellent'.[3]

On 19 December, the British Ambassador in Washington wrote to Lord Russell to say that William H. Seward, Lincoln's Secretary of State, had begged him, as a personal favour, to be allowed to read the dispatch before it was communicated to him officially, as 'so much depended on the wording of it'. Mr Seward was pleased to find that the Prince Consort's phrases were 'courteous and friendly, and not dictatorial or menacing'; and on the 26th he replied, on behalf of his government, that reparation was due to Britain and that the four prisoners would be 'cheerfully liberated'.

This polite and sensible news reached Queen Victoria on 9 January – twenty-six days after the Prince Consort died. His doctors were mostly old and they were led by Sir James Clark, remembered for his folly in the case of Lady Flora Hastings.* It was not until 7 December that they realized that the illness which was killing him was typhoid fever – the disease which, by sad coincidence, had killed his beloved cousin in Portugal a few weeks before. The delay in diagnosing the fever, which had begun about the time of his visit to Cambridge, later caused indignant criticism within the medical profession.[4] But while the royal doctors professed optimism, and the Queen prayed for his recovery, the Prince Consort alone knew that he was dying.

On Sunday, 8 December, he asked to be moved into a bigger room, and he wished Princess Alice to play a chorale. He listened to the phrases of *Ein' feste Burg ist unser Gott*, which he remembered from his boyhood. He looked 'upwards with such a sweet expression, and with tears in his eyes'; but then grew

* See pp. 37–38.

irritable – a symptom of his disease – and said, '*Das reicht hin*' – 'That is enough.'

In the evening the Prince was calm again, and when the Queen read *Peveril of the Peak* to him he followed the story with interest. Even in these days of hope and fear, the Queen did not go to bed without writing in her diary. On this night she wrote, 'He was so pleased to see me . . . stroked my face, and smiled, and called me *liebes Frauchen*. . . Precious love! His tenderness this evening, when he held my hands, and stroked my face, touched me so much – made me so grateful.'

On 13 December, Dr Jenner had to tell the Queen that the Prince's state might lead to congestion of the lungs. Next morning was fine and, at seven o'clock, while the sun was 'just rising and shining brightly', she went to his bedside. She recalled, 'The room had the sad look of night-watching, the candles burnt down to their sockets, the doctors looking anxious. I went in, and never can I forget how beautiful my darling looked, lying there with his face lit up by the rising sun, his eyes unusually bright, gazing as it were on unseen objects, and not taking notice of me.'

Unknown to the Queen, the Prince of Wales had arrived from Cambridge during the night – too late for his father to recognize him. In the evening the Queen sat beside the bed again, and her husband spoke to her for the last time: he whispered '*Gutes Frauchen*,' and then 'gave a sort of piteous moan'. She did not cry when she was with him, but every hour or so she went to the next room in a 'terrible burst of misery'. She said, over and over, 'The country; oh the country. I could perhaps bear my own misery, but the poor country.'

While the Queen was out of the bedroom, about eleven o'clock at night, Princess Alice leaned over her father and then whispered to Lady Augusta Bruce, who was beside her, 'That is the death rattle.' She brought her mother into the room; the Queen knelt beside the bed and held the Prince's hand, but it was already cold. The breathing became faint and the Queen whispered, 'Oh, yes, this is death. I know it. I have seen this before.'⁵ She fell on the dead Prince and 'called him by every endearing name'. Then her ladies supported her and led her into the next room, where, for a moment, she was crumpled and dazed. Then her courage came back: she sat up and asked for her children, and when they came she told them she would fight and live for them and for her duty.

The Queen sent for the doctors and consoled them for their failure. Then she turned and saw the Prince of Wales beside her. She believed that he was partly to blame for his father's death because of his immoral ways, and their relationship was to be threatened for many years; but in this sad hour he embraced his mother and said, 'I will become everything you wish.' He promised that his whole life would be devoted to her comfort and to an endeavour to diminish her grief.

Then the Queen's ministers came, among them Lord Palmerston, whom she had once thought of as her enemy. When he saw her sitting on the sofa, fighting her agony, he 'wept bitterly'.

CHAPTER TWENTY-THREE

1861-1863

Queen Victoria was forty-two years old when the Prince Consort died. Less than a year before she had danced with her sons during a party at Frogmore. Now she was a solemn woman, pledged to grief for many years to come. She cried, 'There is no one to call me Victoria now.'

The Queen was tortured by what doctors of the next century described as a 'nervous breakdown', and her children, her Court, and her ministers, watched her in alarm. She tapped her forehead and said, 'My reason! my reason!'; and remembering that King George III had suffered his years of madness in Windsor Castle, it was considered wise to move the Queen to Osborne, where there were no dark ghosts to encourage her melancholy. But the obsession continued: she wrote to Queen Augusta of Prussia, 'I could go mad from the desire and the longing.' This fear was to endure for a long time: eighteen months later, when she was threatened with a change of government, Queen Victoria harped on the theme in an audience with Lord Clarendon. Lady Clarendon recorded the scene during which the Queen said 'she knew she would go mad' with worry, and that 'three times at Balmoral she had thought she was going mad'.

At Osborne, the gardens were stark and dead, and every morning the Queen sat by a window, looking over the frosty earth and the winter stretches of the Solent. The little black-dressed figure, with what her children called her 'sad-cap' on her head, was estranged from her people and her family. She wrote to Lord Russell on 10 January, 1862, 'The things of this life are of no interest to the Queen.' Ten days after her husband's death, she had written to King Leopold, '. . . please God! I am to see you so soon . . . *no human power* will make me swerve from *what he* decided and wished – and I look to *you* to *support* and *help* me in this.' But she seemed afraid that her uncle might try to resume his old part as her adviser, and she added, 'I am *also determined* that *no one* person, may *he* be ever so good, ever so devoted among my servants – is to lead or guide or dictate *to me.*'

The Queen's peril, in her extravagant grief, was in her relationship with the Prince of Wales. Lady Clarendon wrote in her diary that the 'serious misfortune' Lord Palmerston saw, 'looking ahead', was the Queen's 'unconquerable aversion' for her heir. Lord Clarendon dared to speak to her on the subject, and found the situation 'worse than he expected'. It was, he said, 'a positive monomania with her. She got quite excited while speaking of him, and said that it quite irritated her to see him in the room.' Then came the pathetic sentence, 'I believe the poor boy knows of his mother's dislike of him, but seems to have the good taste not to speak of it.'

Two months after his father's death the Prince of Wales sailed for Egypt and the Holy Land. While he was away on his journey, on 26 May, 1862, Queen Victoria wrote to Queen Augusta of Prussia:

> I only lived through him, my heavenly Angel. . . Now I feel as though I am dead! I endeavour to do what is right, and try at least to prevent anything which would not be according to his wishes, but alas, the vital power is finished. Disheartened, I continue my gloomy, sorrowful life alone. . . I try to comfort myself by knowing that he is always near me, although invisible, and that our future union will be even more perfect and eternal! But my nature is too passionate, my emotions are too fervent, and I feel in sore need of someone to cling to securely, someone who would comfort and pacify me!

Slowly the pattern of the Queen's life took shape again. The
Prince of Wales returned to England in June and his mother
thought him improved, and looking so bright and healthy'. Sixteen days later she was still speaking and writing of his being
'most affectionate, dutiful and amicable'.

On 1 July, 1862, Princess Alice was married to Prince Louis
of Hesse. The Queen shut herself off in the chapel at Osborne
so that none of the guests could see her, and she lunched afterwards alone with the bride and bridegroom.

The Queen's courage increased when her eldest son was married at Windsor to Princess Alexandra of Denmark, on 10
March, 1863. She watched the ceremony from Catharine of
Aragon's closet, over the sanctuary in St George's Chapel. Then,
with what Lady Augusta Bruce described as her 'wonderful
grace and dignity', the Queen led the bride and bridegroom up
the steps into the Castle. When the celebrations were over and
the Prince and Princess had driven away, the Queen went down
to Frogmore, to the mausoleum where her husband was buried.
She could look back at the grey towers of the Castle: therein
every monarch but Richard Coeur de Lion had lived, from the
time of William the Conqueror; therein also was the story of
her golden happiness, such as none of them had known. Therein also, she was to grow old – so old that a century would bear
her name. During her life, there had been three kings who ruled
before her, and she was to see three generations of princes who
would rule after her.

Queen Victoria went alone into the mausoleum, to weep, and
to pray. Through the long loneliness of the rest of her life she
was never to waver from the simple Christian certainty that her
husband's immaculate soul was with God.

References and Notes

CHAPTER 1

1. Princess Louise's mother had died when she was born and the Duke had married a second wife, Princess Caroline of Hesse-Cassel, who was childless and able to give all her affection to her stepdaughter.
2. This and subsequent letters from the Duchess Louise to Augusta von Studnitz are printed more fully in the chapter 'The Prince Consort's Mother', in *A Biographer's Notebook*, Hector Bolitho (Longmans Green, 1950).
3. Notes on a conversation with the Duke of Kent, 11 December, 1817. *The Creevey Papers*.
4. Rosenau is now a home for lonely old people and is within a few miles of the frontier of East Germany.

CHAPTER 2

1. Prince Leopold was still receiving an annuity of fifty thousand pounds, settled on him by the British Parliament when he married Princess Charlotte.
2. The author was allowed free access to these papers when he was in Coburg.
3. A full account of the divorce is published in *A Biographer's Notebook*. (See above, Ch. 1, ref. 2.)
4. In *Die Gartenlaube*, No. 3, 1862.

CHAPTER 3

1. Told to the author by the Duke of Connaught. See *My Restless Years*, Hector Bolitho (Max Parrish, 1962), p. 182.
2. This story was half confirmed many years later when an old woman, dying in an almshouse, sent a letter to Queen Victoria saying that her mother, who had been a nurse or servant

to Princess Charlotte, knew that poison had been put in her 'brew' before she died. This story was repeated to the author by one of Queen Victoria's grand-daughters, who believed it to be true.

3. Sir Walter Scott wrote in his diary, on 19 May, 1828, 'Dined with the Duchess of Kent. I was . . . presented to the little Princess Victoria, the heir-apparent to the throne as things now stand. . . . This little lady is educating with much care, and watched so closely that no busy maid has a moment to whisper, "You are heir to England".'

4. Told to the author by the Hon. Mrs Alaric Grant, Woman of the Bedchamber to Queen Victoria.

5. The description of Prince Albert's boyhood is largely based on *Early Years of his Royal Highness the Prince Consort,* by General Charles Grey (1867).

6. In a letter shown to the author by Paul von Ebart, in Coburg, in 1927.

CHAPTER 4

1. When Dean Stanley of Westminster met Duke Ernest, in Egypt, in 1862, he wrote, 'If anything could increase the respect for Prince Albert and the thankfulness for what he has been to England, it may be the reflection of what would have been the difference had the Queen married the elder brother instead. He is going to hunt in Abyssinia and I trust that I may never set eyes on him again.'

CHAPTER 5

1. The latest and fullest account of the life of the Duchess of Kent is in the biography, *The Mother of Queen Victoria,* by D. M. Stuart (Macmillan, 1942).

2. This and other letters from Prince Albert to his brother, covering twenty years of his life in England, are bound in ten volumes and are in the archives in Coburg. The author was allowed to quote from them, and later he edited them

in his book *The Prince Consort and His Brother* (Appleton-Century-Crofts, N. Y., 1934).

CHAPTER 7

1. Princess Beatrice, the Queen's youngest daughter, read these early records after her mother died and she decided to burn them. Private information.
2. Recalled by the Dowager Countess of Jersey in a letter to the author.

CHAPTER 8

1. These scenes are fully described in *Royal Pavilion*, by Clifford Musgrave (Bredon & Heginbothom, 1951).
2. *The Prince Consort, A Political Biography,* Frank Eyck (Houghton Mifflin, Boston, 1959).

CHAPTER 9

1. Claremont, Surrey, had been the home of Prince Leopold when he was married to Princess Charlotte. She died there in November 1817. King Leopold gave the house to Prince Albert in 1840.

CHAPTER 11

1. From a letter written to the author by a descendant of Lord Powys.

CHAPTER 12

1. Lady Augusta Bruce, lady-in-waiting to the Duchess of Kent and later the most intimate of Queen Victoria's ladies. She married Dean Stanley of Westminster. Her letters, describing her years at Court, were edited by the Dean of Windsor and Hector Bolitho, and published in two volumes, *Letters of Lady Augusta Stanley, 1849–1863* (General Howe Ltd, 1927), and *Later Letters of Lady Augusta Stanley, 1864–1876* (Jonathan Cape, 1929).

CHAPTER 13

1. This letter was among documents shown to the author in Coburg. The year, 1846, was written at the top, but there was no month or day.
2. *The Cornhill*, 1951.
3. Queen Marie of Roumania, in a letter to an American friend, commenting on *Albert the Good* as a biography of her grandfather.
4. From an unpublished letter written by Prince Albert to his old tutor, Florschütz, in Coburg.

CHAPTER 15

1. He was Prince Leopold, afterwards Duke of Albany, whose eldest son, Charles Edward, was to become Duke of Saxe-Coburg-Gotha in 1900, on the death of his uncle, Prince Alfred.
2. The full text of this letter, one of the most revealing Prince Albert ever wrote, is published in *Letters of the Prince Consort,* edited by Kurt Jagow (E. P. Dutton & Co., N. Y., 1938).

CHAPTER 16

1. Mr Roger Fulford, in his book, *The Prince Consort* (Macmillan, 1949), has developed this theme, with the help of papers to which I did not have access when I wrote *Albert the Good*. It would be unethical for me to quote from his pages *ad libitum*; but I recommend readers interested in the subject to read the chapter 'He governs us in everything' in Mr Fulford's lively biography.
2. *See Letters of the Prince Consort*, ed. Kurt Jagow (Dutton, N. Y., 1938).

CHAPTER 18

1. *'and Mr Fortescue, A Selection from the Diaries of Chichester Fortescue*, Lord Carlingford, †.6. Edited by Osbert Wyndham Hewett (Murray, 1958), p. 114.

CHAPTER 20

1. This interesting revelation of the mind and character of the Prince of Wales at this time is described in Chapter VI, Vol. I, of Sir Sidney Lee's biography of King Edward VII.
2. The Queen's fear of madness was real: haunted by the example and the blood of King George III, she frequently expressed her fear, especially after the Prince Consort died. See p. 229.
3. Extract from a letter (25 January, 1878) from Lady Bloomfield to the Dowager Marchioness of Ely. Martin, Vol. IV, p. 16.
4. Country Life Ltd, 1964.

CHAPTER 21

1. See Chapter 1, p. 5, and *Overture to Victoria,* McKenzie Porter (Redman, London, 1963).

CHAPTER 22

1 & 2. The full story of the Prince's escapade is told in *King Edward the Seventh,* Sir Philip Magnus (E. P. Dutton & Co., Inc., N. Y., 1964).
3. The author is indebted to Sir Owen Morshead, late Librarian at Windsor Castle, and to the Librarian and Keeper of the Papers at the Foreign Office, for the texts of the *Trent* dispatch.
4. The controversy among the medical profession over the delayed diagnosis of the Prince's disease is recorded in *The Lancet,* 21 December, 1861, p. 599; 28 December, 1861, p. 621; 4 January, 1862, p. 14; 11 January, 1862, p. 47.
5. The account of the Prince Consort's death is largely based on a letter written by Lady Augusta Bruce, who was present during the anxious days. See *Letters of Lady Augusta Stanley,* edited by the Dean of Windsor and Hector Bolitho (Gerald Howe Ltd, 1927), pp. 239–248.

Bibliography

ALBEMARLE, 6th Earl of: *Fifty Years of My Life* (Macmillan, London, 1876).

ARGYLL, 8th Duke of: *V.R.I. Her Life and Empire* (Harmsworth Bros., Ltd, London, 1901).

ASHLEY, A. E. M.: *The Life and Correspondence of H. J. Temple, Viscount Palmerston* (R. Bentley & Son, London, 1879).

BAILLIE, Albert, and BOLITHO, Hector: (Ed.) *Letters of Lady Augusta Stanley* (Gerald Howe, London, 1927).

(Ed.) *Further Letters of Lady Augusta Stanley* (Jonathan Cape, London, 1929).

BENSON, A. C., and ESHER, Viscount: (Ed.) *Letters of Queen Victoria, First Series, 1837–1861* (Murray, London, 1908).

BENSON, E. F.: *As We Were* (Longmans, Green, N.Y., 1932).

Queen Victoria (Longmans, Green, N.Y., 1935).

BOLITHO, Hector: *Albert the Good* (Appleton-Century-Crofts, N.Y., 1934).

(Ed.) *The Prince Consort and His Brother* (Appleton-Century-Crofts, N.Y., 1934).

(Ed.) *Letters of Queen Victoria from Archives of House of Brandenburg-Prussia* (Yale University Press, 1938).

The Reign of Queen Victoria (Macmillan, N.Y., 1948).

BUNSEN, Frances, Baroness: *A Memoir of Baron Bunsen* (Longmans, London, 1868).

CONNELL, Brian: (Ed.) *Regina vs. Palmerston* (Doubleday, Garden City, 1961).

CORTI, E. C.: *Leopold I of Belgium*, Tr. Joseph McCabe (T. Fusher Unwin, London, 1923).

D'AUVERGNE, Edmund B.: *The Coburgs* (Stanley Paul & Co., London, 1911).

DAVIS, Frank: *Victorian Patrons of the Arts* (Country Life Ltd., London, 1963).

EBART, Paul von: *Luise, Herzogin von Sachsen-Coburg-Saalfeld* (Minden, 1903).

ERNST II, Duke of Saxe-Coburg-Gotha: *Aus Meinen Leben und Aus Meiner Zeit* (English translation: Remington & Co., London, 1888–90).

EYCK, Frank: *The Prince Consort, A Political Biography* (Houghton-Mifflin, Boston, 1959).

FULFORD, Roger: *The Prince Consort* (Macmillan, London, 1949).
See also *Greville.*

GREVILLE, Charles: *The Greville Memoirs, 1814–1860.* (Ed.) Lytton Strachey and Roger Fulford (Macmillan, London, 1938).

GREY, Hon. Charles: *The Early Years of H.R.H. The Prince Consort* (Harper & Row, N.Y., 1867).

HOBHOUSE, Christopher: *1851 and the Crystal Palace* (E. P. Dutton & Co., Inc., N.Y., 1937).

JAGOW, Kurt: *Letters of The Prince Consort, 1831–1861.* Tr. E. T. S. Dugdale (E. P. Dutton & Co., Inc., N.Y., 1938).

JERSEY, The Dowager Countess of: *Fifty-one Years of Victorian Life* (Murray, London, 1922).

LEE, Sir Sidney: *Queen Victoria, A Biography* (Smith, Elder & Co., London, 1902).
King Edward VII, Vol. I (Macmillan, N.Y., 1925).

MAGNUS, Sir Philip: *King Edward the Seventh* (E. P. Dutton & Co., Inc., N.Y., 1964).

MARTIN, Sir Theodore: *The Life of The Prince Consort,* 5 Vols. (Smith, Elder & Co., London, 1875–80).

McCARTHY, Justin: *A History of Our Own Times* (Harper & Row, N.Y., 1879–80).

McCLINTOCK, Mary Howard: *The Queen Thanks Sir Howard* (Murray, London, 1945).

PARKER, Charles S.: (Ed.) *Sir Robert Peel, From His Private Papers* (Murray, London, 1899).

STOCKMAR, Ernst Freiherr von: *Denkwürdigkeiten Aus Den Papieren Des Freiherrn* Christian Friedrich von Stockmar (Brunswick, 1872).

STRACHEY, Lytton: *Queen Victoria* (Harcourt, Brace & World, N.Y., 1921).

See also *Greville.*

TORRENS, W. M.: *Memoirs of The Right Hon. William, Second Viscount Melbourne* (London, 1878).

VICTORIA, Queen: *Leaves from The Journal of Our Life in The Highlands* (London, 1868).

More Leaves from The Journal of A Life in The Highlands (Smith, Elder & Co., London, 1884).

See also *Benson, A. C.,* and *Bolitho.*

WYNDHAM, Mrs. Hugh: (Ed.) *Correspondence of Sarah Spencer, Lady Lyttelton, 1787–1870* (Murray, London, 1912).

INDEX

Gloucester, Dss. of: 124
Gotha: 1–3, 18, 80, 101, 133, 167–8
Grant, John: 207
Granville, 2nd Earl: xii, 130, 180
Gravesend: 179
Great Exhibition of 1851: x, 111, 117,
   119–20, 123, 125–8, 137, 188, 200;
   see also Crystal Palace
Greece: 98, 120
Gregory xvi, Pope: 34–5
Grenadier Guards: 218
Greville, Charles: 22, 42, 44, 46–8, 52,
   56, 67, 73, 100, 116, 118, 126, 130–1,
   142, 151, 156, 167, 196–7
Grey 3rd Earl: 120
Grey, Sir George: 115, 211
Guizot, François: 78, 83
Gujrat: 105, 112

Hancock, John: 210
Hanover: 60, 183
Hardinge, 1st Viscount: 141, 162
Harrisburg: 210
Harrow School: 137
Hastings, Lady Flora: 37–8, 226
Haustein, Alexander von: 10–13
Heidelberg: 219
Helena, Pss.: 93, 143
Henry ii, King: 108
Henry v, King: 194
Henry vi, King: 154
Higginson, Gen. Sir George: vii
Hong Kong: 74
Hyde Park: 119, 123, 125–7, 164, 173,
   176, 190

India: 31, 67, 90, 112–13, 135, 139,
   173–7, 180–1, 183–4, 215, 220
India Bill (1858): 175, 177, 180–1, 203
Inkerman: 148
Ireland: 50, 66, 72, 88, 90, 95, 100,
   103–5, 114–16, 218, 222
Irish Coercion Bill (1846): 92
Isabella ii, Queen of Spain: 78, 83–4
Italy: 98, 186–9, 195, 206, 211, 213,
   215, 220; see also Sardinia

Jamaica Constitution Bill (1839): 38
Jenner, Sir William: 227

Jersey, Countess of: 50
Jerusalem: 138

Kabul: 67
Kamiesh (Crimea): 148
Kean, Charles: 107
Kensington Palace: 6, 8–9, 14–17, 25–
   6, 29, 212
Kent, Duke of: morganatic marriage
   to Mme de St Laurent, 5; marriage
   to Pss. Victoria of Leiningen, 2,
   5–6; death, 8–9; 64, 206
Kent, Pss. Victoria, Dss. of: marriage,
   2, 5–6; and Prince Albert, xi, 7, 43,
   98–9, 118, 191, 216; and Queen
   Victoria, 6, 9, 15–17, 21–2, 26, 29–
   30, 32, 43, 55, 60, 71, 89, 99, 158,
   178, 191, 195, 216–18; and King
   Leopold, 9, 16; and Conroy, 8–9,
   16–17, 21, 30, 60; and Baroness
   Lehzen, 8, 17, 60; and Pss. Bea-
   trice, 198; death, 216; 222
Ketschendorf Castle: 11–12, 18
Kew: 76, 219
Khyber Pass: 67
Kingston, Ontario: 208
Knight, Charles: 15
Königswinter: 165
Kossuth, L.: 128–9

Lee, Sir Sidney: 111–12, 188, 193
Lehzen, Baroness: 8, 17, 30, 32–3, 40,
   52–3, 59–60
Leigh, 2nd Baron: 50
Leiningen, Pss. Victoria of: see Kent,
   Dss. of
Leopold i, King of the Belgians: ix,
   9, 13, 118, 206; first marriage, to
   Pss. Charlotte, 4–5, 20; and Prince
   Albert, 20–1, 24–5, 39–41, 45, 56,
   87, 89, 103, 218; and Queen Vic-
   toria, 26–7, 32–4, 40, 44–6, 49, 53,
   58, 63–4, 70, 77, 82–4, 89, 93, 107,
   109, 112, 115, 119, 130–2, 136–7,
   153, 156, 187, 191–2, 195, 212–13,
   217–18, 230
Leopold, Prince (Duke of Albany):
   136, 144, 158
Leopold, Prince, of Saxe-Coburg: 78
Le Tréport: 77
Lewis, Sir George C.: 156
Lieven, Pss.: 21